Conversations with Larry Brown

Literary Conversations Series
Peggy Whitman Prenshaw
General Editor

Photo credit: Tom Rankin

Conversations with
Larry Brown

Edited by
Jay Watson

University Press of Mississippi
Jackson

Introduction

Larry Brown liked to tell interviewers and other interested listeners that he had gotten a late start as a writer. Indeed, "A Late Start" was the title of the first major literary address he gave before a public audience, at the Fifth Biennial Conference on Southern Literature in Chattanooga, where he was honored in 1989 as an emerging talent on the regional and national literary scene. Brown's choice of title was no accident, and no exaggeration. He was twenty-nine years old and a full-time firefighter in Oxford, Mississippi, when he decided to try his hand at writing fiction. An avid reader since childhood, he had come to wonder how people made books and whether it was the kind of thing you could learn to do if you applied yourself to it. As he told Kay Bonetti in 1994, "I wanted to know how people went into a room and sat down and created a book out of their imagination or memory or whatever—created this book where nothing had existed before, a tangible object you could pick up and hold in your hand. How did people do that?" In this way began one of the more celebrated and unlikely careers in recent southern letters.

If that career began belatedly, it also ended prematurely, with Brown's sudden death in November 2004, at the age of fifty-three. Only sixteen years separated the publication of his first book, the story collection *Facing the Music*, and his death. The loss to his family and loved ones is of course incalculable, and one wouldn't want to trivialize it, but the loss to literature is nearly as staggering. To begin to put it in perspective, had Brown's fellow Lafayette Countian William Faulkner passed away at fifty-three, we would have no *Requiem for a Nun*, no *A Fable* or *The Town* or *The Mansion*, no *The Reivers*. Had Faulkner's career ended only a decade and a half after his debut novel, we would have no *Go Down, Moses* or *Intruder in the Dust* as well. Or, to cite the example of a contemporary with whom Brown is often compared, had Harry Crews lived only sixteen years beyond the publication of *The Gospel Singer* in 1968 (when Crews was thirty-three), southern literature would be missing such hard-boiled classics as *The Knockout Artist, Body,* and *Scar Lover*.

Brown made good use of the time allotted him. His oeuvre includes five novels, two short fiction collections, a memoir of firefighting and his early writing years, a collection of personal and autobiographical essays, a number of uncollected stories, and a stage adaptation of his Vietnam novel, *Dirty Work*. At the time of his death he was working on two additional novels and a massive screenplay about the life of Hank Williams. The Brown catalog also includes several dozen literary conversations, from lengthy formal interviews to feature articles or profiles that draw significantly on interview material. Despite living in a rural area ten miles from the small town of Oxford, maintaining a busy writing schedule, and, during the first decade of his career, holding down a dangerous and physically demanding job while frequently moonlighting on top of that (he compiles an epic list of part-time jobs for Orman Day), Brown was generous with his time, making himself available to print journalists, radio hosts, TV personalities, documentary filmmakers, academics and freelancers, fellow writers, even high school students. He was interviewed by Jane Pauley for NBC's *Today* show, and by Terry Gross for her National Public Radio program, *Fresh Air*. What may have been his final interview was published online.

This volume brings together seventeen of the most significant conversations with Larry Brown, ranging from 1988 to 2004. They are arranged chronologically according, whenever possible, to the date when they were conducted rather than the date of publication. Most follow a conventional question-and-answer format. Brown gave half a dozen major interviews for literary journals and magazines; all are reprinted here. They are joined by some shorter pieces for newspapers or trade publications, by several items I have transcribed from other media, and by a pair of interviews that have never been published in any form.

One of these unpublished items, the first piece in the collection, is a telephone interview conducted by Jackson *Clarion-Ledger* reporter Gary Pettus as part of his background research for a 1988 feature article that appears to be the earliest published "conversation" with Brown.[1] The origins of the 6000-word interview typescript, which now resides with the Larry Brown papers at the University of Mississippi's John D. Williams library, are somewhat mysterious. Pettus himself has no memory of recording the interview, and there is a consensus among those who knew Brown well that he would have lacked the technical know-how to record it himself. Nevertheless, the typescript appears to have been the work of Brown himself. I have opted to include the full interview over Pettus's 1000-word profile not only for its greater wealth of detail but for the revealing glimpse it offers of a young writer, on the eve of literary celebrity, half-awed and half-bemused by the recognition and by the publicity-generating apparatus that are starting to descend upon him. Without a doubt Brown is still feeling his way into the interview process in his exchanges with Pettus. He would soon enough become old hat at the promotional interview, but here, though characteristically accommodating and courteous to his interlocutor, he sounds tentative, self-conscious. On a related note, because it was likely Brown himself who typed up his conversation with Pettus, I have deviated from my editorial practice elsewhere in this volume of silently correcting mechanical errors and have instead allowed idiosyncrasies of grammar and punctuation to stand. Critics, reviewers, and Brown's own writing peers often point to his pitch-perfect ear for southern working-class dialect and idiom as an important source of the authenticity so many readers have found in his work. Here we can see him attempting to render for himself the rhythms of his own speaking voice, in a manner consistent with his exercises in fictional dialogue.

A word or two of background is in order for some of the other pieces in this collection before turning to a more general appraisal. By far the largest group of Brown conversations consists of feature profiles for large-circulation, big-city newspapers. Over the years such articles, sprinkled selectively with quotations from Brown, have appeared in regional publications such as the *Atlanta Journal-Constitution*, the *Times-Picayune* of New Orleans, the Memphis *Commercial Appeal*, and, of course, the *Clarion-Ledger*, and in national outlets such as the *New York Times*, the *Chicago Tribune*, the *Los Angeles Times*, the *Washington Post*, even *USA Today*.[2] Because these articles were so often timed to coincide with book releases or promotional tours, however, they often tend toward the formulaic—especially in the early years when Brown was still fighting fires, an angle that reporters were seemingly powerless to resist and rapidly worked to death. For this reason, I have chosen to represent the "author's profile" genre with a pair of articles from Oxford's weekly arts and entertainment paper. These pieces, both authored by local gonzo journalist and radio personality Jim Dees, appeared with the publication of *Father and Son* in 1996 and *Fay* in 2000, but they manage for the most part to avoid book-release boilerplate. They are funny and freewheeling, offbeat and improvisational, more than a little gonzo themselves. In the company of another local writer, Brown enjoys himself, takes chances. There is nothing quite like these two performances in the large archive of Brown conversations.

Nor is there anything like the 1997 radio session that brought Brown, Barry Hannah, and Brad Watson—a trio of Mississippi native sons—into an Oxford recording studio for an hour of lively dialogue about the craft of fiction and the writerly life in front of a live audience. Though Hannah is the self-appointed master of ceremonies, presiding over the occasion with great wit and flair and live-wire intelligence, the three writers take turns bringing each other out, discussing each other's works with insight and obvious admiration. At ease with his fellow storytellers, Brown talks candidly about writer's block, favorite means of procrastination, and the surprisingly liberating pressures of meeting deadlines, which he says have produced some of his best writing. He is also comfortable enough to let Watson and Hannah take the reins at times. We should be aware, then, that part of what we are *hearing*, in exchanges from which Brown's voice is absent, is his genuine pleasure in listening to, and simply sharing the moment with, such gifted colleagues. That pleasure is contagious, the setting relaxed and intimate. As one of the session producers put it to me in a private e-mail, "if you listen carefully, you can hear the ice clinking in their glasses."

Perhaps the most unique item in the entire collection, however, is the interview material transcribed from Gary Hawkins' marvelous documentary, *The Rough South of Larry Brown*. The film contains dramatizations of several Brown short stories, but its emotional center is to be found in the voices of Brown and his wife, Mary Annie. In footage taken over several years, Hawkins shoots the couple separately and together, sometimes speaking to the camera and sometimes directly to each other; but the film's skillful editing works to create an ongoing conversation between the two, a moving and sometimes testy dialogue on vocation, family, and fame. Emerging from this dialogue is a portrait of Brown that captures his drive and dedication to his art without neglecting the strain that a writer's life imposes on those who are closest to him and love him most. His voice is wry, compelling and careworn, but the voice of Mary Annie Brown is the film's true touchstone and revelation. It is an unforgettable voice: plain-spoken, unflinchingly honest, in its occasional criticisms of Brown as well as its fierce loyalty to him. One of the most important gifts that Hawkins has given us in his film is access to that voice.

All but one of the interviews collected here have been reproduced in their entirety. The exception is Day's 2004 dialogue with Brown on working-class writing and identity, which was originally part of a larger forum that also featured writers Dan Chaon, John McNally, and Susan Straight. The four writers responded to Day's questions separately, by correspondence; their replies do not comment on or significantly engage one another. Extracting Brown's part of the interview thus poses little risk of altering its meaning or otherwise compromising its integrity, so I have chosen to publish it alone.

Throughout these pages Brown for the most part sticks closely to topics with which he is personally familiar: his childhood and family history, his firefighting days, his fictional craft and technique, his travels and experiences as an established writer and, later, as a teacher of writing, and the farm, forest, and small-town landscapes of north Mississippi. He can be amazingly precise, for instance, in recounting the genesis of particular novels and stories. The image that launched "Facing the Music," one of Brown's first and finest stories, came to him as he sat at a traffic light in Oxford. A dead dog by the side of a county road provided the germ of "Boy and Dog," and the story's unique form (it is arranged in five-word paragraphs that give Brown a poet's control over line) was the result of a self-conscious decision to come up with some technical innovation worthy of Donald Barthelme. Another work began with the vision of a woman in tears in her living room because her son refused to leave his room. Why wouldn't he leave his room? The answer became *Dirty Work*. And the childhood tragedy that warps Glen Davis of *Father and Son* came directly from the tale of an accidental shooting that circulated in Brown's rural community.

Because Brown so rarely oversteps the limits of his own expertise, the reader of these conversations will find little on the subject of politics, the broad currents of world events, or the writer's role in society. His pronouncements on art typically focus on the artist's moral and aesthetic responsibilities rather than on his political ones. When he does reflect on the larger forces of history, economics, or politics, it is usually in terms of their concrete impact on the local milieu he knows best. Asked by Wayne Pond to describe the most significant changes the South has experienced over the previous generation, Brown has less to say about the Civil Rights movement, for instance, or even about the Vietnam War than about "physical changes in the land . . . such as the reduction of acreage that's being farmed, the reduction of a lot of the hardwood timber that was once around everywhere, where a lot of it has been clear-cut, logged off, and now is on pine plantations." (He develops this point at greater length in a memorable passage from his interview with Bonetti.) The removal of agricultural acreage from production was not an abstract issue for Brown. Nor was it a matter of physical geography alone. It was also a powerful social factor that radically altered southern labor arrangements, forcing sharecroppers and tenant farmers off the land and into the towns and cities in search of a better life. This, as Brown tells Tom Rankin, was precisely the path taken by his sharecropping father when he moved his family to Memphis in 1954 and hired on at a trailer company. In this way Brown's family history and native landscape both bear eloquent witness to the legacy of economic modernization in the twentieth-century South—a legacy, of course, that he has also traced in such fictional works as *Joe* and *Father and Son*.

The most notable exception to Brown's general reticence about world affairs is his April 2002 interview with Keith Weston of WUNC radio in Chapel Hill. Here, having returned to the scene where, six months earlier, he had delivered the Thomas Wolfe prize lecture, Brown shares his impressions of one of the defining public events of our contemporary moment: the September 11 attacks on New York and Washington. As it happens, Brown was in Toronto at a film festival on the day of the attacks, and the massive lockdown of the U.S. air grid in the wake of the disaster left him stranded there for several days. He finally got out by taking a bus to, of all places, Manhattan, arriving at the Port Authority terminal. The cityscape he encountered was eerie, surreal:

> The night we were there, we went down to the Hudson River, and we started seeing these enormous tents that had been set up, like a two-story tent. And they were full of nothing but powdered concrete that they had hauled out of there. They had to dump that stuff somewhere and so they dumped it down by the Hudson River, just mountains and mountains of concrete. And of course you could see across the river where all the lights were set up for the rescue operation in that empty space where they used to be standing.

It is worth noting that even here Brown refrains from political commentary, from any larger analysis of terrorism, ideological conflict, or U.S. preparedness.

He focuses, as always, on what he was there to observe firsthand: the all too literally concrete details of the destruction. And its human toll as well. For Brown's thoughts are also, as we might expect, with the New York City firemen who perished in the collapse of the Trade Towers. Flying out "past the remains of the towers" on the Monday after the attacks, he muses on "all the firefighters who were buried underneath that and what it took for them to do what they did, to go up when everybody else was coming down." That last phrase in particular is vintage Brown. In spare yet dead-on language, it says everything there is to say about his missing comrades. Their fall becomes a kind of apotheosis: they went up when everybody else was going down.

Brown's 9/11 story is unique, but any collection like this one risks a certain degree of repetition across and even within interviews. Interviewers have their tried-and-true questions, reporters their pet angles, and writers themselves their favorite stories, themes, and turns of phrase. Brown is no exception. A recycled description or twice-told tale, however, can offer a window onto his literary sensibilities. Take for example Brown's account for Don Swaim of his maiden voyage into fiction:

> Well, the first thing I wrote was a novel about a man-eating grizzly bear in Yellowstone National Park. This is the God's honest truth. I'd never been to Yellowstone National Park, and I wrote this terrible, terrible novel. And I thought it was good, and it would be published, you know, and I sent it off up here to New York, and got my first rejection slip. You know, it took me about five months to write that novel. It was like 327 single-spaced pages. I didn't even know you were supposed to double-space back then.

It's a funny story, and Brown enjoyed telling it—to Swaim, Bonetti, Rankin, Hannah and Watson, Bob Summer, Dorie Larue, and any number of other interviewers over the years.[3] What prompted him to tell it over and over? Beyond its obvious entertainment value, I would suggest, lies a more substantial point, which has less to do with the size of the doomed manuscript, its sensational subject matter, or Brown's initial ambition to write pulp rather than serious fiction, than with the fact that, as Brown himself explicitly notes, *he had never been to Yellowstone National Park*. As a storyteller, in other words, he had made the fatal mistake of relying purely on invention instead of applying his imagination to the stuff of memory, experience, and observation. He had not yet absorbed the lesson he would later attribute to Stephen

King, one of his idols: "that all your human experience—your memory, everything you ever heard or saw, everything anyone ever told you about, all of that stuff—is like a well, and you drop down into that well every day for your fiction." Brown's well was sunk deep in the same ground Faulkner once called his little postage stamp of native soil. Yellowstone lay half a country away. Subsequent forays into fiction would do their literary prospecting closer to home.

With his Yellowstone anecdote, then, Brown is evoking the early, error-prone stages of a writing apprenticeship. Indeed, apprenticeship is one of the central themes that emerges from this collection. The word pops up in interview after interview: with Pettus, Summer, Larue, Day, Susan Ketchin, Michael Manley, Keith Weston, Charles Blanchard, and Marc Fitten and Lawrence Hetrick. It was a crucial concept for Brown, one he liked to frame in quantitative terms: the two long years before anything he wrote was accepted (the first story he placed appeared in a motorcycle magazine), or the eight years before his first book was published; the hundred short stories from which he drew the ten comprising his first collection; the five novel manuscripts that preceded *Dirty Work*; the thousands of pages he typed and retyped himself (Brown had an elephant's memory for page counts; throughout his career, he could rattle off the exact length of just about any manuscript he had ever worked on); or, to boil the whole thing down to essentials, the million-odd words he estimated it took him to arrive as a writer.

Clearly, this deep and remarkably concrete belief in apprenticeship helped sustain Brown through years of rejection and disappointment. As Hannah puts it in these pages, sounding slightly awestruck, "Nobody I know would be rejected over ten times without folding up. Really, I don't know many people who'd take it, can take it." Brown's conviction that a writer must pay his dues, that a thing worth doing took time to do well, that with hard work and dogged persistence he would improve and become worthy, helped him "take it." "I think I wrote thirty-nine short stories in 1983," he tells Swaim, "and none of them were published." Still, he pressed on. No wonder his most characteristic advice to beginning writers was to keep struggling, to learn to write by writing, as he had. His notion of apprenticeship valorized that sense of struggle, gave it meaning and context.

Implicit in this notion is a related concept of writing as craft. Though it brought him a better life and great personal satisfaction, Brown did not romanticize his vocation. He was of the "perspiration" rather than the "inspiration" school regarding literary success. "I don't think I was born with any talent," he tells Bonetti point-blank. A lifetime of blue-collar jobs and hard manual labor—picking cotton, bagging groceries, deadening timber, cutting and hauling pulpwood, driving trucks, answering telephones, fighting fires, cutting people out of wrecked automobiles—had predisposed him to approach authorship less as a matter of genius, the spinning of tales and visions, than as a matter of careful construction and repair. Remember, he took up writing because he wanted to learn how people *made* books, created material artifacts out of words. It is not surprising, then, how often he compared the activity of writing to carpentry, bricklaying, or house building (see Summer, Bonetti, Rankin, and Hawkins). Indeed, at more than one point in his career, the labors of writing and building alternated directly in a mutually reinforcing rhythm. He began *Dirty Work* in 1986, immediately after completing work on a new house for his family; the months of construction work had energized him and given ideas time to gel in his mind. Similarly, in many of the interviews surrounding the publication of *Fay* in 2000, Brown seems as eager to talk about the writing cabin he was building for himself beside a small pond near Tula as he is to discuss the challenges of creating a female protagonist for his new novel. In this context, what apprenticeship represented for Brown had far less to do with initiation into a mystery than with the training that results in the creation of durable, functional, meaningful objects. The durability of his work was important to him. As he told Hawkins in 1999, in words that have acquired a haunting resonance since then:

> There's only so many books I can write in my life. You know, I'm going to die at a
> certain age. I don't know what that age is, but while I'm alive I want to write as
> much as I can. And I want it to be good. I figure if my health continues and all I
> probably still got twenty more years of writing in me. That'd be good. To be writing
> at sixty-eight, that'd be nice. I'd be relaxing by then. Sure. Yeah, but I hope my
> books survive. You know, I hope that they're still being read after I'm gone. That's
> probably about the most you can hope for. Is for them to stay in print. Like
> Faulkner and Flannery O'Connor, people like that, you know.

We're not so far here from Faulkner's own self-penned "obit and epitaph too," with its own hints of an artisanal awareness: He made the books and he died.[4]

A concept of apprenticeship also implies the presence of masters and guides who offer support, instruction, and wisdom. For Brown (and, we come to realize, for Mary Annie), writing was often a lonely endeavor, but it was also informed at every point by the dialogue between Brown and his literary influences. It is important to remember that reading was a vocation, a true calling, for Brown long before writing was. Encouraged by his mother, he read voraciously as a child, drawing inspiration and sustenance from classical mythology, bible stories, the Grimm brothers, Poe, Hemingway, the adventure stories of Melville, Twain, London, and Zane Grey, and the "boy and dog" fiction of James Street, Jim Kjelgaard, and Fred Gipson. Brown's list of literary "heroes," as he liked to call them, is extensive: in addition to the figures just cited, it includes Faulkner, Welty, O'Connor, Hannah, Barthelme, Crews, Cormac McCarthy, Tobias Wolff, Charles Bukowski, Raymond Carver, and Stephen King. These are the masters from whom Brown learned his trade.

There are also those figures whom Brown sometimes referred to as his "saints," who offered him advice, assistance, and assurance along the way. Writer Ellen Douglas, who taught Brown in a creative writing class at the University of Mississippi in 1982, helped point him in the right direction. He could already put together a good sentence, she told him, but the crucial stage in finding his voice would be discovering where his true subject matter lay. By introducing Brown to *The Norton Anthology of Short Fiction*, she opened his eyes to a world of literary possibilities beyond the thrillers, crime stories, and supernatural tales that were his early models. Local bookstore owner Richard Howorth (now in his second term as mayor of Oxford) read many of Brown's early manuscripts and helped convince him to trust in his own literary instincts. In particular he gave Brown confidence in "Facing the Music," the story that became his breakthrough into serious fiction. Sympathetic magazine editors at *Outdoor Life* and *Twilight Zone* wrote Brown letters of encouragement whether or not they accepted his work. Hannah, who moved to Oxford the same year Brown published his first story, took an early interest in the young writer and championed his work in several early newspaper profiles. Richard Ford met Brown at a reading in Jackson (Ford's reading, not Brown's) and helped bring his stories to the attention of journal editors. Perhaps Brown's most trusted guide and collaborator over the years, however, was his editor at Algonquin Books, Shannon Ravenel, who worked with him on all but one of the books he published during his lifetime. Again and again he points to her editorial acumen, her belief in his talent, and the objectivity she helped bring to his writing and revision process, as key elements of his success. (Among other things she convinced him that the dramatically appropriate place to begin *Dirty Work* was over 150 pages into the original manuscript, and she supervised the excision of hundreds of pages from the *Fay* typescript.) As this rich gallery of mentors and guiding angels suggests, writing was always a product of conversation for Larry Brown.

The sense of struggle intrinsic to Brown's idea of apprenticeship may be one source of another important theme that runs through these interviews, and that is the role of conflict in his narrative aesthetic. For Brown, fiction is driven by character, and character is driven above all by adversity. "I try to start with trouble on the first page," he told Hawkins, and he was even more blunt with Bonetti: "If you don't have problems in your characters' lives, then you don't have a story." The point is ironclad, non-negotiable, and it is one of the only issues on which Brown approaches anything resembling a didactic tone. He no sooner dreamed up his characters than he cast about for ways to heap trouble on them, to weigh them down with impossible choices, a process he referred to as "sandbagging." As he told Manley in 1994,

> My characters usually know the difference between right and wrong. They know what the right things are to do, but that might not be what they want to do. It might be because they want to go out drinking or out whoring around instead of staying home and keeping a job and working. And they've all got some kind of struggle, because if you don't lay some kind of trouble on them, if they don't have some conflict, then how are you ever going to have a resolution or an ending. What you've got to do is to make things on them as tough as you can and that's what I consciously try to do. I do what I call "sandbagging" and make things as hard on them as I can so then I'll see how they're going to react and what's going to happen and what the story's going to be about.

Similar statements can be found throughout the volume. For Brown, then, sandbagging his characters was an aesthetic strategy, drawing the reader into the action of the story, but it had an ethical dimension as well. He wanted to find out what his protagonists were made of—whether they would rise to the challenge of adversity, whether they would make good choices or just easy ones—and he knew his readers would want to know these things, too. Many of his most memorable characters are beleaguered in just this way: Leon Barlow of "92 Days," the unnamed protagonists of "Samaritans" and "Wild Thing," the shattered veterans of *Dirty Work* or the unsinkable Gary Jones of *Joe*. Adversity allowed Brown to take the true moral measure of his people. As in the work of Flannery O'Connor, trouble in excess was the peculiar grace they received from their creator.

One of the pleasures of putting together a collection such as this is acknowledging the many people who have helped it come to fruition. I am grateful to Seetha Srinivasan and Walter Biggins of the University Press of Mississippi for initially proposing this project to me and for shepherding it through the production process. Joan Hall shared her experiences editing a volume for the Literary Conversations series, which helped me a great deal as I plotted my approach to this collection. Tom Rankin was an invaluable source of advice, encouragement, and factual information about Brown. He put me on the track of several of the interviews that appear in this volume, and it was he who suggested that I pay a visit to the Mississippi Department of Archives and History in Jackson, where the courteous staff introduced me to the subject file on Brown, a treasure trove of clippings from every stage of his career. Tom also read and commented on a draft of the introduction, and he supplied the photograph for the cover of this collection. It is difficult to overstate his generosity or to thank him enough.

At the John D. Williams library at the University of Mississippi, I received assistance from reference librarian John Cloy, who helped make my search for Brown-related materials a more efficient and productive one, and from Jennifer Ford, director of Special Collections, who provided me with a copy of the unpublished Gary Pettus interview that opens this volume. At the Center for the Study of Southern Culture, Ann Abadie offered useful recommendations and helped jog my memory about local newspaper items, question-and-answer sessions, and public readings involving Brown. It was Ann who hooked me up with Brown biographer Jean Cash of James Madison University, who graciously shared materials with me and has been a friend of this project from its inception. Oxford attorneys Hale Freeland and John Moses helped me track down biographical information that closed a few gaping holes in my Brown chronology.

I am also grateful to the many persons, publishers, and presses who granted me permission to reprint material for this collection. Whether or not that material ultimately appears in the volume—space considerations prevented me from using all of it—I remain deeply appreciative of your generosity and your support for this book.

I owe a special debt of thanks to Gary Hawkins. He knows why.

My deepest thanks go to my wife, Susan, and my children, Katherine and Judson. Your love—and your conversation—continues to nourish and challenge me. You give me a ground to stand on, a place to come home to. In the end, what else matters?

Perhaps the most unexpected pleasure of editing this volume has been that of transcribing audio and video recordings of Larry Brown in conversation. Expecting a carpal-tunnel nightmare, I instead found myself delighting in the sound of my subject's voice. The voice is well-matched with the face: craggy, weathered, unpretentious, and unmistakably southern. Whiskey, cigarettes, and the Mississippi hills have put gravel in it. The pace is easy and contemplative, the tone low and even, punctuated now and then by a soft chuckle, often at his own expense. It is a voice all the more precious for having been silenced too soon. I hope at least some of its pleasures manage to translate to the printed page.

This volume is dedicated to the memory of Larry Brown.

JW

Notes

1. See Pettus, "Writing His Way to the Holy Grail," Jackson *Clarion-Ledger* (23 August 1988), 1C, 3C.

2. Examples include Peter Applebome, "Larry Brown's Long and Rough Road to Becoming a Writer," *New York Times* (5 March 1990), C11; Berkley Hudson, "Country Boy Hits Big Time," *Los Angeles Times* (17 September 1989), "View" section, pp. 1–7; Fredric Koeppel, "Author, His 'Tragedy,' Spring from Same North Mississippi Turf," Memphis *Commercial Appeal* (22 September 1991), and "Brown Tours with Rabbit Factory," Memphis *Commercial Appeal* (14 September 2003); Susan Larson, "Keeper of the Flame," New Orleans *Times-Picayune* (2 October 1996), E1–E2; Danny McKenzie, "Oxford Writer Stays Same While Literary Fires Brightly Burn," Jackson *Clarion-Ledger* (6 February 1994), 1B; Bob Minzesheimer, " 'King of White Trash,' Characters Share Thirst for Life," *USA Today* (5 April 2000), 7D; Don O'Briant, "Apprenticeship Is Over," *Atlanta Journal-Constitution*

(14 December 1988), K10, and "Writer Larry Brown in Faulkner's Footsteps," *Atlanta Journal-Constitution* (9 April 2000), L1; Gary Pettus, "Brown: 2nd Novel Better than 1st," Jackson *Clarion-Ledger* (27 September 1991), E1; Mary T. Schmich, "Getting a Late Start," *Chicago Tribune* (19 June 1990), section 5, pp. 1–2; Michael Skube, "Straight from the Heart," *Atlanta Journal-Constitution* (29 September 1996), M3; Billy Watkins, "Hot Career Move: The Oxford Fireman-turned-author Is Building a Strong Base of Fans," Jackson *Clarion-Ledger* (24 December 1996), 1D, 2D, and "Larry Brown," Jackson *Clarion-Ledger* (23 March 2000), E1, E3; Teresa Weaver, "Larry Brown: Mounting Tension Is Crucial to Storytelling," *Atlanta Journal-Constitution* (28 September 2003), Q4; and Judith Weinraub, "The Back-Roads Blue-Collar Artiste," *Washington Post* (9 December 1990), F1, F4.
3. See for instance Applebome and Schmich.
4. See *Selected Letters of William Faulkner*, ed. Joseph Blotner (New York: Random House, 1977), 285.

Chronology

1951	William Larry Brown born July 9 in Oxford, third child of Knox and Leona Brown. At the time of his birth, the family is sharecropping for Chester Stanford in the Potlockney community of southeastern Lafayette County.
1954	The Browns move to Memphis, where Knox Brown begins work at the Fruehauf Trailer Company. During the Memphis years, Knox will also work at the Mid-South fairgrounds, and Leona will work for the Camp Electric Company and for Katz Drugstore.
1964	The Browns return to Lafayette County from Memphis.
1968	Knox Brown dies of a heart attack.
1969	After graduating from Lafayette County High School, Brown works at the Chambers stove factory in Oxford, where his father was working at the time of his death. During this year, Brown also meets Mary Annie Coleman (b. September 26, 1955).
1970	In November, Brown enlists in the Marines and spends Christmas in boot camp at Parris Island, South Carolina.
1971–1972	After basic training, Brown is stationed first at Camp Lejeune, Jacksonville, North Carolina, and then at the Marine Barracks, Philadelphia, Pennsylvania, where he hears stories from wounded veterans at the NCO club that will provide material for his novel *Dirty Work*. Throughout his tour, Brown sends money home to help his younger brother maintain his college deferment from the draft.
1972	After completing his tour, Brown returns to Lafayette County and to his job at the stove factory.
1973	Brown begins work as a firefighter at the Oxford Fire Department in December.

1974	Brown marries Mary Annie Coleman August 17. At the time of their marriage she is working as a secretary in Oxford.
1975	Son Billy Ray born June 5.
1977	Daughter Delinah born but dies in infancy.
1979	Son Shane born August 14.
1980	In October, Brown decides to try his hand at writing fiction. He spends five months on his first manuscript, a novel about a marauding grizzly bear in Yellowstone National Park. At the time he is working his regular shift at the fire department and, on his days off, at Comanche Pottery, Oxford.
1982	Daughter LeAnne born June 29. In February, Brown's story "Plant Growin' Problems" becomes his first to be accepted for publication, in *Easyriders* magazine. Brown meets writer Barry Hannah in Oxford. During the fall term at the University of Mississippi, Brown audits a creative writing class taught by novelist Ellen Douglas. Douglas assigns stories from *The Norton Anthology of Short Fiction*, and Brown begins to shift his emphasis as a writer from pulp fiction to serious literature.
1983	By his own estimate, Brown writes thirty-nine short stories during this year. None are accepted for publication.
1984	*Fiction International* accepts "Boy and Dog," Brown's first work to be published in a literary magazine. Brown takes another creative writing class, led by John Osier at the Memphis public library. He begins work on the manuscript that will eventually become the novel *Joe*.
1985	"Facing the Music" is accepted by *Mississippi Review*. Brown meets writer Richard Ford in Jackson.
1986	Brown is promoted to captain at the Oxford Fire Department. From March through August, he works on a new home for his family in the Lafayette County town of Yocona. The house includes a writing room, separate from the main living space. In August, Brown begins work on the manuscript that will become his novel *Dirty Work*. On November 8 he gives his first public reading at the Lafayette County courthouse. Barry Hannah serves as master of ceremonies.

1987   "Facing the Music" published in *Mississippi Review*. The
            story gets the attention of editor Shannon Ravenel at
            Algonquin Books, who contacts Brown about the possibility
            of publishing a collection of his stories.
1988   Brown's story collection *Facing the Music* is published by
            Algonquin Books in September. The *Greensboro Review*
            awards its 1988 Literary Prize to Brown for "Kubuku Rides
            (This Is It)."
1989   *Facing the Music* wins the annual Mississippi Institute of
            Arts and Letters award for literature, and "Kubuku Rides
            (This Is It)" is selected by Margaret Atwood for *Best
            American Short Stories 1989*. In April, Brown gives address,
            "A Late Start," at the Fifth Biennial Conference on Southern
            Literature in Chattanooga. In September, Algonquin pub-
            lishes *Dirty Work*, and Brown is interviewed by Jane Pauley
            on NBC's *Today* show. In October, he is interviewed by
            Cable News Network and begins work on a stage adaptation
            of *Dirty Work* for a PBS American Playhouse production in
            New York. Late in the year, Brown begins the fire station
            journal that he will develop into the memoir *On Fire*.
1990   Brown retires from the Oxford Fire Department on
            January 6 to concentrate full-time on writing. From
            January until September he works on a long story, "A
            Roadside Resurrection," for the *Paris Review*. He wins the
            annual Author's Award from the Mississippi Library
            Association for *Dirty Work* and is a fellow at the annual
            Bread Loaf Writers Conference in Middlebury, Vermont, in
            August. Algonquin publishes the story collection *Big Bad
            Love* in December.
1991   Brown returns to Bread Loaf as a faculty associate in August.
            Algonquin publishes *Joe* in September, along with an appre-
            ciative essay from noted critic Cleanth Brooks, "An Affair of
            Honor: Larry Brown's *Joe*."
1992   Visiting writer at Bowling Green State University, Ohio,
            January through May. *Joe* wins the Southern Book Critics
            Circle Award for fiction. Brown is once again a faculty asso-
            ciate at Bread Loaf in August, and during the fall academic

term he is Richard H. Thornton Writer in Residence at
Lynchburg College, Lynchburg, Virginia.

1994   Brown's stage adaptation of *Dirty Work* enjoys a ten-night
run in January at the Arena Theater in Washington, under
the direction of Richard Corley. *On Fire* published by
Algonquin in February.

1995   The stage adaptation of *Dirty Work* is performed at the
Dallas Theater Center. Brown begins the journal that will
develop into the title essay of *Billy Ray's Farm*. Brown plays
a small role in *100 Proof*, an independent film shot in
Kentucky.

1996   Visiting writer at Centre College, Kentucky, in January and
February. Algonquin publishes novel *Father and Son* in
September.

1997   Brown travels to Park City, Utah, for the premier of *100 Proof*
at the Sundance Film Festival. *Father and Son* wins the
Southern Book Critics Circle award for fiction. Brown is the
first two-time winner of the award.

1998   Brown serves as a creative writing instructor at the University
of Mississippi, Oxford, from January to May. He begins
working on a pondside writing cabin on property he owns
near Tula in southeastern Lafayette County.

1999   Brown gives the keynote address for the University of
Tennessee, Chattanooga Perspectives Series in February. He
is one of ten writers to receive the Lila Wallace-Reader's
Digest Award, a three-year grant that requires the recipient
to develop an affiliation with a nonprofit organization of his
choice. Brown chooses the Oxford-Lafayette County library
and establishes the Larry Brown Writers Series, which brings
writers Andre Dubus III, Jill McCorkle, Jim Grimsley, and
Mark Richard to Oxford for public readings. Brown spends
the fall semester at the University of Montana as the inaugu-
ral Kittredge Writer in Residence.

2000   In April Algonquin publishes Brown's novel *Fay*, and *The
Rough South of Larry Brown*, a documentary film directed by
Gary Hawkins, premiers at Duke University.

2001   Algonquin publishes *Billy Ray's Farm: Essays from a Place
           Called Tula* in April. The film version of *Big Bad Love* is one
           of three American films selected for the Cannes Film Festival
           in France in May.
2003   Brown's novel *The Rabbit Factory* published by The Free
           Press in September. Brown is also working on a screenplay
           about the life of country singer Hank Williams.
2004   Brown dies of heart failure at his home on November 24. At
           the time of his death he was nearing completion of a novel
           manuscript, "The Miracle of Catfish."

Conversations with Larry Brown

Interview with Larry Brown

Gary Pettus / 1988

This interview was conducted August 18, 1988, as part of the background research for Pettus's profile of Brown, "Writing His Way to the Holy Grail," Jackson *Clarion-Ledger* (23 August 1988): 1C, 3C. The sixteen-page typescript resides with the Larry Brown papers, Special Collections department, John D. Williams Library, University of Mississippi. Used by permission.

Pettus: Is [*Facing the Music*] your first book? How long have you been writing?
Brown: Yeah, that's the first one, sure is. Almost eight years. I started in 1980.

Pettus: Have you published anything before?
Brown: Yeah, I've been publishing short stories since about 1982. You still there? Okay, I heard a click. I didn't know.

Pettus: Where have you published?
Brown: I've published mostly in literary magazines, the small quarterlies. I haven't been published in any of the big magazines in New York yet.

Pettus: Had you written earlier in your life than 1980?
Brown: No, that was when I started. I just started all at once.

Pettus: You never wrote anything when you were younger?
Brown: No, never did, really, other than just, you know, stuff your teacher wanted you to write. I never had really tried it until I was twenty-nine.

Pettus: What made you start writing?
Brown: Well, I've always been a big reader all my life. I just got more and more involved in reading stories and novels and things as I got older and finally one day came, I decided I was going to try it for myself. I'd always wondered if I could do it, but I never had really sat down and tried to do it and when I started I just kind of made up my mind that I was going to go ahead and do it until I published something. But it took a good while. It's kind of hard to explain.

Pettus: How did you begin?

Brown: I just started doing it. I sat down and wrote a novel that took me about five months to write. That was the first thing I put out. I sent it off to New York and it was sent back, I sent it off again and it was sent back. I gradually began to read more and more of what I call literature. The whole thing kind of just dawned on me after a good while, how much you had to write to really learn how. But I decided I would go ahead and do it anyway.

Pettus: So reading helped you?

Brown: Well, both, yeah. Reading and writing both. I guess it's a different apprenticeship period for any writer. You know Faulkner had one I think about five years, something like that. It's just a very gradual process where you learn more and more and more about the whole deal. About both sides. From the publishing deal and the writing deal, too.

Pettus: What is the hardest part of it?

Brown: Well, you've gotta write enough and read enough to be able to know when your own work is good enough. I don't think you can really appreciate a really good piece of work until you have sat down by yourself for a number of years and tried to do it yourself. I think that's what literature, the best writing, is all about. To come to the highest, the very highest form of the art of writing. I think it just takes time and it's a slow process and I think I'm still learning it, too. I don't think I'll ever get through learning it. Because everything I write now is not published. Everything I write is not good enough to publish.

Pettus: So you do still have difficulty publishing some of your work?

Brown: Oh yeah. Yeah, I do. I still have some difficulty convincing editors around the country. I just have a hard time publishing my stuff. My stuff will go around sometimes . . . I've had stories taken after fifteen rejection slips. That takes a couple of years, to get fifteen rejection slips on one story. So I've had kind of a hard time getting my stuff accepted. It's still not being totally accepted.

Pettus: Why do you think that is?

Brown: Well, I think my stuff kind of strikes a little chord of fear in some people. They don't want people to see it or read about it. I don't know. Some of the things I write about . . . I guess, I don't know. I've heard every excuse. There's that end of it and then there's the other end of it. It's so hard to get published in New York. Now. Just because of the way everything is in the publishing world. I've had stories that were read at *The New Yorker* and rejected and then taken almost immediately by a small literary quarterly. And it's not easy to get published in them. That's where the best stories, the best literature, that's being written in our country is published every year. And all of the poetry. So it kind of makes you think, you know, why worry about what they're gonna do in New York, what they're gonna publish? You just have to kind of . . . what I do is I read what I like to, I read the quarterlies I like to and don't really worry about my stuff not going over big commercially. I try to just do the best work I can.

Pettus: Do you have anything placed right now?

Brown: Well, no, I had a letter from an editor in New York that my agent sent me, it was one of the biggest magazines there, and they've been reading my stuff for years, and they've come very close several times to taking a story. It's always something different, this reason, that reason. I think the main thing is you've got to get your name built up big. They want to sell magazines, they want to sell a lot of issues. I don't know if they're afraid to take a chance on an unknown writer or what. And it happens sometimes. They will take stories by an unknown sometimes. I just haven't lucked out yet. There's a lot of luck involved in it.

Pettus: How do you find time to write?

Brown: Well, I don't have much. I'll tell you my schedule. I get off from the fire department one morning at seven. I drive home and change clothes and then go to my store by eight o'clock. Then my mother comes over and lets me off at 9:30. I come home and I try to write until 1:30. Then I go back to the store and stay till 7:00. And if I'm going to write anything at night I do it then. Mostly what I get to do is done in the middle of the day from 9:30 until 1:30. That's twenty days a month. The other ten days are taken up by my duty at the fire department. I don't write up there. I know that boy took some pictures yesterday of me with my pen on the tablet and all, but I very rarely do that up there. There's too much noise and all.

Pettus: Do you write in longhand?

Brown: No, I don't do too much handwriting any more. I usually do all mine on the typewriter. I used to, a long time ago.

Pettus: Did you know how to type when you started?
Brown: Yeah, I took typing in high school.

Pettus: And you get off in the morning?
Brown: Yeah, seven in the morning. I'm on duty twenty-four and off forty-eight.

Pettus: And you write some at night?
Brown: Well, sometimes, if I'm not too tired and I feel like it and everything's going right.

Pettus: Do you have any trouble writing? And do you write fast?
Brown: Once I get involved with something I do. Once I get to rolling somewhere, I write really fast. I don't really do a whole lot of revision, but there are also a lot of nonproductive times when I'm just sitting there looking at the machine and trying to think of what I'm going to say next. I try to edit myself as well as I can when I first write it because I don't like to come back and spend a lot of time revising. That's not one of my strong points.

Pettus: Do you write for a reader?
Brown: No, I don't think so. I think I write for myself, what makes me happy, I figure will please somebody else. I mean you're writing for your reader, but you've got to write for yourself first. You know if you like it, after you've spent that much time on it, you know that if you like it then somebody else is bound to like it too.

Pettus: Why are your characters like they are?
Brown: You mean from the poor side of town? Well, that is because probably most of my life that is the kind of people I've associated with and still do. I come from a very humble beginning myself, you know. My father was a sharecropper when I was born in 1951, down at Potlockney. Potlockney, Mississippi.

Pettus: Can you spell that?
Brown: I'm going to have to guess. Let's see. This is an old Indian name. I think it's P-O-T—they're gonna kill me if I misspell it—L-O-C-K-N-E-Y. I'm hoping that's right. There's no sign anywhere. It's on a few maps, not all of them.

Pettus: Do you think that writing ought to be about people who are higher in society?

Brown: I think your greatest literature comes from exactly those kind of people. Common people. The working man and the working woman. The best stuff is really about people's innermost feelings, and it doesn't really matter what level of society they're on. They can have any job or do anything if you make your characters real and give them the feelings they're supposed to have, you know, the moral feelings they're supposed to have. That's where you get your stories from. About the situations they get themselves into. I don't really know how to explain this, but I was born in the country and was raised in the country, and I still know a lot of country people, and I live in the country myself. I hear them every day talking, and I know what their lives are like, and that's what I write about. I know what my life's like. It's pretty similar to most of theirs.

Pettus: You live at Tula?

Brown: No, that's where my store is. I live at Yocona now. I've been over here about fourteen years. I married a girl from over here and we live on her mama's place. We just built us a house over here about two years ago.

Pettus: Have you been influenced by Faulkner?

Brown: Oh yeah, heavily influenced by Mr. Faulkner. That was one of the things I talked about when I gave my reading at the Faulkner Conference here a couple of weeks ago. I got up and I talked about how I started reading him when I was sixteen which is true. And I read a short portion from "The Bear." I told them that I had not really followed the course of most contemporary writers which is to go to a university and get an MFA degree in creative writing. What I have done is just read all the good literary books I could find and then write on my own. I had one writing course at Ole Miss in '82 under Ellen Douglas. You know she's got a new novel out, *Can't Quit You, Baby*. She was my teacher in '82. And she helped me a lot. She encouraged me, she read my early work, which was a lot of times awful, you know, but she encouraged me anyway. I think I was writing my third novel then, I believe, and she just told me to stick with it, just hang in there, you've got what it takes. So. That's basically how it came about. I just kept working and ignored the rejection slips, which is what anybody's got to do who's going to make it writing, they've got to just keep writing and just put the rejections back and send the story out again.

Pettus: And when will your novel [*Dirty Work*] be published?
Brown: Well, we haven't talked about a date yet. I know they're going to publish it but I don't know when. I've been working on it for about two years and I'm doing the fifth draft on it now. And hopefully this one's going to be the last.

Pettus: Is it similar to any of your earlier novels?
Brown: No, it's entirely different. This is number six here.

Pettus: Did you try to get the others published?
Brown: Oh yeah, I tried to get all of them published. But now I can see that they don't need to be published. They're not good enough. I can see now that everybody else was right years ago. See, I just didn't know it myself. That's the process you go through.

Pettus: Are you embarrassed over your earlier work?
Brown: Yeah. I wouldn't let anybody read the first novel I wrote. I would not want anybody to see it because I'm too ashamed of it now. I think, my God, how could I have written anything so bad and expected somebody else to publish it? It's a humbling experience, you know?

[*The interviewer's question was not recorded.*]

Brown: Okay, just take your time, I've got plenty of time. I'm just sitting out here in my room. I've got a little room here on the end of the house. When we designed our house, we just kind of drew our own house plans, and I've got myself a little room out here on the other end of the house, across the carport, where I'm completely isolated from the main part of the house. That's where I do my work. I felt like I had to have that if I was going to build a new house. I had to have a place I could go to. I've got three children and they keep the television going all the time and something's going on all the time in the house, so this is where I stay when I'm trying to work.

Pettus: How long have you been married?
Brown: I've been married fourteen years yesterday.

Pettus: Congratulations.
Brown: Thank you.

Pettus: What do your friends, and your fellow workers at the fire department think about your success?

Brown: Well, they're beginning to get pretty excited about it. Of course the boys at the fire department and my family have all been knowing about it for years because I've been doing it for so long. And I'd had some minor successes in years back when I had stories published in different magazines and things. They've all gotten pretty excited now that the book has come out and all. 'Cause that's like the majors, finally getting a book out. But in a way, you know, they've kind of taken it in stride, too, because they've been knowing what I've been attempting for so long, and they're glad to see me finally break on through. So they're excited, they're happy for me. I've got a lot of people pulling for me.

Pettus: Are there any other writers in your family?

Brown: I don't think so. I don't believe so. My mother, and my brothers and my sister, they're all big readers, but I think I'm the only one who ever tried to go into writing.

Pettus: Were you influenced by your parents?

Brown: Yeah. Yeah, we all kind of got to liking that early. We always read. All our lives. We'd see Mama doing it when we'd be little, you know, books, magazines, whatever. I guess we just kind of latched onto it after her. My daddy wasn't a reader, now, he didn't read at all.

Pettus: What was your early life like?

Brown: Well, I was born in Oxford, but I was raised out at Potlockney until I was about three, and then we moved to Memphis and lived up there for about ten years, then came back down here, and I've been back down here ever since. Except for two years I was in the service. I've lived at either Tula or Yocona for most of my life.

Pettus: You were in the marines, right?

Brown: Yeah, I was in the marines.

Pettus: Did you go to Vietnam?

Brown: No, I never did go over.

Pettus: When did you join?
Brown: I joined in 1970. Stayed in until '72.

Pettus: What made you join?
Brown: Well, when I was nineteen, that was when they had the lottery system going. That year, my birthday came up number one. And I was already classified 1-A. That was back when you'd get your physical and all when you were eighteen. Get classified. So the lady who ran the draft board called my mother and she told her, she said, "Now Larry's got about two weeks before the army drafts him, he's gone, you know, so if he wants to join another branch, like the Navy or the Air Force or the Marines, he'd better do it now." And I just decided that since I was going to have to go anyway, I'd join the marines. I figured they were about the toughest thing going. That's what I wanted to join. So I joined up.

Pettus: Do you think now it was a good thing to do?
Brown: Oh yeah. It was a great thing to do. Oh yeah, I wouldn't take anything for being in the marines for two years. Some of the best experiences of my life were in there. I was young then, single, yeah I had some good times back then. After I got out of Parris Island. Man, that was the bad place, there. That's where you don't want to go.

Pettus: Then you came back here?
Brown: Yeah, came back here, got married after a while, started raising a family. I started working at the fire department in December of '73. I've been there ever since. I've been there almost fifteen years. I made Captain finally.

Pettus: How long have you been a captain?
Brown: Oh, I've been a captain I guess about two and a half years, something like that.

Pettus: How did you get into being a fireman?
Brown: Well, at the time, it just looked a lot better than what I was doing. I was driving a fork lift in a stove factory. At Oxford. The hours seemed a lot better. The pay wasn't great, but I knew I could work another job on the off days and make more money that way, so that's what swayed me. I had to go to that. It was a hard place to get on, and it was and still is a very desirable place to work. I mean we've got our own department, we're kind of just out

there on our own, most of the time. When something bad happens, we take care of it. We take care of the town, take care of the university. It's just a good feeling. It's a good job to have when we do something right and stop a fire. There's no feeling like it because you've helped somebody.

Pettus: And you were working in a stove factory?
Brown: Yeah, a stove factory. I was driving a truck on the weekends, too, driving a truck up to Nashville and back just about every weekend. I was putting in about sixty or seventy hours a week.

Pettus: How many are you putting in now?
Brown: Let's see. I'd have to figure on it awhile. I'm putting in a lot. I can figure it right quick. I put 240 hours a month in at the fire department. It'd be . . . let's see . . . probably eighty-something hours a week.

Pettus: Does that count the writing time?
Brown: No, that don't count the writing. I have to do that with what's left over.

Pettus: How big is your store?
Brown: It's just a little small building. Not very large at all. Just a little small country grocery store. It's the only one we've got in Tula now.

Pettus: Do you sell a lot of groceries?
Brown: Well, not a whole lot. Mainly cigarettes and gas, chips and cokes. Stuff like that. We make sandwiches and stuff. We try to feed the deer hunters in the winter. We open up a little early and cook stuff for lunch and all that. We have a lot of customers who a lot of them are our friends, people we know and so forth, and we try to feed them when deer season's open. Everybody comes by there and eats.

Pettus: Do you think you'll keep writing about your area?
Brown: Yeah. Yeah, I think so. I've got a lot of stuff I still want to do about this place. I'm doing some of it now, but there's a lot in the future I want to do, a lot of stories I haven't even thought about writing yet. I wouldn't want to go anywhere else, I don't think, and stay any long period of time. This is my home and there's plenty here to write about. It's like Faulkner said, you know, his own little native postage stamp of soil.

Pettus: Do you know other writers?

Brown: Well, you meet people when you get a book published. More people that you have to talk to. It's just a gradual process, but I've got a lot of friends, and I've got a lot of friends I've met like just a few years ago, when my stories started to be published, who really liked them and stayed with me and encouraged me. All of those, they're just so glad for me. It's a great thing to have the support that I've got here in Oxford, because there are a lot of my friends here who are really behind me.

Pettus: Who has helped you more than anybody?

Brown: Well, the person who's helped me most is Richard Howorth, probably. He owns Square Books in Oxford. Richard got five hundred copies of my book early. Algonquin shipped him five hundred because I was reading at the Faulkner Conference and then we had my book party the next day. We sold a lot of books and now all these people, you know they're academic people, they're going back and telling their friends about it. I've already got two more offers for readings next year, from other colleges, so it's been a really positive thing.

Pettus: How has writing changed your life and could you stop?

Brown: Well, no, I couldn't live without it. It's going to eventually change my life to the way I want it to be. I hope. Which is what I've been trying for for so long, to be able to write full time. That has always been my goal.

Pettus: That would change your life?

Brown: Yeah. Change it drastically. Go from working so much to working none. I don't call this work because I love to do it.

Pettus: You don't think it's work?

Brown: I don't think it is, to me. I have too much fun with it. I mean there are times when it goes bad, sure. You want to shoot yourself because you can't think of anything to write for a couple days.

Pettus: Is it harder than it used to be?

Brown: I don't know. It's gotten easier, the older I've gotten, and the more I've written. I figure now I've written close to a million words. I used to figure it up every once in a while. Figure up 400,000 and go back a little later and figure some more, but it's been so long since I've figured and my pace has stayed pretty much the same, that I figure I'm getting close to a million words. That's a pretty good bit of typing.

Pettus: Is there any autobiography in your work?
Brown: Well, I think just about everything that I write has a little, a tiny bit of autobiography in it. I mean some stuff I will invent totally out of my imagination, and it may be only a phrase or a few words, but most of the time there'll be something from my life in there. Something I heard or saw, and remembered, most of the time. My editor says that's dangerous, for me to take so much stuff from my own life. She says it's kind of scary, sometimes, the way I take stuff from my own life. She thinks it takes a lot of bravery to do that, but it doesn't bother me.

Pettus: Do you think other writers do that?
Brown: Well, they may do it. I'm sure that's probably basically true. For most people, most writers. You've got to draw it from somewhere, you know. Stephen King says he draws from his well every day.

Pettus: When is the publication date of your book?
Brown: It's not going to be officially released until September 15. See, Richard just had these five hundred advance copies. Algonquin just kind of did us a favor and got some down here early.

Pettus: Have they sold well?
Brown: We've sold over three hundred in about two weeks. It's going good.

Pettus: What about "Boy and Dog"? Was that autobiographical?
Brown: Naw, I just kinda (huh huh huh) went a little wacky writing that one. It's a very strange story. It was published in *Fiction International* back in 1984. San Diego Press out there. I was trying to do something . . . I'm a big fan of [Donald] Barthelme. I was trying to think one day, now what could I write in some style that he's never written in before? I finally came up with telling the story in five words each on the line and one under another like a poem. I started writing it and it just came to me. I enjoyed it, though.

Pettus: Something that he hadn't done?

Brown: Right, something that he had not done. Because he had written so many stories in so many different styles, I mean just completely unorthodox styles, that it looked like he had covered just about all the ground anybody could cover. He's still doing it, but I was just trying to think of something a little different, and that's how the story came about. I've written different stories maybe in imitation of some of the people I admire, but nobody has really picked up on any of that too much. I don't think they've really made the comparison between me and my heroes and my heroes' style and my style.

Pettus: What about "Old Frank and Jesus"? What made you write in that style? And in that time frame?

Brown: Well, that time just kind of came to me. That's the oldest story in the book, by the way. That story was written in 1984. That frame of time, during the Vietnam war, in the sixties, and the Beatles, when they were big, and the kids were rebelling, and the parents didn't like it, that's just the time frame that hit me for the story. I mean, something different happens every time I sit down to write a story, like a . . . kind of like the Holy Grail once you get after it, that's all you want to do. That's all I want to do, is write. And I'm just glad that I finally found out what I want to do. And that I'm starting to have some success at it. That's the main thing. I was kind of really searching for a way to pull myself up out of poverty, and debt, for the rest of my life. And I thought, why don't you try this? Maybe this is something you're good at. I just kind of kept believing, and it's finally starting to happen. That's about the best way to explain it, I guess. I mean I didn't have any education, you know, my parents didn't, either, and I just felt like I was going to go nowhere with my life if I didn't get out and try to do something. I'd always liked reading and I decided to try writing.

Pettus: How old are you now?

Brown: I'm thirty-seven. I just turned thirty-seven back in July.

Pettus: Well I've enjoyed talking to you, Mr. Brown.

Brown: Well I've enjoyed talking to you, too, Gary, sure have.

Pettus: I appreciate all the time you took with me and I love your book.

Brown: I'm glad you like it, I sure am. Okay. Thanks a lot. Bye bye.

Book Beat Interview with Larry Brown

Don Swaim / 1989

This interview was conducted September 27, 1989, at the CBS Building, Manhattan, for the nationally syndicated CBS radio program *Book Beat*. Excerpts from the interview were used in a pair of *Book Beat* segments that aired on November 6 and 8, 1989, on WCBS-AM, New York, before being nationally syndicated by the CBS Radio Stations News Service. Audio text of the unabridged interview from the Donald L. Swaim Collections (MSS #177), Robert E. and Jean R. Mahn Center for Archives and Special Collections, Ohio University Libraries, Athens, Ohio. Transcript by Jay Watson. Used by permission.

DS: Let's talk about Larry Brown. I was reading this little booklet called "A Late Start," and I guess what this means is that you got a late start as a writer.
LB: Yeah.

DS: Why? Why did you get a late start?
LB: Well, I probably didn't start as early in life as most writers do. I was twenty-nine before I started. It just kind of hit me one day to finally try. I had been thinking about trying to write for a long time, and I finally just decided to undertake it about nine years ago. I'd been a reader all my life, you know, and had always loved books and reading. And I'd been wondering about how people taught themselves how to write and I decided I would just finally try to start learning how.

DS: You grew up in a working-class household, is that right?
LB: Mmm-hmm, yeah.

DS: What did your family do?
LB: I've been a firefighter for about sixteen years. My father did all kind of different jobs when I was growing up. You know, I'm from like you said a

15

working-class background. He farmed early on when I was born, when I was real small. That's what he'd been doing when I was born.

DS: Were they, I guess—is the term a migrant worker? The characters in *Dirty Work* certainly worked in the fields. How do you describe them? As migrants, or what?

LB: Well, he was sharecropping when I was born, which is where you hire on to work for a man and you use his land and he furnishes the tools, the equipment, the fertilizer and seed and all that, and you repay him with part of the crop.

DS: You grew up a good portion of your life in Memphis, didn't you?

LB: I lived there for about ten years, from the time I was three to thirteen.

DS: Did you do a lot of reading when you were young?

LB: Yeah, I did quite a bit. I started reading pretty prodigiously when I was small, and I always kept it up all my life.

DS: When you graduated from high school, if I read some of the publicity material, it didn't occur to you at that time to go on to a higher education, did it?

LB: No, it didn't really. About the only thing I was concerned with was just getting out and getting me a job and buying myself a car. I wanted to have a way to go and I didn't have any way to go, and I knew I couldn't have one until I went to work. So I didn't really have any interest in any higher education. I was mainly concerned with just getting out of school, getting through it, getting finished with it.

DS: Now in *Dirty Work,* the two protagonists of the book are Vietnam veterans. You served in Vietnam, didn't you?

LB: No, I never did serve in Vietnam. I was in the Marine Corps from '70 to '72, but I never did go to Vietnam.

DS: What kind of duty did you have in the Marine Corps?

LB: I stayed at Camp Lejeune for about half the time, in a guard company there. And then I was at Marine Barracks, Philadelphia, for about thirteen months, where I finished my tour.

DS: That sounds like an easy military career.

LB: (Laughs.) Yeah, it wasn't too bad.

DS: How did you get into the Marine Corps? Did you enlist?

LB: I enlisted back when the draft was going on. They had the lottery system, and they pulled everybody's birthday out one at a time, 365 days out of the year. July 9 is my birthday, and that year they pulled it out number one. And so I had already been classified, I was 1-A, and I knew I was going. So I just decided to join the Marines. I knew I wouldn't have any choice if the Army drafted me. So I went ahead and joined the Marines while I still had a choice to pick what branch of the service I wanted to go into.

DS: Why the Marines?

LB: I guess I wanted to see if I could make it, and they seemed like the toughest thing going. And I wanted to be in the best, you know.

DS: What happened after your two years in the Marines?

LB: I came back to Oxford. I went back to a job I had at a factory there in town, and about a year later I got on with the fire department, where I've been working ever since. I got on there in '73. And I married, raised a family, and then about 1980 I started trying to write seriously.

DS: What took you to Oxford to begin with?

LB: Oxford is only about ten miles away from where I was raised. Oxford is where I was born, and that's where all my family are. It's home, you know, my home.

DS: There's a fairly large literary shadow over Oxford, isn't there?

LB: Yeah, Faulkner. (Laughs.)

DS: In addition to your own, I mean.

LB: Well, I don't know how big mine is so far, but yeah, there is a big literary heritage there because of Faulkner and the university and all that. There's several writers who live in town there who are well known. Barry Hannah and Willie Morris both live there.

DS: So you joined the fire department, and—obviously it's not a volunteer fire department.

LB: No, it's a professional department.

DS: What was it like? What has it been like for you on the fire department, especially since you are spending a great portion of your time writing? I mean, do you get razzed by the other firemen, or what?

LB: No, I think they're pretty happy with what I've done. I brought some recognition to my department with my work and everything. I've had a pretty good bit of publicity about it, and they're happy to see me succeeding with my work, because I've been doing it for so long. They've been knowing about it for a long time. So they're glad to see me succeeding.

DS: You're a captain, though, now. They can't really razz you very much if you're a captain.

LB: No, they can't say too much. (Laughs.)

DS: (Laughs.) So about eight or nine years ago you started testing the waters in terms of writing. You had no experience, no formal training. Of course it is stated that it's almost impossible to teach anybody writing, that a writer has to learn it himself in some form. But you wanted to write, so tell me about your first effort.

LB: The first thing I wrote was a novel about a man-eating grizzly bear in Yellowstone National Park. This is the God's honest truth. I'd never been to Yellowstone National Park, and I wrote this terrible, terrible novel. And I thought it was good, and it would be published, you know, and I sent it off up here to New York and got my first rejection slip. It took me about five months to write that novel. It was 327 single-spaced pages. I didn't even know you were supposed to double-space back then. (Laughs.) I mean it was terrible, and I was crushed when it came back, you know, that they didn't publish it. But that was just kind of the tip of the iceberg. I decided, well, maybe I don't know enough to get one published. I'll write another one. And so I started another one, and I started writing some short stories. And then after about two years it dawned on me, this is going to be a lot longer haul than you figured on when you started out. But I just kept going. I had the belief that if I stayed at it long enough I would eventually learn how to do it right.

DS: So what was this process? You stayed at it long enough, but when you finished a story you looked at it? It's kind of difficult to appraise your own work, isn't it?

LB: It is when you start out. You don't have any objectivity at all. That's one of the hardest things to gain, some objectivity about your own work. You know, you're jaded by what you write yourself, and you don't really hold it up to what you admire. Or I didn't when I was starting out. And that was really one reason that I started reading more and more literature and finding out what it meant to read literature and how hard it was to write literature. So writing helped me become a better reader, because I started reading better and better writers. I started reading the best writers I could find, contemporary literature, stuff that was being published now. So it's just a long slow process for me, a combination of reading and writing both.

DS: Some teachers of creative writing often suggest to their students that they find an author they like and try to imitate that author or that style. Did you try that approach at all?

LB: Yeah, I used to try to imitate William Faulkner. I thought that was the way to go back then. But I found out that that's not it. You've got to write in your own style. You've got to find your own voice and your own way of telling stories. And that's what probably everybody who is trying to learn how to write is searching for, his own voice, how to be unique.

DS: Does he search for his own voice, or does he just settle into a pattern that emerges as his own voice?

LB: I don't know. Some people may. I try not to do the same way, the same thing each time. I try to be different with a piece of work. I like to experiment with the language and try and write in new forms occasionally. I like to mess around with the language all I can and not be stuck in just one particular pattern.

DS: You kept writing these short stories, and finally you got one published, didn't you?

LB: Yeah, I got one published in '82, in *Easyriders* magazine, the motorcycle magazine in Malibu, California. And I thought I had it made then. I thought I had broken through and I would sell everything else I had thereafter. But that wasn't the case. It was about two more years before I placed another story, and I was writing just all the time. I think I wrote thirty-nine short stories in 1983, and none of them were published.

DS: What did you do, just send these out to various magazines?
LB: I sent 'em everywhere. I kept stories out ten or twelve at a time, all the time, everywhere.

DS: You mean you group them in a batch you send out to a single publication?
LB: No, one to each different magazine. I would send ten or twelve out at a time, to ten or twelve different magazines.

DS: And they'd all come back.
LB: They'd all come back, yeah.

DS: I was talking to the short story writer Bobbie Ann Mason, with whom you may have something in common, to a degree, because her last novel was *In Country*, which has been filmed, also about Vietnam. And she was telling me, she was sitting right where you are, just a few months ago, and she was saying that even to this day the majority of her stories are rejected. One out of every dozen stories she sends off to the *New Yorker*—she has success with the *New Yorker*, but they'll turn down a dozen for every one. So she says her approach is this: she says, one, don't get discouraged, and two, have an ample supply of postage and envelopes. And she just keeps sending them out to the *Southern Review* and to various magazines. And she says eventually, it might take a couple of years, but eventually most of her stories have found a home.
LB: Yeah, I agree with that. If you believe in a piece of your own work strong enough, it doesn't matter how many rejection slips it collects. To me it just means that the right person hasn't seen it yet. And I don't let that discourage me.

DS: You finally got a number of short stories published. They were collected into a book, weren't they? Tell me about that.
LB: Yeah, that was my first book I published last year, called *Facing the Music*. And I wrote most of those probably in about a three- or four-year period from late 1984 through early 1988. And many of them had been rejected many times. One story in that collection had been rejected fifteen times. But all of them, I felt good about all of them, the ones that I wanted to put together for this book. When Shannon Ravenel first contacted me about trying to put one together, she asked if I had enough stories to publish in a

collection. And I said, yeah, I've got about a hundred, how many do you want to see? But I was kind of just kidding, I said I've really only got probably about ten or fifteen that would be good enough to publish. And from that group we came up with this collection of stories.

DS: I assume that the story you sent to *Easyriders* magazine was not in the collection?
LB: No, that was not in there. (Laughs.)

DS: (Laughs.) Well, now we're almost up to date with *Dirty Work*. This is your new novel, published by this wonderful little publishing house called Algonquin Books, and they have so much interesting literature that they send up. And I know they have a contract recently to distribute their books through the Workman Press, which was a good thing for them. Tell me how *Dirty Work* developed as a book.
LB: I built a new house in 1986. I took about six months off from writing anything at all, to build this house. And I moved to it in August of '86, and I moved the table into my dining room. And I sat down the first day I was in that house, and I started writing a story about a guy who had come back from Vietnam and he stayed in his room all the time, he wouldn't go out and see anybody. His face was all messed up from shrapnel damage and all, and he didn't want anybody to see him. So that's initially where I began *Dirty Work*, and I took it through about three drafts over the next, probably, year and a half. And in the meantime now we put this first collection together. But after the collection was published, and I had the third draft ready, I showed it to Shannon Ravenel, my editor, and I started working on it even harder. And we sent pages back and forth, back and forth, back and forth, and I started working on the story more, refining it more, and carried it through about two more complete drafts. And by the time I wound up with it I had thrown away about six hundred pages, besides what appears in the book. And the whole process of writing took me about two and a half years.

DS: You kept the narrative very tight. But one good thing you had with Shannon Ravenel, you weren't working in a vacuum, you did have some help.
LB: Right.

DS: And so you got a different perspective as you—

LB: It's a lot better to have her working with me than to just be by myself, because she's got her own objectivity about it. She's just a wonderful editor, and she cares so much about the work, and she wants it to be as good as it possibly can. She can point out to me my mistakes in a constructive way that helps me see what I need to work on harder and what I need to strengthen, what I need to de-emphasize, or whatever. And it's not an easy process. We had arguments about certain things in there. But we were both working toward having a good novel, a novel that I could finally publish. Because I had written five others before this one, and none of them had been published. So this was just kind of like the culmination of all the years I had spent trying to learn how to do this. She helped me finally put this book together.

DS: Well, let's hope it's not the culmination!

LB: Well . . . (Laughs.)

DS: Let's hope you have many more books in you. When you write, some teachers say, forget grammar, forget spelling, forget punctuation—just get the story on. Was this your approach?

LB: Yeah, that's my idea. There's a lot of stuff in there that's not grammatically correct. Just the way Braiden talks, the black character in there. I like to go with dialogue the way it sounds in the ear, rather than how it's supposed to be on the page. I want to write it so that the reader hears it in his ear like how it would sound coming out of somebody's mouth.

DS: Oh, that's why I like to write dialogue that way, too, because you're not bound to any grammatical rules.

LB: Right, you can do anything you want to with it that way.

DS: Now here is the story of two Vietnam veterans, both in the hospital, one without legs and arms, the other with a shattered face and mental problems because of the bullet that hit him, for which he was treated in the Philippines. Such a sad story. Did you know how it was going to come out at the end?

LB: Yeah, I had an idea. I had a pretty positive idea of how it had to end as I was going through it. One of these characters was kind of modeled after a guy that I knew when I was in the Marine Corps. And of course Braiden, he came along later. I originally started the novel about the guy who stayed in his room all the time, but Braiden came along much later. But eventually, through writing the story, writing it over and over I figured out how everything was eventually going to turn out. And that's usually the way I work. I don't often know what I'm trying to say when I start writing it, but by writing it and refining it I find out what I'm gonna do with it. I can never finish anything in one draft. I usually revise quite a bit.

DS: You have wonderful reviews—they sent a lot of these up here—a lot of interesting articles. I guess you're quite a celebrity now in Oxford?
LB: Well, I don't know. (Laughs.) They're pretty excited about me being on the *Today* show tomorrow. They're all up in the air about that. Everybody's—

DS: Are you nervous?
LB: Not too bad I don't think. I don't think I'm too bad over it now.

DS: (Laughs.) That's all right. They're only going to give you two and a half minutes.
LB: Yeah. (Laughs.) It can't be too painful, can it?

DS: They never really talk about the art of writing anyway. I mean, they'll probably ask you about your career as a fireman, a fire captain, and how do you reconcile writing and. . . . How *do* you reconcile writing with being a fire captain? (Both laugh.) But I guess you work shifts, don't you?
LB: Yeah, I work a shift. I work twenty-four on, forty-eight off. And I don't mix the two. I work when I'm at home, and that's the only time I work. Usually when I'm on duty, if I'm not doing anything, if we don't have a fire going or some training or something, I sit there and read. And that's where I catch up on all my reading, that's when I'm on duty.

DS: But you might go all day without a fire, right?
LB: Yeah.

DS: Ten-hour shift?
LB: Mmm-hmm.

DS: Why can't you do some writing there, or would they frown on it?
LB: No, they wouldn't frown on it. It's usually that there's too much noise going on, a card game or television or somebody hollering at somebody or something. I work with some kind of wild boys, you know. It's kind of noisy around there sometimes. (Laughs.)

DS: (Laughs.) You've been making some appearances at literary conferences, haven't you? What's that like for you?
LB: Well, it's real nice. You know, it's nice to get up in front of people and read my work and hear them applaud. It's a really, really good feeling to take what I've been doing on the page and get up and read it and have people appreciate it. It's a great feeling, it really is.

DS: Are you at the point now where you're sharing notes and comments with other writers about the craft?
LB: I'm beginning to have quite a few younger writers asking me for help through the mail. And I'm trying to help them when I can, when I think they deserve some help. I mean, I try to be honest with them and tell them, well, this is good or this is not good or you need to do better. I know what I went through looking for help when I was starting out, and people were very generous to me with their time. And so I'm trying to help them as much as I can, too.

DS: A lot of criticism—for example, rejection of stories or rejection of novels—is simply an opinion, someone's opinion. It doesn't mean too much. I mean, the tales are myriad of stories that have been turned down over and over and over and they'll pop up and they'll become a critical success or even a best-seller. It happens all the time.
LB: Yeah. Yeah, it's pretty common. Sure is.

DS: Did you read *Sophie's Choice* by William Styron?
LB: No, I haven't read that one, sure haven't.

DS: Well, you ought to read that because there's a section in that book at the beginning where Styron had come to New York from his native Virginia, and was working at McGraw-Hill, which then occupied an ugly green office building on West 42nd Street very close to the river. (They're now on Sixth

Avenue.) And it was a publishing house, and still is to a degree, which was very conservative, and people always wore suits and ties, and Styron wasn't really like that. But he was an editor there, and one day a manuscript came in, and he looked at this book—he was giving them trouble anyway, because he was kind of a maverick, he would always come in carrying the New York *Post*, which was then a very left-wing newspaper. So this manuscript came in, and he said, "This is awful." He wrote a critique, he said, "This is terrible, this is about a bunch of Norwegians sailing the Pacific on a raft." He said, "This has absolutely no interest to anybody." Well, the manuscript went to another publishing house and turned out to be Thor Heyerdahl's *Kon-Tiki*, which was a worldwide best-seller, and finally McGraw-Hill said, "Enough, Styron, enough!" and they let him go.

LB: (Laughs.)

DS: But even Styron's opinion about this manuscript was an opinion. And somebody else picked it up and made a best-seller out of it.

LB: Yeah, there're so many things you don't have any control over even if you are writing on a competent level. Even if you have a good story, you can always send it off and have the wrong person see it, a person in power, a person who has the right to accept it or reject it, and just because that person doesn't agree with it that particular day, he sends it back home. And it's hard then, and that's what makes you uncertain, and that's one of the scariest things about it when you're starting out. You've got to have somebody else reinforce your opinion that your work is good. I had that happen to me several times, but there's really not that much you can do about it. Just, if you believe in it, keep sending it out. Keep sending it out.

DS: So I guess your advice to struggling writers is try not to get discouraged, keep sending them out.

LB: Yeah, yeah, just keep on. If you believe in yourself, and if you want to apply yourself hard enough, I think anything is possible.

DS: Well, Larry Brown, *Dirty Work*, it's a beautifully done novel. I am sure it's not going to be the last one. Congratulations.

LB: Thanks a lot.

DS: Thank you.

Larry Brown: Proceeding out from Calamity

Susan Ketchin / 1991

Originally published in *Southern Quarterly: A Journal of the Arts in the South* 32.2 (Winter 1994): 95–109. Reprinted in Ketchin, *The Christ-Haunted Landscape: Faith and Doubt in Southern Fiction* (Jackson: University Press of Mississippi, 1994): 126–39. Used by permission.

My interview with Larry Brown took place over the course of three meetings, in the Mississippi towns of Tula and Taylor and in Durham, North Carolina. Though we had met before this, our talks about religion and fiction began in July 1991, when my family and I came to Mississippi for a visit on the occasion of Brown's fortieth birthday.

Having met Richard Howorth (to whom the story "Facing the Music" is dedicated) at his Oxford store, Square Books, my husband and I followed him to Taylor, about ten miles south of Oxford, to surprise Larry at a catfish place where Mary Annie, his wife, had told us they would be eating supper. Kudzu was growing two or three stories high on both sides of the state road between Oxford and Taylor. There were no billboards, roadsigns, or markers to guide us along the twists and turns on the backroads—nothing for miles, it seemed, but dark kudzu in the summer twilight.

Taylor Restaurant is situated at a sharp bend in the road; it and a one-room post office constitute most of downtown Taylor. Worn, sagging wooden steps lead to its narrow porch. One solid wooden carpenter's bench sits outside the entrance; on the other side of the black, double screen doors is the drink box. People come here from all around to eat catfish and drink beer, especially on Friday nights after work. Huge live oak trees— "must be two hundred years old," someone said—brood over the sandy sideroads and walks. We waited in the heat in the gravel parking lot (though it was past seven in the evening, it was still over 90 degrees and humid) until we saw Mary Annie and Larry go inside. A moment later, we walked in to find them in a booth in back.

Larry Brown is a slightly built but strong and wiry-looking fellow, whose face shows years of hard work and pain. He has fine features (a long thin nose, sad hazel eyes) and sunburned skin from many years in the Mississippi sun.

Sitting at a long wooden table big enough for the eight people who had gathered to celebrate, we ate fresh, fried catfish, french fries, cole slaw, hush puppies, and homemade fried apple pie. The slatted floors creaked as customers walked to and from the combination bathroom/broom closet in back; ropes of exposed wiring crawled up the walls to the pressed tin ceiling and over it like snakes toward two or three overburdened outlets. Stark puddles of light emanated from bare bulbs in the high ceiling.

The waitress brought platters of fried fish, as fast as the owner could fry them, to the tables from the grill that ran the length of one side of the room. Initials and hearts, names and platitudes, were carved all over the boothbacks and walls. Larry was in a bemused and philosophical (though by no means solemn) mood. He talked readily about the meaning of his fiction, and of the good life—what it takes, who's got it, who doesn't, and why; after about the third platter of food and that many pitchers of beer, we concluded that truth in fiction, and truth in friendship, not to mention truth *in vino*, figure prominently. Our booth was near the jukebox; we played "I Fall to Pieces" and "You Don't Know About Lonely 'Til It's Chiselled in Stone" for Larry— Patsy Cline and Vern Gosdin easing him into his forty-first year.

That fall, Brown came to give a reading from his novel *Joe* at the Regulator Bookshop, an independent bookstore in Durham. Dressed in his usual Lee jeans, baseball cap, tweed jacket, cowboy boots, and a Flannery O'Connor t-shirt (he opened his jacket to display the front—a large caricature of O'Connor clutching a Bible, with a comical-looking peacock in the background), he smoked Camels and looked a little nervous. "I always hate it on the road," he says. "I don't sleep too good away from home."

People began to drift in for the reading an hour and a half early, some visiting a moment or two with Brown, a few asking him to sign books. The store owner showed us a sun-filled room in back where we could talk quietly for an hour or so before the reading. As always, I was struck by Brown's quiet manner—he speaks in a low, soft Mississippi accent, an undertone of sorrow everpresent in it; his hazel eyes seem to look far off and deep within as he talks. When he speaks about ancient myths and the lure and power of storytelling in ancient cultures, it strikes me that he's been there. He is an "old soul."

Ketchin: Let's talk about "Facing the Music." People not only seem to react very strongly to that story, but there seems to be a remarkable disparity in their reactions. Some decry it as unrealistically bleak; others see it as a story about redemption—or at least that its ending redeems the bleakness by suggesting hope in the midst of loss. What were you thinking as you wrote this story and what is your reaction to it now?

Brown: It's true that most of the stuff I write about does come from things I've seen, or lived through myself—with the exception of "Facing the Music." It's funny. People think that story is autobiographical. I get letters all the time about that one from people consoling me and my wife about "her mastectomy." But this story is really about pain and loss wherever you find it. I just believe that my fiction, anybody's fiction, is simply supposed to illuminate the human condition, tell us something about ourselves. I did see it as having a hopeful ending.

Ketchin: Your fiction does seem to reach its fullest power when you are writing about what lies at the heart of human suffering. One of the most powerful scenes in your first novel, *Dirty Work*, occurs when Jesus comes to Braiden at his hospital bed. As Jesus lights a cigarette for him, the paralyzed Braiden asks how long he must continue to suffer. This scene portrays a startlingly human Jesus who suffers along with the world in sorrow and grief.

Brown: Some people get upset about that scene. They want to know whether the scene is actually occurring. Is Jesus actually there, or is it a vision, or something in Braiden's mind? To tell you the truth, I don't know. Braiden—he's helpless. He's tired. He wants suicide. But he has no way to do it. He doesn't think it's wrong any more. He believes in it. By that I mean, he believes God is merciful, and that he's suffered enough; he can't stand any more. He longs for death. It's not a sin in his case. I can understand Braiden. But I believe the Lord don't ever put more on you than you can bear.

Some people just have harder lives than others. I've got an aunt who I figure is probably one of the most devout Christian people that there is in the world. I know a lot of other people who profess to be that, but who don't live life—I don't believe they live it—or practice their religion the way that she does, and her mama before her, my grandmother, all my aunts. Some people have such a harder time than other people do, some people have to pay more in life, I don't know why.

Ketchin: It makes you understand why one might consider giving up, or suicide. Some of your fiction seems to deal with this notion.

Brown: For a long time, I've been trying to understand suicide, and I do see how it is not a sin for some people, in some cases. The story "Old Frank and

Jesus" is drawn from a man who used to cut my hair. One day, he borrowed a pistol and shot himself through the head. I knew him well—I'd picked cotton with him and things like that. There was no outward indication of any trouble. That was when I began imagining, What is the pressure? What would cause someone to do that? Years later, I learned that he had been losing his land to taxes. He'd lost twenty, thirty acres. Mr. P. in the story was concerned with two things he couldn't understand: How could anybody be so mean to Jesus? How did he let his wife talk him into shooting his old dog? That kind of despair was what I was thinking about in "Samaritans," too. Since then, I've known others who were caught in something like that.

Ketchin: Does the story end in despair?

Brown: I was thinking about despair when I wrote that story. Mr. P. was at the end of his rope. There was no help for him, the pressures were too much. I wanted to show how the loss of love can bring it on, can bring on very strong emotions. Grief can kill you, I mean literally, it can. When Harry Crews talked about his boy drowning, he said you think you are going to die. That you couldn't survive that. Most of the time, you can, but sometimes you can't. When our baby died, in 1977, I didn't think I would survive. It was a very rocky time . . . tough. You meet other people who have suffered the same thing. It comes up in conversation—it's the same each time—you never get over it.

But my fiction is about people surviving, about people proceeding out from calamity. I write about loss. These people are aware of their need for redemption. We all spend our time dealing with some kind of hurt and looking for love. We are all striving for the same thing, for some kind of love. But love is a big word. It covers a lot of territory. I try to tell it in a fresh, new way, to be innovative.

Ketchin: Several of the titles of your stories refer to biblical images, maybe in an ironic way. Tell me about the origins of the titles "Old Frank and Jesus" and "Samaritans."

Brown: Even though "Samaritans" has a suggestive title, it's not a "message story." I wanted it to say a lot of things, some contradictory. Like, it's about the futility of helping people who do nothing to help themselves, the outcasts of society. But it's also about that it's a good thing to try. That's what Jesus would have done. It's an ironic title.

Ketchin: Partly because it's in the plural. Only one character in the story actually acts like the Good Samaritan of the parable, yet the title suggests that other people in the story, including the itinerants, could be considered Samaritans. Do you see your stories as growing out of a particular view of God and humankind?

Brown: I'm asked about this a lot of times, and I always say I think it's evident in my work, in some of it anyway. I don't take a specific stand about things like that, but it's in there, in certain stories, in certain models. I think a lot about God in the humanity of Jesus, like with the conversation between Braiden and Jesus. It helps me. But most of my stories aren't directly concerned with religion—except for "A Roadside Resurrection." Now that is a religious story. It's about a real faith healer, someone who really heals the afflicted. It's all about faith and trust, where they come from. This famous healer has lost his faith, but no one knows it yet. It has humor in it, too. There is an ex-Elvis impersonator who needs healing.

Ketchin: It is, in fact, a very funny story.

Brown: I've always thought being able to write humor is the mark of a superior writer, but it's going to ruin me. People think I'm mocking their beliefs, and I'm not. I have a strong belief in God.

Ketchin: Tell me more about that. What do you believe are the origins of your belief, for instance?

Brown: I was raised in the Methodist church in Memphis. That's where all my cousins, aunts, and uncles went. When we moved, we went to a country church, Mama's church, for a while. We belong to a Methodist church here, but I don't go like I should. My faith has gotten deeper over the years. It seems to have developed because of the suffering I see—of mine and of others. I believe suffering is here to make you strong. See what you can endure. Some are weak, some are stronger.

Ketchin: It is often said that your experiences as a firefighter shaped your vision as a person and as a fiction writer. How about your beliefs?

Brown: I write about life-and-death situations in my nonfiction book that I am working on now, *On Fire*. Sometimes things would happen where you'd get put in an utterly helpless position. When it was really bad was when everybody would be looking at me: What we gonna do, Captain Brown? So, when you've got the rank, and you're drawing the pay, it's up to you. Somebody's life can be in your hands, and it's a heavy responsibility.

The bad thing is, you've got fifty or a hundred people standing there watching you, watching every mistake you make, ain't going to miss a thing. They ain't going to walk off and leave. And you got to do something. And you're going to hear all this noise, people second-guessing you afterward. I could hardly stand to do it, sometimes, the situation would be so bad, but I had to kind of detach myself from my feelings about what the person was going through. In most cases, I could not concentrate on their pain, I could only concentrate on the speed and efficiency of my crew in removing the person from the situation, so that they could go to the hospital.

Ketchin: If you thought about their pain, you wouldn't be able to move them because it would hurt them too much.
Brown: That's right. And you know, you sometimes have people there screaming, "Y'all are killing me, you're killing me!" What can you do? You're there to try to help them and remedy the situation. But it's a very nerve-wracking business to be in. But it wasn't the excitement that I left, it was the boredom. The hours sitting there with nothing going on, and I was wishing I was home writing.

Ketchin: You got caught between two worlds?
Brown: Yes. But I didn't back off from anything I ever got sent to. I always preferred to be the first one there, so that I could size it up, and figure out what was going on, whether I had to call in more people, or certain pieces of equipment, or whatever.

Ketchin: Many southerners speak vividly of the time when they were "saved" as being as emotionally intense an experience as they have ever undergone. Have you had such an experience?
Brown: I've felt I've been saved many, many times. No joke. Once, when I worked as a fireman, my partner, a black guy, and I worked a long time together—for hours, one night, to get someone out of a car that was wrapped around a telephone pole. It was a boy who had this terrible, terrible wreck. Inside the city limits. Normally, you wouldn't have that bad an accident inside the city limits. I can't remember whether this boy was running from the police, or what, but he'd wrapped his car completely around a telephone

pole. It was on the right side of the street, headed the wrong way, so the driver's door was up against this pole. His chest was all broken up internally, he was bleeding out the mouth, ears, nose, and everywhere else. This nurse was in the seat with him, trying to clear his airway with a piece of surgical tubing, which was steadily getting clogged with blood. So the boy was in real danger of dying right there, but there wasn't any way for him to come out. His legs were in this door behind him, and his body was lodged over up against the shifter. That's what had him caught. This nurse was screaming at me to do something; I was in charge of the crew. But I just couldn't see any way to bring him out. He was going to lay right there and die before we could get him out. Only thing I could see was that he couldn't come out sideways, he'd have to come out straight up. So I said, Okay, we'll chop the windshield out, reach in and bend the shifter off of him, and bring him out.

That's what we did. We covered him up in a blanket and took our fire axes and chopped around the windshield, pulled it out, and throwed it out on the street. I climbed up on the hood and reached down for the shifter, but I couldn't bend it. So, Mack was there, the black guy who worked with me. I told him to get up here and help me. I said, "Put your hand on top of mine, let's bend the shifter, that's what's got him hung." He nearly crushed my hand with his, but the thing started moving. We bent it on over. We both fell down into the floorboards, but we got it off of him. Then we put the backboard on the boy, pulled traction on it, and brought him on out. They loaded him in the ambulance, took him on down to the hospital. He lived, too. When things like that happen, it makes you really realize the preciousness of life. The whole rescue depended on the strength of this one guy's arm pushing the gear shift out of the way.

It's about life and death—the real thing. I had another experience one time like that that I would call a conversion experience. It was a truly religious experience. When my partner—that black guy I was telling you about—died, he died while he was rabbit hunting, real quick. Had a stroke. I went to his church for the funeral. And the ladies coming in, and they're starting to sing; they don't have any hymnals in their hands. It was in the summertime, and it was this church, way way out in the woods. I mean off this sure-enough tiny pig trail. We had to take the fire trucks up there, and it was muddy. It was really bad. And the place he was buried in was a really scrubby little piece of pitiful land with these stunted trees and weeds and just wasn't a pretty place to be buried. But they all had this faith, and the way it came out was that this preacher stood up and started preaching and then he got to moving and he got to kind of rocking and rolling and people started getting excited. They'd jump up and holler, "Amen! Yeah brother, tell it!" You know, we were just sitting there just looking around with our white faces. And it just made me see how strong they were, how much faith they had, and it also made me realize that God ain't got no color. It's something I wouldn't ever forget. One God, no particular color, one God for everybody.

Ketchin: Your fiction reveals this same intensity of feeling.
Brown: All kinds of things have a deep meaning to me. All kinds of experiences. They move me. When I write, all I'm doing is trying to tell a story. Above all is the art. Your art must evolve from your experience and it must evolve as art.

Ketchin: You have told me that some folks have criticized the violence, the alcoholism, and the graphic language and so on in your work. They point to the "brutality" in your work, its sexism, and the so-called "antireligious" nature of it.
Brown: I can't be concerned about who's going to think what. I try to make as good a story as I can, and let the chips fall where they may. I can't write to please others; I must please me. I must trust my own judgment, and above all, I must be honest. Your art must evolve from your honesty, your experience. If they are seeing only negative things in my fiction, then they aren't reading it right, not seeing what's there.

Ketchin: What do you think impels you to create fiction?
Brown: At around age thirty, I realized that I was still being bossed by someone else. I had done about everything I could think of, being a fireman, setting out trees, a carpenter's helper, and so on. I was married and had three kids by then. I realized I must do something else with my life, make something of myself. I had always loved books and reading; it was what I cared most about. I figured writing was the only thing I could teach myself to do on my own.

I checked out books from the library by the armload—Flannery O'Connor, Raymond Carver, William Faulkner, Harry Crews, Cormac McCarthy. I found out that I wanted to write "literature," the kind of stories that I had read over and over again. At first, I thought it would be simple.

It's not. I think everybody who wants to write well has to go through an apprenticeship, with a blind faith that says you can't take no for an answer. In a way it was like the Marine Corps—it's all in your mind. To be successful in boot camp or in writing, you must become an automaton: keep going, keep working, keep believing. And I've always believed in the trash can as a valuable tool. I burned a novel one time.

Ketchin: You did not.
Brown: Burned it in the back yard. I sure did. I felt like I had to.

Ketchin: How come?
Brown: Wasn't any good. And there wasn't any saving it. I had it finished and it didn't work. I said I believe it's a kindness to take that into the woods and burn it, lose it forever. I think the main thing was that in destroying it, I knew that I was never going to see it again or be able to. Once I made that decision, it was irrevocable. That work was up in smoke just like the paper was.

Ketchin: Did burning it free you?
Brown: Yes. I wrote two more bad ones, wrote five bad ones altogether, before *Facing the Music* was published. Over time I came to love the act of writing, the inventing, the imagining of a character. Now, it's not even work, and when it's going well, it's pure recreation.

Ketchin: Let's talk more about "A Roadside Resurrection." It has just recently come out in the *Paris Review*. What are some reactions you've gotten to that story?
Brown: People seem to be spellbound by it. It's the idiot, I think. In fact, I'm spellbound by it. It's a wild story. The writing of it was a process of discovery, one of those things that just started telling itself. The first draft took a week—it was really cooking, burning to be finished. The rhythm of the words developed a life of its own; it assumed its own way of being told. I revised it at least six times to take out stuff and tighten my control on the language. The story just came—it was as if I were just a transmitter.

The main character, the youthful healer, is ambiguous. He's lost his faith. He is caught up in a dilemma. What is he going to do? Has God turned his face away from him? Flenco, the ex-Elvis impersonator's wife, is on a quest of faith, too, but she doesn't get what she wants. She believes if she can just find him then everything's going to be okay. But the faith healer has no awareness that this woman's looking for him. It's not even a part of his life.

Ketchin: Tell me about the ending of the story. The crosses on the roadside— what did they suggest to you?
Brown: The crosses at the end of the story are a mystery to me. You see them all over the South, along the sides of roads and interstates. I've seen them in Mississippi, Alabama, Georgia. Nobody knows where they come from. Who puts them up? Nobody ever sees them being put up. It's a great deal of trouble—they're huge, like telephone poles.

Ketchin: It may be stretching it a bit, but just as those crosses might be seen to be imposing a startling image of faith on the consciousness of those who are driving by, do you see your stories as possibly posing startling problems of faith for the reader?
Brown: Yes, I do, sure do. I think any literature, if it's going to be any good, has to be about right and wrong, good and bad, good versus evil. Like my novel, *Joe*. Joe must do something bad to get rid of the evil in his world. He must do what he does (he gives them plenty of warning, too), but he must do what he does as a moral imperative. Even though he wasn't directly affected, Joe felt he must take care of the problem. Joe knows that evil is real, not some abstraction. Whatever good is in this world has to have teeth in it if evil is to be dealt with.

Ketchin: Is there redemption in this suffering, any hope for these characters?
Brown: You can't tack a happy ending on tragedy. Braiden in *Dirty Work*, for example, loves his life. It was what he wanted all along. But his problems are too much. He wants release. In his case it is not a sin to seek suicide. The ministers I've talked to about this story agree with me. God wouldn't punish Braiden; God would pity him. Braiden has a strong, unwavering faith in God. He seeks release and peace.

Ketchin: Why do you think so many southern writers write about religion? Somehow it always seems to come up, whether it's Faulkner's sermon in *The Sound and the Fury*, or the three crosses and the faith healer in "A Roadside Resurrection," or simply in a title that gets you thinking, like "Samaritans."

Brown: Well, I think in my case religion crops up so much because I heard it all my life. From the earliest times I can remember, I was in the church, raised in the church, went to Sunday school, vacation Bible school, church on Sunday night, church on Sunday morning, all that stuff. And my whole family was heavily involved in it. I think probably the reason it crops up in so many other southern writers' works is for the same reason. Because they were exposed to so much of it at an early age, it makes an impression on them.

Ketchin: Harry Crews has said that he feels matters of life and death, and suffering and meaning, so deeply that he has to write about them in his fiction, sort out these emotions through his characters. The characters themselves start talking to him about their struggles.

Brown: Yeah, I've seen other writers that are doing it, too. Cormac McCarthy's got a couple of lines—this preacher is travelling around, doing this talking, and he said, "A blind feller hollered out one day and said, 'Look at me' (and he only had one leg). He said, 'Look at me, legless and everything; I reckon you think I ought to love God.' And the feller said, 'Yeah,' said, 'I reckon you ought. An old blind mess and legless fool is a flower in the garden of God.'"

Ketchin: Fiction, you were saying, has to be about some kind of moral problem or faith problem. Southern writers seem to say that about fiction more often and more openly than writers of other regions do. Notable southern writers, you and others such as Robert Penn Warren and William Faulkner, have talked very compellingly about the moral imperative of fiction, that is, that it must deal with these ultimate questions of good and evil, life and death.

Brown: Yes, that's what my fiction is about and I guess that's what religion is all about, too. The basic concept is either to be good or to be bad. And in order to be good you got to fight the bad. So those are the issues that most of my characters are struggling with. They are struggling to be good people. They know the difference between good and bad, and right and wrong. They don't always do what's right, because they're imperfect, like all of us. Like all people. And I try to give my characters those human traits that we all recognize and all have and all feel. I try to make them as real as I can. And therefore, very simply, a story's about a person who has a problem, and he or she will either resolve that problem or they will not resolve that problem. The problems may be many-faceted, especially in the course of a novel. In a good novel there is always something going on: either they are not satisfied with their life, or they have some major problem that's disrupting their life. I mean if you go along happy-go-lucky, one scene to another, nothing ever happens, there's never any trouble, everybody in the world is nice and treats everybody with kindness, that's not representative of the real world, and it's not representative of a real novel, either. It's got to be a major struggle. More than one, nothing simple.

Ketchin: And you pile them on, too.

Brown: Yes, I pile 'em on. I think you should sandbag your characters—load 'em up with as much as you can, then see what they do. That's why I make things so tough on them. I want them to have some kind of conflict going on within themselves and with the other characters around them. I think the thing to do is pull the character in early in the first few sentences and keep him. And once you get him by the throat, don't let him go. Don't let him go until you're finished with him. The way I look at a novel, the way I tell a novel's finished, is the point when I think I have done all I can for them, have helped the characters as much as I can, helped them all I can.

Ketchin: And these characters mostly, well, all of them except Wade in the novel, *Joe*, and that idiot-monster in "A Roadside Resurrection," it seems to me, are basically well-meaning people.

Brown: I have some bad people in my stories, but they're there as antagonists. They're the ones who are making the problems.

Ketchin: And even Wade is human.

Brown: Yeah, he's human. He doesn't have very many redeeming human qualities about him—

Ketchin: Can't think of any.

Brown: Can't think of a thing.

Ketchin: He's incorrigible, yet, it doesn't come across as if it's being done for effect. He, unfortunately, is all too human.

Brown: He's got some concerns. But his are mainly selfish, pertaining to himself only.

Ketchin: Atavistic, primitive concerns. Right now, I am reading in *Joe* where Wade has killed a black guy for his food coupons. Wade laid his hands on something in the grass, picked it up and knocked the man's brains out.
Brown: Yeah, Joe and him have difficulties, a hard time.

Ketchin: In the book I'm doing, I'm ascribing a chapter title to each author which will try to capture what each author is about. Reynolds Price, for example, said that most of his characters might be termed "saintly outlaws," that is, good-hearted people who live and act, nonetheless, outside the norms of society. Harry Crews talks about the writer as shaman or healer in a society because he sees that the sacred role of the writer in the community is to tell stories about who we are. How would you describe your characters or your role as writer in this regard?
Brown: Some of my work is on the other side of reality sometimes. Maybe you would want to describe my work in terms of myths and dreams. *Dirty Work* involves so much myth you're not able to tell what's real and what's not, sometimes.

Ketchin: Myths and dreams.
Brown: Yes, and that's the way I want it to be. I wanted the reader to be uncertain what really was occurring, what was fantasy and what was reality.

When I read the *Iliad* and the *Odyssey* when I was little, on my own, it got me thinking in terms of myths and dreams; I was really into Greek mythology, all the battles and gods, what each one did and what each one was responsible for. They formed the core of my belief about storytelling.

Ketchin: What do you see as the importance of storytelling?
Brown: I think people depend on storytellers down through history to carry on the stories of things that came before. When Alex Haley went all the way to Africa chasing down his ancestors, he got finally to that village where Kunta Kinte was from and the guy there told the story that many years ago, there was another person in our tribe named Kunta Kinte who went into the woods to get wood for a drum and we never saw him again, and that was the day they kidnapped him and put him on a slave ship and brought him to America. That was the storyteller's job, to keep all the information and to relay it—the whole history of not only his tribe but also the individual families and what all had happened before. And once he made that

connection, he knew irrevocably that this was his family; he knew where he was from and thus who he was.

Ketchin: Before we go, can you tell me how you think living where you do, in Yocona, Mississippi, has shaped your writing?
Brown: Well, for one thing, I'm the real native son of Oxford. Faulkner wasn't from around here. He was from Ripley, sixty miles away. Seriously, though, living in the country shapes my whole life and work. My writing is formed by the people, by the lives they lead around here, and the land. In the country, you can swim, fish, ride your bike on dirt roads. I hate cities. I lived for ten years in Memphis, and I was not happy. Things here are peaceful, quiet, no hassles. When I spent some time in Los Angeles, I got downright scared. It's depressing.

That's where my fiction comes from, I think. I use everything: memory, imagination, and what people have told me. Like with "Waiting for the Ladies" —the guy in that exposed himself at a dumpster. There was a real guy like that and I followed him once. He was simply not right in the head.

Publishers Weekly Interviews Larry Brown: The Former Firefighter Talks about His Long Apprenticeship as a Writer

Bob Summer / 1991

From *Publishers Weekly* 238.45 (11 October 1991): 46–47. Used by permission.

In 1980 Larry Brown decided to become a writer, although this son of a Mississippi sharecropper had failed senior English in high school and had little in his hardscrabble background that hinted of a literary bent. Nevertheless, ten years later, Algonquin Books of Chapel Hill has published his well-received short story collections *Facing the Music* (1988) and *Big Bad Love* (1990), as well as *Dirty Work* (1989), hailed as the most powerful anti-war novel since Dalton Trumbo's *Johnny Got His Gun.* But if the unanimous prepublication raves for *Joe*, a novel that Algonquin will release this month, are harbingers of what's to come, Brown's reputation and readership are poised to expand dramatically.

Brown's unusual track record indicates that he did indeed have a talent for writing when he attempted eleven years ago a (never published) novel about a man-eating bear in Yellowstone National Park—a place he had never seen. But the forty-year-old ex-marine and former fireman emphatically disagrees.

"There's no such thing as a born writer," he contends. "It's a skill you've got to learn, just like learning how to be a bricklayer or a carpenter. You've got to write X number of words before you can write anything that can be published, but nobody is able to tell you how many words that is. You will know when you get there, but you don't know how long it will take."

That's hindsight learned the hard way, as Brown acknowledges on a hot morning in August before he returns to Middlebury, Vermont, for the Bread Loaf Writers Conference, this time as a faculty associate. Dressed in camouflage pants and a T-shirt, the compactly built Brown lounges on the sofa in

the living room of the ranch-style house he built himself six years ago in the
rural Yocona—locally pronounced "Yockny"—community south of Oxford,
Mississippi. The room is neat, showing no telltale signs of his three children
(ages nine, eleven, and sixteen), all occupied elsewhere after putting in a
brief, polite appearance. Against one wall stand bookcases filled with works
by Flannery O'Connor, Cormac McCarthy, Harry Crews, Raymond Carver,
Richard Ford, and Charles Bukowski. On the opposite wall hang the certifi-
cate of appreciation he received from the city of Oxford and other framed
items given to Brown by his fellow firefighters when he resigned in 1990 after
seventeen years of service.

Adjacent to the kitchen across the connected carport is his small office,
where a Royal electronic typewriter sits on his desk next to a pile of cleanly
typed manuscript. Tacked above are pictures of Elvis Presley and James
Dean and a list of people whose support Brown deems fundamental to his
writing career. These "saints" encompass, among others, an *Outdoor Life* editor who sent him early letters of encouragement; Richard Howorth, propri-
etor of Square Books in Oxford; and Shannon Ravenel, Brown's editor at
Algonquin.

"People keep telling me I should get a computer," Brown admits, but he
remains comfortable with his Royal, which in itself reflects the long way he
has come. He used a portable Smith-Corona, borrowed from his wife Mary
Annie, to compose the Yellowstone novel he expected to inaugurate his writing career. "It had lots of sex and violence," he recalls of that neophyte work.
"I thought that would sell." At the time he was reading "Stephen King, Louis
L'Amour, big blockbuster bestsellers, stuff like that. I've always liked to read;
I got that from my mother. When I was a kid I had my school books, which
I didn't care much for, and my library books—hunting stories, fishing stories,
cowboy stories, Zane Grey—nothing you would call literature. It took me a
long time even to learn what literature was."

That realization was still to come when, in the late 1970s, weary of a string
of dead-end jobs that supplemented his fireman's income, Brown jumped
into "the thing [writing] to see how far I could go with it. I had been wondering how books get written and if someone could teach himself to write. And I
thought I could make some money from it. Of course, I didn't know what I
was doing. I didn't even know about double spacing. I typed that whole novel
single spaced, 327 pages. I worked on it every spare moment I could find for
about seven months."

But his efforts brought only rejection letters until Brown put away the ill-fated novel. Finally, two years later, the magazine *Easyriders*, after rejecting "three or four others," bought a story about a biker. Another two years went by before *Fiction International* accepted a narrative poem (later included in *Facing the Music*); a few years later *Twilight Zone* took a horror story.

Brown's problem, as he gradually came to realize, was that all the writers' self-help books that he'd been studying could not find his voice for him. Learning of a short story course taught by Ellen Douglas at the University of Mississippi in Oxford in 1982, he made an appointment with the much-respected writer to see if he could audit. "She was very nice," Brown remembers, "and asked what I had written. I told her that I had written three novels, none of which had been published, and close to a hundred stories. So she let me in. She was real encouraging and turned me on to writers I should be reading. Miss Douglas gave me a much better idea of what literature was and made me see what I needed to be working toward." During this time Brown awoke to his subject matter: the harsh, often bitter lives of rural people of lower economic status and limited expectations, circumstances he describes with unflinching honesty.

When talking about writers who have had the most impact on him, Brown conspicuously omits William Faulkner, the Mississippian who transformed the Oxford area into Yoknapatawpha County, Faulkner's own postage stamp universe. In no respect except their shared birthplace does Brown believe that he can be paired with Faulkner, despite critics' almost invariable tendency to do so. Though Brown is pleased by the comparison, and observes, "Of course, all Southern writers work in Faulker's shadow," he feels it is erroneous to call him a Faulkner disciple. "Mr. Faulkner and I don't have much in common, really, besides dealing with the same kind of people in the same area. I'm writing at a much later date. And he wrote about so much that went back before his time. I don't get into that. I write about the here and now."

Nor is his work to date autobiographical, Brown says. He is saving the circumstances of his own life for a nonfiction book that will deal with "fighting fires, hunting with my boys, fishing in the pond over at my place in Tula—a little of everything." Brown does admit, however, to fashioning his fiction out of everything he has seen or heard: "I mix it all in my imagination. Stephen King said something like, 'You sift through your mind every day and pull it all out of the well.' That's the way it is for me."

And if Brown's gritty world of down-and-outers struggling to live up to their own codes of honor seems bleak, as some reviewers have observed, then so be it. "I understand how readers can think that," he acknowledges. "I think I'm a pretty happy guy, so I really don't know why some of my stuff takes as dark a turn as it does. But I'm trying to grip my readers as much as I can, hoping to get them hooked early and keep them involved. I try to sandbag my characters; I load them with as much as they can take, because that's what a story is all about. You've got a character who's in trouble, and he or she is either going to find their way out, or not. Life is hard for lots of people, and the guilty aren't always the ones who get punished."

But what his unrelenting eye sees is pierced with a redeeming humane sensibility. Last year when he was a fellow at Bread Loaf, the African American writer Reginald McKnight asked Brown to get together and talk about *Dirty Work*. For that novel, Brown had drawn on his memories of the time when he was stationed at Philadelphia's Marine Corps barracks, spending hours in a nearby bar listening to disabled veterans of the then-raging war in Vietnam (he himself was fortunate enough not to see active duty). Brown surmised that one of the main characters, a black veteran maimed in the war, had captured McKnight's attention. Indeed, McKnight's first question was "How the hell do you know how to write like a black man?"

As Brown recalls, he replied, "You know, I've lived around black people all my life, I've worked with black firemen, I was in the marines with blacks, I've listened to them talk." But what McKnight really wanted to know was " 'How do you know how they think?' I told him the novel took a lot of work and was rewritten five times to make it as authentic and convincing as I could."

Writing *Joe*, his fourth book in four years, was no picnic either. Longer than *Dirty Work*, *Joe* came harder and slower. "From the first," Brown discloses, "I was trying to tell a story in a way I had not done before. I was trying to make the landscape—the area where I live—an integral part of the story. I started it in '84 or '85 and wrote a good bit of it but then set it aside. I would pick it up from time to time and do a little more and think about where it was going. At one point I put it away to concentrate on *Dirty Work*, but I always had it within reach." The ending, especially, gave him trouble, and he wrote several versions before deciding that "there was really only one way to end it, although everybody might not be happy with it." Already, Brown says, he has heard talk about the fate of the novel's most repellent character.

Joe was the first of Brown's work that did not require extensive revisions. When Shannon Ravenel (to whom he has been devoted since she excitedly contacted him after reading his story "Facing the Music" in a 1987 issue of the *Mississippi Review*), received the manuscript last January, she called to tell him it was "wonderful," an assessment readers are now reinforcing. By August Liz Darhansoff, Brown's agent, had sold foreign rights in England, Sweden, and Holland. For the first time in his career Brown awaits an auction for mass market rights. Also brightening his horizon is the forthcoming production of his adaptation of *Dirty Work* for PBS's *American Playhouse.* And next fall Richard Corley, who in June of this year directed a production of three of Brown's stories at Manhattan's HOME for Contemporary Theater and Art, will visit Yocona. "He has an NEA grant," Brown notes, "and he wants to spend time working with me on another project."

Coming also is publication this fall of a story commissioned by the *Paris Review,* which Brown considers the most prestigious magazine to publish him so far. Although his fiction has appeared in numerous other respected literary reviews, he has been unable to break into *Esquire* and the *New Yorker.* When the latter returned "Kubuku Rides (This Is It)," which was later chosen by Margaret Atwood for inclusion in the 1989 *Best American Short Stories,* Brown recalls that the rejection notice "said the ending was pretty good, but the overall story was monotonous."

Brown most likely keeps such reproofs in mind while working with students at Bread Loaf. When you criticize a student's writing "you're messing with something that has come out of somebody's heart and soul," he believes. "I tell them if it doesn't work this time, they've got to keep trying and believing in themselves."

Interview with Larry Brown:
Bread Loaf 1992

Dorie LaRue / 1992

From the *Chattahoochee Review* 13 (April 1993): 39–56. Used by permission.

The Bread Loaf Writers' Conference takes place every mid-August at the Bread Loaf campus of Middlebury College in the Green Mountain National Forest of Ripton, Vermont. At the 1992 Breadloaf Writers' Conference, Larry Brown was one of the associate staff. I interviewed him in the Barn, the huge, drafty edifice of notched wood and stone that has not changed significantly in the last half century and is the general social area for students and staff. That day was misty and cold and the Barn's fieldstone fireplace, tall as my head, was ablaze. I met Larry, dressed in camouflage and cowboy boots and his ever-present cap, in one of the comfortable corners where it gave us a semblance of privacy. I had seen Larry before at various get-togethers, or spotted him at readings lounging outside the Little Theatre in one of the wicker chairs, so, I guessed, he could listen and smoke. He was a popular teacher, accessible, funny, totally committed to his students. He was known to leave functions early or refuse late socializing so that he could mark short stories. His books *Facing the Music* (which won the Mississippi Institutes of Arts and Letters Award for Literature), *Big Bad Love, Dirty Work* (which received a Mississippi Library Association Award) and *Joe* were selling briskly in the campus book-store even before his reading on Friday night. Larry, a former fire-fighter, born in Mississippi, had read from a work in progress based on his experiences with the Oxford Fire Department.

L: In your childhood did you think that you'd be a writer?
B: Nah, it never crossed my mind.

L: When did you first start thinking about it?
B: I started around the time I was twenty-nine, just wondering how people learn how to write, how they went into a room and sat down and wrote a

book where nothing had existed before. I'd always been a big reader all my life, ever since I was a little kid, one of the main pleasures I had in life. And I just began wondering if a person could teach himself how to do that, to sit down and start writing. So I thought about it a good while and finally—my wife had a portable typewriter, an old Smith-Corona—I sat down one night and started writing a novel. That was in 1980.

L: Who were your influences as a child? Not necessarily writers—but who were those people you found interesting? Did you have any helpful influences? Parents, teachers?
B: My mother was a big influence on my reading. She's who I got that love from. But my father didn't like to be around anybody who was reading. I can remember her sitting there in a chair reading a magazine, as he walked in the room, she'd pull up the cushion and hide the magazine 'cause she knew it'd aggravate him.

L: He was threatened by it?
B: Yah, he just didn't believe in it or thought it was a waste of time. He just didn't have any use for it at all. But we all read, all of his children.

L: How did your family and friends react to *your* books?
B: Well, it's been pretty favorable. I dedicated my second book, *Dirty Work*, to my mother and my father. And Mother didn't know that I had dedicated it to Daddy 'til I carried a copy over there and signed it for her. They have liked my work, you know. I think they were a little stunned maybe when I finally published a book. They knew I had been writing, but I don't think that they realized how serious I was about it, that I'd been doing it for eight years. But I didn't talk about it that much. I mean, they knew I was writing stuff and sending it off, and occasionally publishing something in a magazine. But it was just every couple years, I'd get a story. I was just struggling through those apprenticeship years, and all. You don't know how long it's going to take. It took me eight years.

L: What, if any, contemporary writers interest you? I saw you buying a book of poetry the other day.
B: Yeah, I bought Jud Micham's book of poems. I think one of the best ones who's come along lately is Lewis Nordan. He published three collections of

short stories. My favorite living writer is Cormac McCarthy. He's published his sixth novel back in May. That's like six since 1965. And I think he's probably the greatest living writer we've got. I'm a big fan of his work and have been for a long time. But when I was young I read just about anything I could get my hands on. I read a lot of Greek mythology. That was one of my favorite things. I read Faulkner when I was about sixteen. And stuff like the *Iliad* and the *Odyssey*, Mark Twain, all that kind of stuff.

L: Did anything from that come out in your work, any of, say, the ideal hero?
B: Probably just the fact that I think tragedy is probably the highest form of drama. That's the one thing that my readings impressed on me in all the stuff that I've read. But when I was a teenager and when I got older I read a lot of different stuff. John D. McDonald—I was a big fan of his Travis McGee books. Later on, as I got to my twenties, I was reading Stephen King and mostly, well, it's what you'd call commercial stuff, not any literary books. I didn't really start reading any literary books with the intent of reading them to learn from them until after I started writing myself. And, I kind of found out through that process what kind of a writer I wanted to be. At first I was writing just all kinds of stuff. The first novel I wrote was about a man-eating bear in Yellowstone National Park. The next novel I wrote was about a bunch of guys in Tennessee raising a big patch of marijuana. And I wrote a supernatural novel. And I wrote a hunting novel. And a boxing novel.

L: This is all before *Facing the Music*?
B: Yeah, all before *Facing the Music*.

L: How many is that?
B: Five altogether.

L: Five novels that are unpublished? Are you going to try to go back and get any of them?
B: Nah, they're up in my attic, tucked away.

L: Just learning experiences.
B: Yeah, just chalk them up to experience. I think that's what you've got to do. Of course in your early years, you don't have any objectivity about your work and you send everything off with the hopes of getting it published. Which

I did. I sent off my novel to all these publishers in New York City, and I tried every magazine in the country, literary magazines as well as the "slicks" of New York. Just all over the place, just trying to publish anywhere I could. And I published my first story in a motorcycle magazine in 1982. In *Easyriders*. I think I had about thirty rejection slips in. But then, I thought had really broken through by publishing that one story and thought it would be easy from then on. But it was two more years before I had another story taken.

L: Well, I'm curious to know how you go about your writing—What are your sources of energy—talking to people, observing unobtrusively?
B: Observing people.

L: Where do you go to observe?
B: Gosh, just everywhere. Uptown, out in the country, bars.

L: I bet that country store you worked in helped, didn't it?
B: Yeah, you hear a lot of stories in there. I heard a lot of stories, got a good bit of material out of all that—people just coming in and talking. They'd just come in and talk to you for an hour, two hours sometimes. And just listening to people because, one thing you find out is that they're always telling stories about something. What happened years ago, last week, last year. And if you just listen to it, you can hear anything, get a wealth of material.

L: Your style is reminiscent of Raymond Carver. Did he influence your work in any way?
B: Yeah, he's a big influence. I started reading him probably around '83, maybe '84, somewhere around there. I took a writing course in 1982 at the University of Mississippi under Ellen Douglas. I was just in the class. I wasn't a student. I wasn't enrolled at the University. But I went to her and I asked her if I could get in. And she wanted to know what I had written. I told her I had written three novels and about ninety short stories, and she said I could get in. And then I started going to the bookstore there in town that had opened up—an independent bookstore—and I began to see that there was a lot of titles there by contemporary writers who I was familiar with. So I started reading all those people and finding out more and more about what was being published, and the books that were being published then. And so that's what I tried to concentrate on. Carver was one of the main ones.

L: Your background in the early stages of your writing was not academic.
Do you feel this enhanced your writing?
B: Well, I didn't know any of the rules and what to break and what not to
break. I kind of got my eyes opened to some of the things I was doing wrong
when I took that writing course in '82 at the University. That lasted about
twelve or fourteen weeks. And she [Ellen Douglas] was really a great teacher.
She had all these accurate insights into your manuscript. And she kind of
pointed me in the right direction. One of the things she did was comment on
the people I had never heard of, like Conrad and Dostoevski and Ambrose
Bierce. She'd assign us all these stories to read out of the *Norton Anthology of
Short Fiction*. I had never encountered these stories before. I had never heard
of Katherine Anne Porter before, I had never heard of Flannery O'Connor
before. And I found all these wonderful writers, some of them had been dead
a long time. I really had my eyes opened to what was going on.

L: You answered one of the questions I had for you Friday with your reading:
What works do you have in-progress? You read some of your nonfiction,
which is based on your experiences as a firefighter. Would you like to tell me
a bit about what you plan to do with this?
B: Well, I started working on this one actually before I quit the department.
I think I started writing it sometime in the fall of '89. Then I left in January
of 1990. And it started just out of boredom and not being able to sleep at the
fire station in the early hours of the morning. I would just be lying back there
for a while, awake. And then I said, "Well might as well get up and write
something." And I had just finished reading Rick Bass's *Oil Notes*, and I liked
it a whole lot and enjoyed the style that he used, autobiographical. And I just
thought I'd give it a try. So I've been on it now drawing close to three years.
And I've got about 200 pages of it.

L: So, we may see it soon, then?
B: Well, I hope so, I hope so. I've been involved with a bunch of little projects
and haven't been able to devote the time I need to. I've been teaching and
working on my play and my screenplay and some other stuff.

L: You're working on a play as well? Is it based on one of your novels?
B: It's based on *Dirty Work,* yeah. That's the name of the play. It's two acts
that run about two hours and fifteen minutes; and we've got about, I think

about fourteen characters. And we're going to do a three-week workshop production in January and February at the Arena Stage in Washington, D.C. I gotta move up there for three weeks. Then we'll have a paying audience at the end of hopefully, a full run.

L: *Dirty Work* has been cited as one of the definitive novels concerning the personal effects of Vietnam on the individual. Is any of it autobiographical? Were you in Vietnam or were you too young for that?
B: Nah, I went into the Marine Corps in '70 and got out in '72, but I never did go to Vietnam.

L: Would you give me some background on the writing of *Joe*?
B: Well, let's see. I started working on that book around '85 or '86, a long, long time ago. And then put it aside. Wrote a good bit of it, then I put it aside to build a house. And then I, during the process of building the house, got the idea for a novel about a guy that stayed in his room all the time and wouldn't come out because his face was all disfigured in Vietnam. And I stopped writing completely for six months to build that house. That was in '86. And then as soon as I had the house finished and all, I started in March and had it finished in August. And as soon as I had a chair to sit in and a table to set my typewriter on, I sat down and started writing the story about the guy. But as it turned out, I had to put *Joe* completely aside for two and a half years because I got so heavily involved in this other novel. And during that time I got my first book contract and I told them that I had a novel, and they wanted to see it later. So, after I had it through the third draft, I showed it to them. But then I still had to do two more drafts. I wrote it five times completely and threw out about six hundred pages. But during that time I was also writing some of the stories that would go into *Big Bad Love*. And then after it came out, after we had it finished, I went back to work on *Joe*, just exclusively on that. And finally finished it, I think around January of last year.

L: I found the style in *Joe* was completely dissimilar to *Facing the Music* and even *Dirty Work*.
B: Yeah, it is.

L: There was a kind of comedic device in most of your short stories, but this book seemed totally serious. Was that deliberate?
B: Yeah, it was. It was an attempt to do something different with the language and the style, to really just use the language almost like a painter, you know,

uses his canvas and his brush and his oil and all of that—to paint as many pictures as I could and to make, try to make the language beautiful and make it say something and make it create all these images. And possibly use the land as a backdrop for all the events told. And that's one thing I wanted to do was to use the land like one of the characters, integral, a backdrop to all the action.

L: Your short stories, too, reflect that love you have of images . . . About characterization—in "Kubuku Rides" and *Dirty Work* you assume the first person voices of a black character. Is this a difficult task?
B: Yeah, it's difficult.

L: "Kubuku Rides" has won an award, right?
B: Yeah, it won the *Greensboro Review* Prize in '88.

L: It just seems perfectly on tune to me.
B: It was rejected very embarrassingly by the *New Yorker*; they said it was "boringly monotonous." Sometimes, you know, when you write the first line, you know you've got the voice. And that's the way it was when I wrote the first couple of lines of that story. I knew that the rest of the story had to follow. I knew that I had the dialect and that the rest of the story had to follow in that vein and be accurate after the first two lines. And that one didn't take me that long to write, but it took me a long time to sell it, to publish it.

L: It's one of my favorites. What exactly is "Kubuku"?
B: Well, it's something that's hard to explain. The voice that I had imagined was that of a young black girl, a writer, telling the story, who had an African name. And this was going to be like the first thing she had done, you know. And it was like a horse coming out of the gate for the first time. And that's just the image that I had of the speaker telling the story. It wasn't Angel telling it; it was somebody else telling it. Not me either.

L: So almost like her spirit, perhaps.
B: Yeah. The way she would talk if she was just sitting there telling it. That's what I tried to re-create on the page.

L: It's perfect. That was the first story I read by you, and I remember opening up the book and reading the first couple of lines and thinking, "Oh, they made a typo in this poor man's book," and then I realized what was going on.

Your use of dialect. Do you see any time during your career when you've consciously modified the way you look at the world?

B: Yeah, I think I've come to look at it a lot more compassionately because a lot of the things that I used to write were about just senseless violence and people hating one another and hurting one another. And I finally found out that they were not the right things to write about, that the things to write about were the truths of the human heart and people and how they reacted and how they try to do the best they can and get along. And I think that's what all good literature is about, about people struggling through problems and trying to do the right thing. But a lot of times my characters don't succeed. And they know right from wrong, but they're not always able to overcome their obstacles. But I try to leave it up to them how to get through them. That's why I guess I make things so tough on them, to see what they're going to do and how they're going to react to all this pressure. That's why I get accused of being so bleak and brutal sometimes, too.

L: Social realism, hmmm? You had one poem published in *Facing the Music*. In lieu of its success, by the very nature of its comedic, yet realistic atunement, why haven't you, or *have* you written more poetry?

B: I've written a lot of poetry, I just have not tried to publish any of it. One thing I guess is that I'm afraid that poetry is just like fiction. It requires as much devotion and studying of the form as any fictional form does. Now in the last few years I have gotten up the courage to show a little of my stuff to some poets I know and they liked it. But I still haven't tried to send any of it out to publish it. To me, poetry is always the emotional response to something that I've seen. I just don't think of a poem about, whatever—you know—trees in the forest or something like that. I see something that impresses me and it stays with me and I have to go write a poem about it. I was coming through the airport in Chicago one day, and I was coming home from here I believe—the first time I was here. But I saw these people sitting in chairs with these long white canes. A bunch of blind guys. And all these people were walking around and nobody was paying any attention to them. And I took another look at them, and they were these huge, stocky built-up guys. And I just realized they weren't just blind guys, they were all blind weight lifters. They had these massive arms and thick necks and big chests, and one of them with like a black cowboy suit and a gold pin in his ear. And all these people in this airport were just flowing around them and didn't even see them. And I thought, "Look what these people have done for themselves. They're blind, but they still transformed themselves into these musclemen." And I had to run over there across the aisle to a little news rack and buy a pen and a pad of paper. I got me a beer and I sat down and wrote that poem right there at the airport. I had to.

L: Do you try to, if you see a situation like that, do you try to talk to people? I remember reading that Carson McCullers used to wander around everywhere, trying to strike up conversations.
B: I just wanted to look at them.

L: In many of your works the characters are lonely, isolated personalities. They're unable to verbalize this to themselves, that they are lonely. Do you see this as a symptom of our society, or do you see. . . .
B: Well, certain groups of society. But it's probably the people, the working-class people that I write about, people who become disillusioned and who have trouble with their women. I always get accused of being rough on women, but I never get accused of that by women. It's always by men. Some of my biggest fans are ladies, you know, and I don't really know where all that comes from, but I just kind of look at people around me and I create these lives and I guess I create their environment too. And I think their environment creates the problems that they have in the world that they live in. And I just go from there. I deliberately try to make it tough on them. I don't know if that answers you very well or not.

L: Yeah, it's a kind of an obscure question. But, your characters are common, their dreams are ticky-tacky dreams. But what they want seems to represent what everybody wants. A niche. A connection with other human beings. You seem to bring that out in your fiction really well. Who do you really think of when you write? You said that you have a lot of women readers. Who do you think of as your audience?
B: Well, somebody who'd go in a bookstore and look around. Somebody who's interested in contemporary literature or somebody who likes collections of short stories and keeps up with what's being published nowadays. People in the South, but really not just them, because I get letters from people in New York City and California and Michigan, all over the place. So I don't really think that it's limited to just region because I have too much

correspondence from people all over the place. I don't know—I guess you
write for yourself first. I guess you please yourself first. But then you begin to
realize that you have people out there who are following you, who have
become readers of your work, and they're gradually spreading the word to
other people. It takes a long time for your work to take off sometimes. My
first book sold, I think, between three and four thousand copies, and then the
next two only sold about eight thousand, and then this last one sold about
twenty thousand. Which is great for me. It's not on the best seller list. . . .

L: And you sold all the paperback rights for all of them, right?
B: Yeah, I was with Harper and Row on the first book. Then I went to Vintage
with two of them. Now I'm with Warner.

L: In *Big Bad Love*, you have ten stories, ten protagonists who live in rural
Mississippi, who like to drive around in pickups with coolers of beer close at
hand. Their marriages are rocky, they prefer local bars to staying at home.
The men are frequently inarticulate. Yet your work has been called one of
redemption and hope. Would you comment on that?
B: Yeah, I kind of go along with that. I try to offer the characters some salvation. I try to fix it where things are not hopeless for them, where they can
make the decisions that will pull them out—although sometimes that's not
possible. Like with Joe, I mean, you know, he's trying to get his act together.
And he's lost his family over all his drinking and trouble and everything. But
I've been told this before—that he is kind of a surrogate father to the boy,
and that's what I intended the reader to get. Although in the end it doesn't
happen for him. But I wrote that ending about five different times. Then I
ultimately decided that I couldn't be faithful to the rest of the book without it
ending the way that it did. I had one happy-go-lucky, happily-ever-after ending, but I said that's not what would have happened, I don't believe, under
these circumstances. Because the old man was so sorry and he was so determined to have whatever he wanted at whatever cost to anybody else, that
I think it was inevitable that that happened.

L: "Ninety-two Days" almost constitutes a novella. The character is a writer.
Oddly enough, I feel the character's trials comforting. Is this autobiographical?
B: Part of it is. Part of it is going back and dealing with the frustration
that I felt so many times when I was trying to publish, although I could

understand why they wouldn't publish me, say, the first five years. But then after, like say 1985, I was writing what I considered some of my best stories—"Facing the Music," "Samaritans," "Old Frank and Jesus," "The Rich"—things like that. And they were still being turned down. And it was not that it was the quality of the work. They had no quibbles with that. I'm talking about maybe they would say "this is a wonderful story and we wish we could publish it, *but* it's too brutal, my boss is not going to like it," etc., etc. And I began to see that even after you got to the point where you were writing publishable work that there could still be obstacles in your way to keep you from getting published. Some of that [in the story] deals with all of that stuff. Nobody can share any of that pain with you. And all of these people who are up here, all these people who are students, are going through exactly what I went through. I think that's the only thing that qualifies me to try to teach any of them—that I've been where they've been. Everybody's got this dream. And the dream is to see your name on the cover of a book, to have your book reviews appear in the paper, and to be able to go over to the library and see it on the shelf. And that's the dream—having your name, even though your name might not mean anything to anybody else, if you get it on a book then, you've got to be taken seriously. You've got some potential. And that's what the whole thing is about, is keeping that hope and that dream alive and feeding it and working hard to reach your goals.

L: In "Discipline: The Trial of a Plagiarist," you use an outrageously comical method of satire. Do you plan to do any more satire?
B: Oh, I don't know. I used to write all kinds of crazy things, and that one, I don't know where it came from.

L: You were having fun with it, weren't you?
B: I was having a good time when I wrote that one. And, I think it was written in '86, as well as I can remember. And again, you know, that's one of the ones nobody would take, nobody would publish it. They just sent it back and said, "You must be out of your mind." But I sent it out so much that I finally quit believing in it and gave up on it. Then when I met Shannon [Ravenel], she wanted to see like fifteen of the best ones I had for inclusion in the first book, and that was one of the ones that I sent her. She said "I think that it's great and I want to include it."

L: Oh, it's perfect.
B: Thank you.

L: One of the characters in "The Apprentice" is a woman writer, and she reminded me of a woman in Ray Carver's "Vitamins." Both are intelligent. Ambitious. Surprising in subtle ways. In this story, too, is a male character who surprises me. He sticks with this woman and he seems less amoral and more articulate than many of your other male characters. And the woman character is much different from, say, Sheena Baby in "Falling out of Love." Would you comment on your voice in your female characters and your male characters? You write in both male and female voice, and inside each voice the range is incredible.
B: Well I write a lot more from the man's point of view, probably just because I'm a man. But I also do like to write about female characters and in some cases use their voice. And, you know, just like, well I'm getting off the beam when I speak on this.

L: Oh no, go right ahead and get off.
B: I was going to comment on Braiden Chaney in *Dirty Work*. I knew for that character to be believable, he had to have the dialogue, the accurate dialogue of a black person. He had to feel the way that a black person feels about the way things were in the war. I don't know how many people know that there was a disproportionate number of black soldiers who fought in Vietnam as opposed to white soldiers. Which the only reason was that so many of them were down at below the poverty level, or whatever, and going in the army was a good thing, or they didn't finish high school, or they got drafted and they didn't have the money and the daddies and the connections to keep them out on college deferment, something like that. That's the main reason. But anyway, the voice you write in, whether it's that of a five-year-old kid or a ninety-year old grandmother—you've got to assume that voice and make that character totally believable. That's why I think first person is so interesting because you can assume so many different voices.

L: So you hear this voice, you said, and it just takes wing . . . Many of your characters have the initials L.B. Do you care to comment on that?
B: That was just kind of, I don't know, something I did for fun, I guess. So many of those stories in *Big Bad Love* have some, some part, you know

however large or small . . . of autobiographical elements and when I was writing these stories, I didn't really have it in my head that there was ever going to be a collection put together. But I just got to giving these characters my initials. I don't know why. But Lewis, Leroy, Leon—I know I call that one Leon 'cause my mama's name is Leona and I've always liked that name. One of Francine's little boys is named Leon, and I told you Leona's my mama. But they're kind of ah, yeah, well, Bukowski's got a character like that—Henry Chinaski—are you familiar with him?

L: I'm sorry, I'm not, no.
B: Well, Chinaski, he was a struggling writer too—and I'm a big fan of Bukowski's—and I was just kind of doing the same thing he was in some of those stories. I wrote another one in that vein that's going to be out in *Southern Review* this fall. It's called "A Birthday Card."

L: I'll be looking forward to that . . . What is the essential element that you strive for in character development?
B: I try to make them fully developed. I try to create people on the page that you remember like the people you met in your life. And to me, that's the ultimate test of a piece of fiction, that character stays with you for the rest of your life—the piece of writing impresses you so much that you remember them like people that you actually met. I think that's the ultimate test.

L: What character of yours do you think that you developed the most fully?
B: The most fully? Probably Walter and Braiden and Joe. I don't know, you don't have as much room in a short story as you do in a novel to create histories, families, a past, to create all the emotions and reactions to a certain situation. But in the course of a novel these people need a childhood, they need memories, they need friends and family that go back through the years, so that they are fleshed out and whole and believable as real people— because the main trick is to get the reader to forget he's reading. You don't want somebody catching stuff here and there saying "This is not right, this is not right." Years ago, whenever that happened to me, I would just keep reading. Now, if that happens, I throw the book away. I can usually tell in the first page or two if I'm in the hands of a good writer or not. I think you've got to grab him early and get him hooked and keep him hooked.

L: Where do you really locate your reader in terms of your fiction? Do you feel like your reader is more of a participant in the action?

B: Yeah, I want him to be. I want him to be right there in the middle. I want it to be like a movie he's watching in his head, and I'm the one who's supplying the pictures. I want him to be seeing everything and visualize everything; and whatever happens, I want him to feel it is as fully as he can, as much as black words on white paper will transmit that. I want it to be as strong as possible.

L: Is that Raymond Carver's influence? His objective point of view like a movie screen?

B: He's the master.

L: In your novels there are visual qualities which suggest your attempt to undo the narrative. Do you feel like there is an established order for a novel?

B: No, I don't think so. Now, when I talk about *Dirty Work*, that's an unconventional novel to my way of thinking because you've got two different narrators. You also have events that are known to the reader that are not known to each of the characters, like Walter's childhood. We know he's just lying there thinking about all this stuff. Braiden's not getting a bit of that. Braiden is having these visits from Hughes and all these other people that are either real or fantasy and nobody is seeing that except Braiden. It's either all in his head or in a place that nobody but him can see. And it goes back and forth in time. Back to Africa—that's all an illusion in his head that he is trying, that is real to him. It's real to him and hopefully real to the reader, too. But Walter's not getting any of that. That's not happening to Walter. It's all happening to Braiden. It's kind of a different way that I was doing to try to tell a story. That didn't evolve right from the first draft at all. That came later, it came slower.

L: How long did it take you to write that?

B: I stayed on it for two and a half years. And see, originally, when I first showed them the third draft, I had all the stuff going on before, 160 pages before Walter and Braiden met, and Shannon said, "This is where your novel starts." I had trouble accepting that, you know. But I began to see what she was talking about. She kept hammering and hammering it through my head. She said we don't know enough about them, we don't know about their childhoods, and we want to know what brought them here. And then I began to figure out that there were so many more things about the story that

I didn't know. And that's the thing about rewriting, that's where you really learn what your story's about. I think now you ought to write it just as fast as you can, just get it down, that's what Carver says, get it down on paper. Then it's time to take it to another draft and toy with it and add things and take out things and do some more drafts. I always do at least three of everything now. I did three drafts with *Joe*, and I always even do at least three drafts of short stories. This long story that I published last fall in *Paris Review*, I started that story in January of 1990, the first thing I started writing when I left the fire department. And the initial writing of it only took a week, hadn't been a week. But, through the next eight months I was still working on it and changing it and revising it, and I wrote six complete drafts of it before I finished it in September. That was one story. Well, that's the process that I've learned, to be very critical of myself and to have to serve as my own first editor, and to not have any word, any single word in it that doesn't fit. To be merciless on yourself. That's what's so hard to learn is to view your work with a cold and objective eye. You can never get completely objective because you wrote it and that's yours. It's always got a special place for you. But you've also got to look at it the way that someone else would look at it, who is not you—some editor who is going to say "yes" or "no"—that's the hard part.

L: Do you have advice for a writer who has a finished book and is trying to break into the market?
B: Well, that's a really tough, tough part, finding a publisher, finding an agent. It's always easier to find an agent after you have a book contract. The catch is that a lot of publishers now will not read unagented submissions. So what you've got to do, if you can't interest an agent in looking at your stuff, then you've got to find publishing houses that will accept over the transom. Some of the best places I would advise people to send to is some of the smaller, newer little houses that are all over the country now. There's some really good ones, and they're publishing some really good writers. And they don't have as much money for advances as the big publishers, but they have good luck with paperback sales, with getting reprinted. Even if they only print, say three thousand copies of your novel, well, if you can sell it to Vintage or Plume or Harper and Row—their Perennial line or something—and get it in paper, it's going to keep living. And there's the hope then that they'll start teaching it in college courses, in contemporary lit. That's what's happened to

me. I'd say just try any place you can, and if you really believe in it, don't give up on it. You hear all these horror stories about books that the publishers had rejected fifty times. There was a guy here on a fellowship, Eddy Harris—the same year I was here the first time—his book about canoeing by himself down the Mississippi River had been rejected fifty times.

L: Is anything easy? Do you find the act of writing easy?
B: Well, to me, it's not really work. It's more like a form of recreation, especially when it goes well. It's not so good sometimes when it's not going well. But the only part I really consider work, is like when I've finished a book and I know that all my corrections are made, but that I've got to type up a clean manuscript with no mistakes—now that's work.

L: Do you have a computer?
B: No, I've got a typewriter. I'm on my fifth one now.

L: You pound all these novels out on a typewriter!
B: Yeah. And I'm kind of a perfectionist. I don't want anybody else doing my typing for me because I might want to change a word right in the middle of writing that final draft. I'm the one that's in my head. And I don't want to turn in any page that has any mistake on it, any misspelled word anywhere. I'm a stickler about that, it's a point of pride.

L: When you were in high school, were you an *A* student?
B: Oh no, I was a terrible student. See, I failed English in my twelfth year in high school and didn't graduate with the rest of my class. Very, very bad on my mother. She had already given me my class ring, and people had given me graduation presents, and all that. And I went in to get my grade and the counselor said, (I had my friend with me, Danny) and he said, "Well you made it Danny, but Larry, you didn't make it."

L: Oh my, like Faulkner!
B: So, yeah, I was pretty crushed about that, but it was my own fault. Been studying by myself, and my term paper on deer hunting got an *F*. Most of the time I stayed out in the woods, out with my dogs coon hunting, when I should have been home doing my homework.

L: Well, those experiences contributed to your novels, so you still have the last laugh . . . Have you found any professional criticism of your work illuminating or helpful?
B: Well, I don't know.

L: Critical reviews?
B: Some people are going to misread any book. Some people have personal axes to grind. Some people write reviews out of jealousy. The best ones give an honest, impartial account about what's between two covers of the book without regard to who wrote it. And 99 percent of the time the reviewers have been very, very kind to me. But I've also had some nasty stuff said about me, me personally, which has no business being in there, but I've always been able to find out the reasons for that—that there was some personal thing that this particular writer had either against me or against my book publishing house or something.

L: Is there any particular historical period other than this one which you'd rather have lived in?
B: Possibly, maybe during the Civil War.

L: Somehow, I knew you were going to say that.
B: I think that would have been an interesting and a hard time to have lived in, too. I just finished reading books, three books, this spring when I was in Ohio on the Civil War. Just a fascinating account of what went on.

L: A little light reading. Okay, last question. Can I ask you what you're going to write next after you finish your nonfiction and your play. Do you have anything in the works?
B: I hope to get back to writing some short stories. That's what I really like to do, but eventually I'm going to have to start another novel. But right now I don't have any ideas for it, just a few things that I have kicking around in my head.

L: I'll wait.

New Southerners: Larry Brown

Wayne Pond / 1993

From *Soundings* 687 (Research Triangle Park, NC: National Humanities Center, 1995). Transcript by Jay Watson. Used by permission.

WP: This is Wayne Pond at the National Humanities Center. Join me now for readings and conversation with Mississippi writer Larry Brown. He's here to read from and talk about his novels and short stories.

LB: This story is as close as I can get to one of my idols, Flannery O'Connor. I wanted everything I could get in here: Jesus, Elvis, faith healing, overweight women, sex, incest, truckers, pickups, goats, pistols, sin and faith and redemption. It took me a week to write it, and eight months to get it to where it is now, and it's about as southern as I can get.

WP: Writer Larry Brown describing one of his recent stories, one entitled "A Roadside Resurrection." Larry Brown will be back in just a moment with readings and conversation. *Soundings* is a cultural affairs service of the National Humanities Center. Major funding for this program comes from the Lila Wallace/Reader's Digest Fund.

Although American society is becoming more uniform, the South retains a cultural distinctiveness unlike any other part of the country. The same thing can be said of a new generation of southern writers whose work portrays social change but also reflects a literary heritage as palpable as a steamy southern summer night. In an exploration of the ideas and images of recent southern writing, *Soundings* now presents the second segment in an occasional series of programs. My guest now is Larry Brown, winner of the 1992 Southern Book Critics Circle Award and the Mississippi Institute of Arts and Letters Award in 1989. To paraphrase another Mississippi writer, William Faulkner, Larry Brown's fiction shows how the past continues to shape the present. Brown is the author of two collections of stories, five novels, and a play. Before he started writing full time, Larry Brown was a captain in the Oxford, Mississippi fire department. He sees southerners living through hard knocks and emotional chaos. But Brown's fiction, however bleak, also offers

62

a margin of hope and humor. In one story entitled, "A Roadside
Resurrection," he presents both a parody and an affirmation of southern life.
"A Roadside Resurrection" is an account of a legendary faith healer, a woman
named Flenco who searches for physical salvation for her dying husband, and
a family harboring a human monstrosity who embodies the darkest side of
the southern grotesque. Larry Brown.

LB: Yeah, that's the first story that I wrote after I left the fire department, and
it did take me about a week initially to write it. But I wound up working on it
for eight months before I got it right, because I kept finding out more and
more things I wanted to say. People have called it wild and crazy and all this
kind of stuff, and I guess that's true. I had a really wonderful time writing
that story. In this story I was trying to make a really bizarre situation that was
believable—

WP: Let me tell you, you succeeded!

LB: (Laughs.) And at the same time I wanted these two stories that were
combined within one story: the story of the healer and the story of Flenco
and her husband, who never quite made their connection, you know. That's
part of the futility of the story, part of it is the futility of her search for this
thing that she hopes to accomplish, and then the situation that the healer gets
himself thrown into just out of the goodness of his acts.

WP: Yeah, this incredible character or monstrosity that he runs into—I want
to come back to that in a moment. Larry, are you making fun of religious
faith in this story? I mean it's possible to read it at that and come away from
it with that sort of feeling. How about it?

LB: To me the story's about faith, and is an affirmation of faith.

WP: And this guy really is a healer?

LB: He really is a healer. He really does have the power, but to get to that
I had to construct what I thought was a believable event, which was a cold-
water drowning, which, you know, just being a firefighter, I knew about that,
that people can survive that. And that faith can do things, because you hear
about all these things that go on. You hear about people who handle snakes
and get bitten and survive, and all the other miracles that are performed. And
so it's partly about all that, it's part of the mystery of the South, some of the
things that go on down here that we pretty much take for granted.

WP: You have a passage where you say that there are people and things in the backwoods of the South that are, I guess, primitive, primeval is the right word to use. And this character, this deformed monstrosity of a son that belongs to these two old people who want the faith healer to work on this kid, that's one of them. Now I've got a friend here at work who read that story and said, "Hey, listen, what this guy's writing about here is original sin." I mean, this demonstrates that people in the South still believe in sin, in the fallibility of humankind. Is that too much of a stretch?

LB: No, I don't think it is. No, I don't think it is, and I'm aware that people like this exist because of the place that I live in. You can still find people living in very primitive conditions. You can still find people living without electricity in their homes, without running water, living like people lived a hundred years ago.

WP: Now what do you want us to come away from this story, "A Roadside Resurrection," feeling? Or let's use a crude word here: a message, a theme. What's going on in your mind?

LB: Well, I really don't consciously, I don't believe, have a theme whenever I'm working on something. I think whatever it is that the story says eventually works its way out through the telling of the story.

WP: So it's up to the reader, is that it? You're just going to let us make up our own minds?

LB: To me the thing is about not only a person having faith not being rewarded, but a person who has lost his faith being reaffirmed. You know, Flenco's case and the healer's case to me as an example of each.

WP: All right. Larry, let's talk about your work as a southern writer. It's always great fun to try to figure out how you connect with the southern tradition, how you come out of it. Let me put it to you this way: How much has the South changed over the past twenty or thirty years? And to the degree that you have experienced those changes or you believe in them, how does that work on you as a writer?

LB: Well, one thing that I've seen as far as physical changes in the land is probably what has impressed me the most, such as the reduction of acreage that's being farmed, the reduction of a lot of the hardwood timber, that was once around everywhere, where a lot of it has been clear-cut, logged off, and now is on pine plantations, as well as the growth of industry.

WP: So in other words the landscape itself makes a difference in the mind of a writer such as yourself?
LB: I believe that it does, yeah. Because once it gets changed, I believe that it's changed irrevocably, that you can't go back to the way that it was before.

WP: What about social change? I mean, for example, I'm going to ask you to read here in a moment from *Dirty Work*, one of your books. What about the experience of Vietnam, and the war? Does that have a particularly southern resonance for you?
LB: I think probably the thing that's happening is the South is becoming more like the rest of the country. I believe it's becoming harder to distinguish it the way it was, say, thirty years ago.

WP: Until somebody comes along and reads with the characters you create in "A Roadside Resurrection"! (Laughs.)
LB: (Laughs.) Talking about stuff like that, I guess I probably just have a vision sometimes of the way that I want things to be in a fictional manner. Or maybe I shouldn't say that, but I guess I just kind of place things so that they work out in the way I want them to for my stories and use that landscape and all.

WP: Let's listen to some of your work here, Larry Brown. I want you to read to me from *Dirty Work*. This is a passage where one character, Walter, wakes up in a hospital and recognizes the man that he's basically going to talk to for the rest of this book, and his name is Braiden Chaney.

[Brown reads from *Dirty Work* and then from "Big Bad Love."]

WP: Now if we subtracted the wonderful way you talk, that great Mississippi accent, and had you read that passage from "Big Bad Love" again, would it be especially southern? I mean, is there anything particularly regional going on here?
LB: Probably not, probably just purely rural. But it could be rural Michigan, as far as I'm concerned in this particular story, because I think a lot of my stuff could be set just about anywhere, where the South doesn't particularly

have an influence on the story. I like to think that they could be set in other places, too.

WP: Now one way to come to your fiction, Larry Brown, is to say that you write as much about questions of class and social station in this country as you do about another of our big questions, probably one of the biggest questions that we face socially, and that's race. How do you come to that interplay in your books?

LB: Well, I try to explore everything from everybody's point of view, whether it's a white person, a black person, a child, a woman, an elderly person, just whomever I'm concerned with, the character I'm creating. And I try to get inside that person's head and know as much about them as I can.

WP: How do you know when you've created the voice that you want to hear coming to you off the page?

LB: Well, I believe that it's established very early in any piece of work. I know when I wrote "Kubuku Rides," one of my short stories, about a black lady who drinks too much, years ago, I knew within two lines that I had established the rhythm and the flow and the sound of that story, and that everything else had to follow those first two lines.

WP: Now that story opens with "Allan come in the door." The husband's coming home, and this woman realizes that she's a drunk. She hates it, but she can't get away from it, and now she's got to face her husband.

LB: Right, yeah. And I could hear—sometimes I hear this voice in my head and I just have to kind of trust and follow it. But I try to assume different voices. I try to assume a different voice for every story.

WP: When you write, for example, in a room by yourself, do you actually say these words? Or is it all on the interior?

LB: I have before, yeah. Usually I will say something aloud to test the dialogue.

WP: (Laughs.) That's wonderful!

LB: To me that's the hardest thing to get right, the dialogue. You know, to make it sound like me and you talking.

WP: Just sitting here talking. I want you to read to me again, Larry Brown. This time you're going to read from *Facing the Music*, a collection of your stories. And here is a passage from "Samaritans." Read to me again.
LB: Okay.

[LB reads from "Samaritans."]

WP: Larry Brown, we've just heard you read from one of your stories called "Samaritans." This is in your collection *Facing the Music*. What's going on here? You're creating a scene of sympathy and empathy between a man and a boy. Is that right?
LB: Yeah, starting off with a character whose wife has left him, and he's hanging out in a bar because he really doesn't have anything else to do. And just through, really through accident, through circumstance, as things often happen, he becomes involved with these people in this old beat-up car who don't have any money and are really downtrodden and down on their luck. And he's sympathetic to their plight, and he thinks they probably need money for food and for gas—they're headed West, you know. And he ends up just being totally conned by these people. And I don't know if there's really a message that I'm trying to say. Some people have said that it's a story about the futility of trying to lend people a helping hand.

WP: Larry, just to generalize about the shape of your fiction—*Dirty Work*, *Big Bad Love*, *Facing the Music*, your novel *Joe*—it's pretty grim stuff.
LB: Mmm-hmm.

WP: Now I could look at you and say, "Come on, you're just having fun with us. You're just trying to do a send-up of really how bad things can get." On the other side, I might look at you and say, "You really believe this. I mean, you really are as pessimistic as this stuff, and as comic, you know all of that darker side of comedy." Who is the real Larry Brown here, speaking to us from these books?
LB: Well, I think what I probably try to explore are the inner strengths of people, and how much people can take and survive. But that is why I make things so hard on my characters. It's been said that I sandbag them before, which is true.

WP: (Laughs.) Absolutely.

LB: I learned that a long time ago. But that works in two different ways. One, if you hook your reader early with what's going on, you've got him, and what you're trying to do is make him forget that he's reading. I want people to be able to get into situations that possibly they've never encountered, and come away changed by what they've read.

WP: But doesn't that create a responsibility for you? Doesn't that put a sort of responsibility on your shoulders? You know, people come to you and say, "Hey, this story changed my life. This made me see the world through different eyes." How about that?

LB: I've had comments like that before, and I have had people come up to me and say, "This story you wrote is about my life." Now that'll make you think twice. (Laughs.)

WP: (Laughs.) Let's move toward a conclusion of our conversation, Larry Brown. We're talking about your fiction. I want you to read to me here a passage from your novel *Joe*. This is the very opening part of the book. Very, very quickly, tell me just the shape of the novel, and then we'll listen to you read.

LB: It's about two different groups of people. There's a group of people who are walking down the road and then there's another character named Joe, who meets this little boy in this family and kind of befriends him. Joe has lost his family; this other family doesn't have any home. And the two meet, and eventually that's what the whole story of the novel evolves out of.

[Brown reads the opening passage from *Joe*.]

WP: Is it important that we understand whether this book has a happy ending or a sad ending? Do you deal in that kind of language in your own mind when you write these stories?

LB: Yeah, and I had probably a tougher time writing the ending of this novel than I had any other one, simply because I was undecided as to what fate Wade should have, who I had tried to make as despicable and disgusting and dirty and foul and nasty as I could.

WP: Man, you did it, you did it! This is one of the meanest people I have read about in fiction in a long time.

LB: To me the whole thing is basically a battle between good and evil.

WP: Do you see the world in those terms, Larry?
LB: I do.

WP: Pretty stark contrast?
LB: Pretty stark, yeah. I believe that evil exists in the world, there's no mistake about it.

WP: Is that because you have a particular set of religious beliefs? Anything that's especially southern at work here? Or how did all that come together?
LB: No, I think it's probably just so much stuff that exists not only in my state or the South or our country but the world, all the ways that mankind can't get along and has never been able to get along. I said one time in *Dirty Work*, Jesus said there has always been wars and there's always going to be wars, and I guess the futility of that is one thing that I try to kind of explore. I believe people ought to love each other a lot more than what they do.

WP: Do you think that your books move us in the direction of that kind of harmony? Is that too much of an exaggeration to put that at your doorstep?
LB: No, I'm trying to create a world that is never going to be perfect but in which people try to do their best with what they've been given.

WP: Larry Brown, I want to thank you very much for coming by the National Humanities Center to participate in our series on contemporary southern writers. Let me tell our listeners about you. Larry Brown, the short story writer, the novelist, your books include *Facing the Music*, *Dirty Work*, *Big Bad Love*, your most recent book is *Joe*, you got a couple of screenplays in the works, and about next spring we can look forward to a book about your experiences as a firefighter?
LB: February, they say.

WP: February of '94. All right, Larry, it's always a pleasure to talk to you. I appreciate your coming by to be on our program, on *Soundings*, and I wish you well in your work.
LB: Well, thanks a lot, Wayne. Good to see you again.

Telling Stories: An Interview with Larry Brown

Michael Manley / 1994

Originally published in *Sycamore Review* 7.2 (Summer 1995): 69–79. Reprinted in *Delicious Imaginations: Conversations with Contemporary Writers*, ed. Sarah Griffiths and Kevin J. Kehrwald (West Lafayette: Purdue University Press, 1998): 118–28. Used by permission.

Larry Brown is the author of two collections of short stories, *Facing the Music* (1988) and *Big Bad Love* (1990), the novels *Dirty Work* (1989) and *Joe* (1991), and a memoir, *On Fire* (1994). His most recent novel, *Father and Son*, won the 1997 Southern Book Award. He lives in Oxford, Mississippi, where he was born and worked for many years as a firefighter and captain of the Oxford fire department.

This interview took place during Larry Brown's visit to Butler University in Indianapolis in January of 1994. Michael Manley was current Editor in Chief of *Sycamore Review*.

Larry Brown is telling a story . . .

Larry Brown: I had some crazy guy show up one time and he was waiting on me when I got there. I'd been over at my place cutting wood. I was hot, tired, dirty, sweaty and I had my overalls on, they were just soaked solid with sweat. Been running the chainsaw all evening. And he was there in this beat-up old car that was just loaded to the top with clothes and stuff. His story was that he had been falsely imprisoned. I started talking to him and he wanted me to write a book or a movie about his life. And that's what some people want. That's one of the reasons I had to get my phone number changed to an unlisted number, because all these people would see me on television or something and they'd call me up and tell me all these wild stories, these horrible stories of persecution. This guy was there, and like I said, my children were there playing basketball. Their momma hadn't come home from work yet. They'd come home from school and were playing basketball in the yard.

My mother-in-law lives right across the driveway. So I talked to the guy for a few moments and I noticed he had a damn tape recorder down in his pocket and he was taping what I was saying. And I finally just told him, "Mister, listen: I'm hot, I'm tired, I'm ready to go take me a shower." And that's really the only time that I've really been worried about anybody. You just can't ever tell what you might encounter out there.

Sycamore Review: You've said that whenever two people get together they start telling each other stories. You're often considered a Southern writer, and many other Southern writers attribute their becoming writers to the Southern storytelling tradition. How does that tradition work in your own writing? How has it affected what you do?

LB: I consider myself a storyteller foremost. Everybody grows up hearing stories passed down from your grandmother, your grandfather, your daddy and all of them. And then if you really start paying attention to people, you find out that they're telling stories all the time. It can be as simple as something that happened yesterday, or something that happened to somebody else. I just take all that stuff I hear and all the stuff I can imagine, my memory and experience of what it is to be alive, and use that to build my stories.

SR: Do you think the storytelling tradition has changed at all?

LB: I don't think so. I was sitting and talking to my son the other night after everybody else had gone to bed. We were just sitting there watching television and talking and I started telling him about something that had happened when I was a little boy. Things I'd never told him before, and he's eighteen years old. He was digging hearing about all of it, "What about this? What about this?" And I'm telling him all about it. We were just sitting there telling stories. And he tells me stories, too, and he tells me some of the funniest stories that I've ever heard. He just cracks me up, all this stuff that he comes home with. All the stuff that's going on with him and all his eighteen-year-old friends. It's wild, great stuff.

SR: In the introduction to *On Fire*, you say that the idea of writing was "a curve ball that you never saw coming." How did you come to that point where you were going to write seriously?

LB: After I'd been into it for a year or two . . . I wasn't really having any success with it, but telling stories was something I really got to enjoy. I got to thinking this was something I'd like to do, to try to make a career out of it, do it seriously. I also finally got to a point where I got a little objectivity about my work and I could see that what I was writing was not nearly as good as the writing I admired most. I saw that there was a big gulf between those two places. That was when it hit me that I was going to have to work even harder, that this was something I was going to have to dedicate my whole life to, my whole being to.

SR: You say you work from your memory and experience. Until *On Fire*, there doesn't seem to be a lot directly taken from the things you'd see every day as a firefighter. Is that material reserved for something down the road?
LB: I'll tell you how *On Fire* happened. It came from not being able to sleep at the fire station, kind of late in my career there. Because we'd have so many runs at night, you'd go to sleep for a couple of hours, but then you'd have to get back up. Then you'd go back, sleep a couple more hours, then go make another run. It totally wrecked my sleep. It didn't wreck anybody else's—they could all go to sleep. What would happen would be that they'd all start snoring and I couldn't go to sleep for nothing then.

So one night I got tired of that, I just decided instead of tossing and turning there all night, I was going to get up and make some coffee and write down everything that had happened that day. And that's when it started, 1989 sometime, when I was still there.

It just became—not exactly a diary, but I began to write about some of the other events that occurred over the years. I started finding out there was a whole lot of material there that might be worth enough to try to make a book out of it. So when I finally got up to about a hundred and twenty pages, I sent all those pages to my editor and said, "What do you think about this? Think we could make a book out of it?" And she said yeah. So that's when I started working on it in earnest. It took me about four years to complete.

People have asked me, "Are you ever going to write a novel about the fire service?" and I've considered it. I've written some openings to short stories, but I don't know. One of these days I might decide to use all that stuff.

SR: You seem to enjoy experimenting with form and voice. In your first collection you seemed to concentrate on voice more, as in "Kubuku Rides." By the end of that book you move into a voice that's closer to the ones in your other books. It seems to be a raw version of your own voice in *On Fire*. How conscious was this progression, and is it still going on?

LB: I think there's a lot of liberties you can take in fiction that you really can't take in nonfiction. To me, in nonfiction you've always got to be totally honest about your feelings about everything, but the thing about fiction is you can assume any role, you can take any stand, you can become any character you want to. Finding your voice is what every writer is looking for. I think really it's more a matter of gaining control of the language and assuming authority so that you can assume any voice you want to and become whatever character you want to. I think early on, in any piece of work that that's got to be established. And after I wrote the first two lines of "Kubuku Rides" I knew the voice and I knew that the rest of the story had to be true to those first two lines. And it was one of those where . . . you remember a while ago when I told you sometimes you get given a story in its complete form . . . that story was like that. It arrived with a beginning, a middle and an ending. I wrote it Christmas Eve day in 1986, and I didn't do anything for fourteen hours but write that story. It came in one long shot, and when I finished the story, it was basically just like it is today. Just a gift.

SR: Was that an exception? You said that you threw out several hundred pages of *Dirty Work*. Do you put that kind of revision into your short stories?

LB: I do at least three revisions of everything now. The story I published in the *Paris Review* a couple of years ago called "A Roadside Resurrection" was the first thing I started writing when I retired from the fire department. But I didn't get that story finished—the initial writing of it only took a week—until September, and I didn't do much else that year but work on that story. It's a long, long story, nearly novella length. I think it went through six complete drafts. I'd work on it, then I'd send it to my editor and she'd work on it, send it back to me and I'd work on it some more. That's the way we work. We send these revisions back and forth and we talk about them. We write notes back and forth until we're both happy with it.

SR: Your story "Boy and Dog" looks to me like something that could've come from your own experience, perhaps during your firefighting years. Did that actually happen?

LB: Well, the reason I wrote that story was because some dogs know not to get in the road and some don't. Sam would've never gotten hit by a car, he just knew better. I've had other dogs killed—over and over and over—by cars in the road because they don't have sense enough to get out of the road.

One day I was driving up the bypass and I saw this dog come walking out of the ditch and there was this Mustang coming down the road about sixty and the dog never looked around, just walked straight into that car—of course it killed him instantly—and I just got this idea. I see something and I think, "Now what if that was me?" or "What if that was my dog?" The way I was working on it was these little short sentences. I didn't write but about a page of them, and they were all behind each other in line as they ought to be, and I said, "Well, why don't I try to change the shape of this and put them one underneath the other and make each one five words long. Make it look more like a poem." That's how that whole thing evolved.

SR: You said once that poetry was the finest form of the language. Do you still write poetry? How successful do you find yourself at that?

LB: I've been writing poetry ever since I started writing. I've never published any of it. I keep getting asked to show some of it to some of my friends who are poets, whose work I respect, but I haven't spent as much time working on it as I have with fiction. I think it really has to be given the time that it deserves. I don't think that I'm a very good poet. I might have written a couple of halfway decent poems, but there's no way I'd call myself a poet because I've got so much respect for it. Poems are stories, but the poet has it down to its finest parts, to the most beautiful parts of the language.

SR: Your work is often called "spare" and you refer to it as "dark." Do you consider yourself a minimalist? You've said that you learned from Ray Carver. Do you ever worry about that kind of labeling? Do you think of yourself as writing in any certain mode?

LB: Carver was a big influence on me, and when I wrote *Facing the Music* it was really in that mode. But I don't really consider myself a minimalist. One of the things I tried to do in *Joe* was describe the landscape in a way that it was kind of a natural backdrop for all the events to unfold against, and it was a constant thing. I always wanted to remind the reader how everything looked and I tried to use my descriptive abilities to the best of my talent. And that book is vastly different from *Dirty Work*, which is vastly different from most of the short stories I've done. But I think that's because you try to do something different each time. You don't want to repeat yourself, keep doing the same thing. And I've discovered that the stuff I'm working on now is different from what's gone before. I hope. I'm trying to develop it more and get it right whenever I'm trying to tell something. There's so many different things you can do with the language. You're unlimited.

SR: Do you always have a character in mind when you start a story?
LB: I'll start with a character in a situation. Sometimes it might be kind of vague what the situation is, but just by writing and developing the character you discover what the story is day by day. If you live with it, carry it around in your head long enough, it's like these people come to stay in your head. Walter and Braiden lived in my head for about two and a half years and I knew the novel was finished when I had helped them as much as I could and there wasn't anything else I could do for them in the story. When the story was over I had to turn them loose, but it was like saying good-bye to two friends because they lived with me all that time. There wasn't a day that went by when I didn't think about them. That's the way it becomes.

SR: How do those situations develop out of the characters?
LB: A lot of people have problems functioning in the ways that they ought to. My characters usually know the difference between right and wrong. They know what the right things are to do, but that might not be what they want to do. It might be because they want to go out drinking or out whoring around instead of staying home and keeping a job and working. And they've all got some kind of struggle, because if you don't lay some kind of trouble on them, if they don't have some conflict, then how are you ever going to have a resolution or an ending. What you've got to do is make things on them as tough as you can and that's what I consciously try to do. I do what I call "sandbagging" and make things as hard on them as I can so then I'll see how they're going to react and what's going to happen and what the story's going to be about.

I think that people in fiction have always got to have reasons for doing what they do. Somebody who pulls out a gun and goes into a bank and robs it has got a reason for doing that. You may not know those reasons. Or somebody's going to rob you, take your money and maybe shoot you—there's plenty of reasons for them to do that, too, but you may not know those reasons. In fiction you've really got to know why the people do the things that they do and you've got to give them some motivation for acting the way that they do. That's another thing I tell my students, "He does this or she does this, but why?" We don't know why she left him or why he had this wreck, but we've got to know. You've got to explore your characters, and that's how you get your reader involved in your story and characters. People ask me what I think is more important, character or plot. I say character. If you create an interesting enough character, the story is naturally going to follow.

SR: Are there any new writers you're interested in?

LB: One of the best I've seen come along in a while is Chris Offut. There's another guy named Thom Jones who wrote a book called *The Pugilist at Rest*. I'm pretty crazy about both of them, and I still read *The Best American Short Stories* every year.

I met a writer named Tim Gautreaux down in New Orleans one night at a book signing down there and his name just rang a bell. I said, "Are you the one who wrote that story about that guy who went around and fixed all those wells in the 1930s and the Depression and met that real mean woman who was gonna kill her husband?" and he said, "Yeah, that's me." I said, "Wow man I think you're just a really wonderful writer." The guy just came in the bookstore, you know. I hadn't ever seen a picture of him or anything, and we just had this great talk. I think if you just keep your eyes open you'll keep discovering these new writers who are coming up. They're going to find a place to be heard. They're going to have their voice heard.

I've been impressed with some of the talent that I see in my workshops. I've seen a couple of students who came out of Bowling Green—one of them got an NEA grant, that's Andrew McDonald. He submitted a story that was the last one we workshopped in Bowling Green, two years ago. I was on the NEA panel but I couldn't vote on it because they're all anonymous submissions but I recognized Andrew's story immediately from the title. So I had to get up and leave the room. But he got the grant anyway. That shows you that the other people saw his talent, too. And I've had several from that class who've gone on to publish in the literary magazines. I had one girl there, Anne Panning, who'd already published when I started teaching her, already had her book of stories accepted with Coffeehouse Press, called *The Price of Eggs*. Anne is really good and she's working on a novel, she's written a non-fiction book. She really didn't need anything from me except a pat on the back. She had been writing half her life—she was only twenty-six when she published that book. Started writing when she was thirteen.

SR: You seem critical of the academic path to writing and sympathetic to the writer who just throws himself into the art. Do you see problems in the way writing is learned these days?

LB: In my way of thinking, the only thing an M.F.A. will give you is the ability to go out and teach creative writing. It's fine and good to go and study with a professional because that's somebody who can give you an honest, informed, accurate evaluation of your work and try to point you in the right direction.

The reason I went was because I was desperate for some help. I had worked for two years on my own and I had knocked on all these doors and nothing was happening. I wanted someone to show me what I was doing wrong. I was writing mystery stories and horror stories and stories about people killing each other over just hatred or little trivial things, and my teacher said, "I don't have any problem with the way you construct a sentence, but your subject matter is what you've got to find and these are the people you've got to read and understand." She gave me the *Norton Anthology of Short Fiction* and said, "You start reading 'Heart of Darkness' and you start reading 'An Occurrence at Owl Creek Bridge' and you start reading 'A Good Man Is Hard to Find' and you'll find out what the things are to write about." And she was right.

I've taught in M.F.A. programs, and really, about all I do when I go and teach is give them my opinion about their work and at the same time tell them, "You're going to get your degree, and that's going to get you a job, some income, and that's fine because you've got to have some income 'cause you're not going to make it on your writing for a long time. But it's completely up to you how many hours you spend locked away in that room, and only the people who write are going to be writers." There's a difference in talking about being a writer and being one.

SR: You mentioned Breece Pancake's book this morning. There's someone the pressure got to.

LB: There's a lot of pressure, and Breece was a good writer. There's no telling what he'd have done if he'd lived. There's no telling what John Kennedy Toole would have written if he'd lived. And Richard Brautigan. A lot of people have succumbed to that, and "Ninety-two Days" and "Discipline" are about dealing with all that frustration and what it's like to want something so bad—and you can't have it and you can't have it and you can't have it and you can't have it—but you keep on after it. I guess it's about the perseverance required to be a writer. "Discipline" was something I dreamed up one day and thought it was an idea that hadn't been tried on before, so I just invented all this stuff. Hack's Prison, these guys going on parole for plagiarism, for copying William Faulkner under the bedsheets at night with a flashlight and stuff. They had to have involuntary sex, they had to put on earplugs and noseplugs and blindfolds, with these obese women who were hairy and sweaty and were whispering, "We're big fans of yours" and told them they were famous and they belonged to a poetry society, and that was his punishment. They wouldn't give him a beer and he had to have this involuntary sex, and this guy was grilling him.

I don't know if you could call it a story. It's more of an exercise, an experiment in form.

SR: How was that one received when you sent it out?
LB: It wasn't received worth a shit. Nobody would take that story, and it was one of the ones I'd sent out so much I finally gave up on it, and then after I had published two books, and was putting *Big Bad Love* together, I had a bunch of other stories I hadn't had published and I showed them to Shannon, and that was one of the ones I showed her and she said, "Oh we've got to publish this." It finally found a home, but no magazine ever took it.

SR: Do you feel your apprenticeship was unusually frustrating or long?
LB: I probably thought it was unusually long, but it probably wasn't really out of line with anybody else's apprenticeship. The only thing that really bugged me was getting to that point in 1985 when I'd written "Facing the Music" and people were telling me, "This is a good story and it's publishable, but we can't publish it. Somebody's going to publish it, but we can't." It was two years down the road before it finally got taken, and then I learned the hardest lesson of all, that you can get to the point where you're writing publishable fiction and still have it rejected for other reasons. It wasn't being rejected because the story wasn't good, it was being rejected because it hurt people too bad to read it. Because it was too honest. And too brutal, some say. And the only way I can really defend myself against any of that is to say, "Well, yeah it's brutal, but I think that it's honest." And what I think you've got to do is share this experience with these people. That's what I'm writing about. That's what the story is about. And you can't just tack a happy ending on things.

An Interview with Larry Brown

Kay Bonetti / 1995

Originally published in *Missouri Review* 18.3 (1995): 79–107. Reprinted in *Conversations with American Novelists: The Best Interviews from "The Missouri Review" and the American Audio Prose Library*, ed. Kay Bonetti, Greg Michalson, Speer Morgan, Jo Sapp, and Sam Stowers (Columbia, MO: University of Missouri Press, 1997): 234–53. Used by permission of the University of Missouri Press. Copyright © 1997 by the Curators of the University of Missouri.

Larry Brown lives in Oxford, Mississippi, where he was born and raised. He joined the Marine Corps during the time of the Vietnam War. Though he was never stationed out of the country, he got to know and hear the stories of many returning disabled marine vets while he was stationed at Camp Lejeune and the Marine Barracks. After his stint in the military, he returned home and worked for the Oxford Fire Department for sixteen years. He resigned in 1990 at the rank of captain to write full-time in a kind of self-imposed apprenticeship that he compares to that of a carpenter. His novels are informed by his experiences with the marines and as a fireman, as well as by the acute kinship with place and family he has acquired living his entire life in Faulkner's South. Brown is the author of a memoir, *On Fire* (1994), and five books of fiction, *Facing the Music* (1988), *Dirty Work* (1989), *Big Bad Love* (1990), *Joe* (1991), and most recently *Father and Son* (1996). This interview was conducted in June 1995, while he was finishing work on *Father and Son*.

INTERVIEWER: You list your hometown as Oxford, Mississippi, where you're still living and worked as a firefighter for sixteen years. Did you actually grow up in the city or out in the country?

Brown: I was born in Oxford at the old hospital up the street from the courthouse, but we lived about twelve miles out in the country. We moved to Memphis when I was about three years old. I lived there ten years and went to school in Memphis until the eighth grade, which was in '64, and then we moved back to Mississippi, and I've been out around here all the time since then, for the last thirty-one years.

INTERVIEWER: What took your family up to Memphis?
Brown: My father came out of World War II in '45, and he farmed for a good
long while, but he was having all of us, and just really couldn't make a go of it
farming. He had a good job waiting for him at Fruehauf Trailer Company in
Memphis so we moved up there. By that point there were six of us altogether,
my mother and my daddy and my two brothers and my sister. We had a
growing family in a short length of time. I was born in '51. My father
came out of the war in '45, and my sister and one of my brothers are older
than me.

INTERVIEWER: I understand your mother was a postmistress?
Brown: She did that part-time until she retired. We had a little store out at
Tula that Mary Annie and I ran for a couple of years. Mother would come in
and take care of the mail every day. The Postal Service was threatening to
close the post office unless we could move it into a building that stayed open
all day long, so I went over and took all the stuff and moved it into my store,
and nailed it all back together, and we opened the post office in the store.
We've still got it out there, too.

INTERVIEWER: Is that the store you've modeled John Coleman's store in
Joe and the store in the story "Old Soldiers" with Mr. Aaron on?
Brown: Actually, ours was a relatively new building. The store that's in
my books was torn down sometime around 1966 or '67, and had been
there for a long time. It had the potbellied stove and the patches of tin on the
floor, and all the bottle caps just ground into the sand, hundreds and hundreds and hundreds of them, and the old slick benches out front that had
been whittled and had people's initials in them because they'd been used
for years.

INTERVIEWER: Where did the love of books and reading come from?
Brown: Mainly from my mother. One of my earliest memories is of seeing
her reading. There were always books in our house. I just grew to love it real
early, I guess—escaping into stories and discovering other worlds. When I
was a child I was a big reader of Greek mythology. I actually read a lot of literature without knowing what I was doing, because Mother bought a set of
encyclopedias, and there was a set of ten classics that came with it. There was
Edgar Allan Poe, and Mark Twain, and Zane Grey, and Herman Melville, and

Grimms' Fairy Tales, and Greek mythology, the *Iliad* and the *Odyssey*, and Jack London. That's eventually what brought me to writing—loving to read.

INTERVIEWER: Was there a point when you started separating things out and making distinctions of taste?

Brown: I don't think I did until around 1982. I had been writing for about two years, pretty much on my own. I had published one short story in *Easyriders* motorcycle magazine. That was my first publication. I was really desperate for some help. So I came out here and went to a writing class that Ellen Douglas taught at the university. She pointed me toward a lot of things that I hadn't seen before, like the work of Joseph Conrad and Dostoevsky and Flannery O'Connor. It was around that time that I began to discover what kind of writer I wanted to be. I had read Faulkner when I was sixteen years old. I really didn't think too much about it, except that "The Bear" was a great hunting story. It was only when I got older that I could appreciate all the other things that story was about, like the encroaching of industry upon the forest, and the way things were changing and all this happening as this young boy comes of age. The gradual reduction of the wilderness, just by the railroad coming through, and people beginning to log the timber off. All that was real saddening once I grasped it later on, but it was only after I started writing that I was fully able to appreciate the value of that story.

INTERVIEWER: You must have recognized it because of the landscape.

Brown: Very much so. It was all very familiar to me. It was right up my alley. When I was sixteen that's what I wanted to do—stay in the woods with my gun and hunt every day and half the night sometimes, too.

INTERVIEWER: I gather that you didn't much like school.

Brown: No, I didn't. I was such a poor student that I failed English my senior year and had to go to summer school to get my diploma. I didn't graduate with the rest of my class. It was very disappointing to my mother.

INTERVIEWER: Why was that? Was it just attitude?

Brown: It was probably a combination of losing my father when I was sixteen and never having any interest in school to begin with. The only interest I had was in getting out of school, getting a job and buying a car, because I didn't have any way to go anywhere. I always had to catch rides with somebody else. I was just itching to get out on my own and start making a living. I didn't think that the future looked very bright at that point anyway because the war was going on. All the boys I grew up with were worrying about it. We'd already had some friends who'd gone over and been killed. I pretty much knew that I was going to have to go into the service at the height of the Vietnam War. I didn't have any long-range plans. I didn't see too much reason to worry a whole lot about what happened in school.

INTERVIEWER: Is Walter James's story in *Dirty Work*, at least in terms of the going away, close to your story?
Brown: In some ways. Of course my father was already gone, then. But one thing that struck me, and why there are references to my father in there, was I saw what a tremendous sacrifice he had made, and that veterans of the Vietnam War made. War is an awful thing, and I didn't understand exactly what his life had been like until I heard him talk about all the hardships that he'd suffered, and how lucky he'd been to come out at the other end of it alive. The guys in *Dirty Work* are actually based on some disabled marines that I met in the early seventies in Philadelphia where I was stationed—guys who were in wheelchairs, who had lost their arms and legs and had made that great sacrifice, too.

INTERVIEWER: You were in the marines during the period of the Vietnam War. Why didn't you get sent overseas? Was it just the luck of the draw?
Brown: I just lucked out. Around the time that I went in, October of 1970, some of the troop withdrawals had already started. Now the marines' policy—I didn't know this when I went in—is, they're the first in, they're the first out, too. A lot of the people who were getting pulled back were in the Marine Corps. The troop involvement was winding down. There were still a few people getting sent over, but from my platoon of thirty-eight men, probably only four or five had to go.

INTERVIEWER: How did you spend your time in the marines?
Brown: I went to the big base at Camp Lejeune, North Carolina, first. Then I got orders to go to Marine Barracks, which is the oldest post in the Marine Corps. It was founded in 1776. It's what they call a dress-blues station. They issue you a set of dress blues—you've seen these marines with blue pants and tunics? What you do is a lot of official duty. There's a big naval shipyard

there. You christen ships, you march in parades, you have to be on all this spit-and-polish detail—things like that.

INTERVIEWER: But you met some disabled vets.

Brown: We had an NCO club behind our barracks. These guys would come over in their wheelchairs, and there was a set of steps there, four or five high. We'd just roll their wheelchairs up those steps and push them back there with us. There were two guys I was most impressed by. One of them didn't have any legs at all, but he had a pair of artificial legs, with pants on and tennis shoes on the bottom. He would come in on a pair of crutches, and you couldn't tell he didn't have any legs. He'd sit up on a bar stool and order a beer. The other guy had the kind of injury that Walter has. He had been shot all the way through the base of his skull. To look at him, he didn't have any kind of disfiguring wound. He was a nice-looking young man about twenty-one or twenty-two years old. But he had blackouts, seizures. They could control it somewhat with medicine, but not to the point where he could remain on active duty. So here was a nice, good-looking young guy walking around, twenty-two years old, on a hundred percent disability for medical problems. All that stuff is based on these real people.

INTERVIEWER: How did you get to know them that well?

Brown: We were marines, too. We were marines and these guys were all Marine Corps veterans, and they were attached to the naval hospital there. I guess they got passes to leave their ward—the ones who were mobile. My friend with the artificial legs had his car fixed up with hand levers. He'd drive himself around, wherever he wanted to go. He had a girlfriend and lived a pretty normal life. That's where all that came from. All the stuff about the weapons and the war I either learned as part of my training, or from talking to veterans of the war. The whole Marine Corps was full of them. The sergeants and everybody were all veterans. Everybody you talked to—the officers—had already been over there and served and come back and been decorated. They were all full of stories. The Marine Corps is full of history. It has a really proud tradition, and they teach you about the great battles the marines have fought in. They show you footage of the first day at Iwo Jima, when they shelled Mount Suribachi for two weeks, and then the first wave went out from those ships and there were three thousand U.S. Marines mowed down and killed the first day—in one day three thousand of them died. You see all that and you get indoctrinated into it. It just becomes a way of life.

INTERVIEWER: You said "I put my father in *Dirty Work*" in that scene between Walter and his dad. To what extent is the portrait of the father in that novel a portrait of your own dad?

Brown: In little ways, here and there. My father never killed anybody and went to the penitentiary or anything. I make up all my characters out of little bits and pieces of real life. But I would like to think that if he and I had been allowed to have that conversation, if he had lived long enough to see me go in, the conversation would have been like that: he would have told me to be careful, and watch out, to try to come back home.

INTERVIEWER: What about the man that runs that country store in Tula—the John Coleman and Mr. Aaron character in "Old Soldiers"? Is that a tribute to, or a portrait of, somebody you know?

Brown: Yes. His name was Norman Clark. He had the store there. He came out of the war just about the same time my father did and he never went anywhere after that. At one point he had a brand-new four-door 1962 Chevrolet Impala. That car sat right across the road and rotted into the ground. There was a period of twelve years when he never left Tula, and Tula's only a few hundred yards long. He stayed in that store every day for thirty-something years.

INTERVIEWER: Did he have sixty thousand dollars in a bank bag? That's what John Coleman says he has in his bank bag when he goes off in the truck—to Joe Ransom's surprise he agrees to go for a ride with him.

Brown: He had more than that! Somebody would bring a check in and say, "Can you cash this check for me, Norman?" He'd say, "Yes." They'd say, "Well, that's a pretty big check now. Sure you can cash it?" He'd say, "Yeah." It didn't matter how big the check was, he could cash it. He had the money in there. And he had that pistol, too. Everybody knew it. He kept his Budweiser in the candy case, too. He didn't mind drinking it hot.

INTERVIEWER: How often do you take people out of the community and out of your life, and transform them into your work?

Brown: In this particular case it was somebody I cared a whole lot about, because I can remember being a little bitty boy and going in his store. He would give me a little pack of candy corn and make some kind of joke about a rooster pecking, or something like that. But then I grew up and spent a lot of time with him. If you went in there by yourself and nobody else was there he would sit down and talk to you and tell you stories. He would tell these great war stories, just like my daddy. But if one other person was there he wouldn't do it. It had to be you and him. I stayed up at the store a lot. It was a little bitty place we lived in. There wasn't much to do sometimes, in the summer. Then I went into the service and came back out. I married and began to raise a family, and he was there in the store. He just died a few years back, from a war wound. He got blood poisoning from a piece of shrapnel that was in one of his leg bones that they never got out.

INTERVIEWER: Is that a sensitive issue for you—using people in your fiction that are modeled on people out of your own life?
Brown: Not really. Even though characters may sometimes be based on real people, what happens is that the story around them will be different. The events will be different and they won't do the same things in my story that they did in real life. They might have a similar lifestyle, but I will invent the rest.

INTERVIEWER: What about the family cemetery, the old house in *Joe,* where the Jones family is squatting. That's the Coleman Place. You figure that out as you're reading the book. Are that little springhouse and the well-tended grave site there real?
Brown: They're all real but they're in different places. The log house was down on a place called Neal Hill many years ago when I used to hunt down there. It's since been bulldozed down. The grave was something that a friend and I found out in the middle of the woods one day deer hunting up in the national forest. There was no structure anywhere around, just these weird little plants like a little protective garden, right in the middle of all these big trees. Just one grave. And the springhouse is something that I remembered from years and years ago. I had a friend, an older fellow I used to coon hunt with all the time. He had an old springhouse on his place. It was ice cold. You don't see those things anymore.

INTERVIEWER: The interesting thing about the use of a detail like that in the novel *Joe* is the kind of atmosphere or reverberation that it helps to create in the character John Coleman. And by extension, in *Joe* as well. It makes the region and this community really sing.

Brown: It's a way to establish history and give some depth to the background of the people. There are old cemeteries scattered in the woods out where I live. Some of the stones go back to the 1700s. These communities died out for some mysterious reason a long time ago. But it's fascinating to me to know that this country was being settled back when the Constitution was being written—that there were people down here in Mississippi, living and building homes and raising families and pretty much exploring this whole country, which was a big wilderness back in those days.

INTERVIEWER: You also move the story, explore character and, in the case of Joe, illuminate the landscape through the world of work. Larry Brown seems to be a person who is fascinated with the daily details of physical work.

Brown: I think it's a hard thing for a man to have to get up every morning and work hard doing some kind of physical labor, like swinging a hammer, all day long. I've had to do that so much myself to support my writing habit. Writing didn't bring in any money. I was doing it all the time, but I wasn't selling anything. I couldn't just come home from the fire department and sit down and write because I had three children to feed. So I'd have to do stuff like build houses and tote bricks, and haul hay, and deaden timber and sack groceries and all the other things that I did. I'm well versed in what hard work is. I really admire the people who do it. A lot of people turn their backs on it, and lay out or become bums or something.

INTERVIEWER: It's interesting how you use it to illuminate character. You learn a lot about Joe Ransom's history from him banging out the fender on that old GMC truck. He says, "I used to be a body man." You wonder if it was in prison or not. The point is, that moves the relationship between him and Gary at that point in the story. It also shows keen observation of detail on your part.

Brown: I listen to people, and I look at their lives and wonder what they're about. Then I begin exploring. I put a character in a situation and I know that I have to have some kind of trouble going early on to involve me in the story, because I'm interested in the way people get through their lives. Joe has had all this stuff happen to him. He's lost his family, his son won't even speak to him, he's been in the penitentiary. He lives by himself. And he's got this work ethic too. He believes that a man ought to get up and go to work every morning.

INTERVIEWER: And he makes a good living.
Brown: He's lucked out and got this job which pays very well, but he has to think about what he's doing, which is killing a living organism, a living forest. He's not happy with what he's doing, but it's a job. I guess he looks at it maybe, "If I don't do it, somebody else will. It's going to get done."

INTERVIEWER: The narrator says, through his point of view, that he's thinking about what he's doing. What is it, in the larger sense of the word?
Brown: The major thing, I think, is destroying the habitat for a whole bunch of wildlife. Hardwood forests support so many different forms of life: deer, turkey, squirrels, all the birds and insects and reptiles that live there. It's a renewable crop every year, this food that comes from oak trees and beech trees and all. The animals gather that up. Squirrels hide it. Predators find their prey there. Hawks and owls and all different forms of life are there. Man uses it to get food from, too. All that gets cut down, and you come back and plant a pine tree on it, and the only thing it bears is a pinecone, with a few little seeds in it. Once you lose that hardwood forest you've lost it forever, because they take so long to grow. You can have a pine plantation ready to harvest in about twenty years. You probably won't have even the first crop of acorns off of oaks until they're thirty years old. Once they're established, and they keep getting bigger and bigger, they provide a huge canopy from the sun. It's shady down there, right now, in the middle of the day, at three-thirty in the afternoon. Leaves fall year after year and choke out the small undergrowth. The big trees are left, and it's just like a floor. The beauty of a hardwood forest to me is unmatched. I think that's what Faulkner was talking about so long ago when he said that the land would accomplish its own revenge on the people. That's true. All that forest has largely disappeared, except for some privately held tracts of land in Lafayette County and what's available up on the national forest. It's gotten to the point now where if you want to hunt you've got to either own some land or be in a hunting club. Things have really changed from what they were when I was eighteen years old and could hunt anywhere in this

county I wanted to, and nobody would tell me there's a posted sign over there.

INTERVIEWER: To what extent were you trying to call attention to issues like that in *Joe*?

Brown: I used to do that for a part-time living. I'm not proud of what I did. I did it simply for the money, to feed my family. I deadened timber in the springtime and the summer, and planted the pines in the winter. It's brutal work. A lot of people can't do it. They come out one day and quit at the end of that day. It's a tough thing to get out there at daylight when it's ten degrees, and work all day setting those pine trees. And it's tough to get out there at six in the summertime, in May, and go down through the woods and run into snakes and yellow jackets and spiderwebs. *Joe* gave me a great opportunity to show the landscape, and to set my characters against it. And to have this larger thing, even larger than the lives that are going on, which is the land. The ground is so ancient. It's the oldest thing we've got. I like to have people picture what is looks like—that distant watershed where all the lines of trees fade into this little blue line that's the end of the horizon. That's what I love. This is my country, and I love this place. I try to re-create it on the page.

INTERVIEWER: In your book on fire fighting, called *On Fire*, you imagined a scene, or you saw this family walking down the road. It became the Jones family walking down the road in the opening pages of *Joe*. Was that the germ of the novel?

Brown: Yes. I started writing it around 1984 or 1985, after I had already written five bad novels and thrown them all away. I burned one of them in the backyard. That was the first image that I had. The image of that family came before *Joe* came. Later on I invented my protagonist. But the opening shot that I wanted was that family walking down that hot blacktop road through a deserted landscape in the middle of the summer, with no place to go.

INTERVIEWER: Where did Joe come in? How did he get in the mix?

Brown: He came as a way to try to save Gary from what his fate would have ordinarily been—probably something bad on down the road somewhere. The kid has never really been given a chance, and his father's not good.

I wanted him to have a chance at a relationship with—not another father, but somebody who could take care of him for a little while. Joe was invented to do that. In the course of working on the story about him, I began to find out that his story was important, too. He had to have a background, a history, a future. This timber job was a logical thing for him to have. He'd lived a good bit of his life already. He'd already had other jobs. He'd had family. And now this is what he was left with. He was left with this job and a dog. That's really all that he has. Once in a while he has a woman, but he doesn't care too much about that. He cares about taking care of the future and trying to get through his life without going back to the penitentiary.

INTERVIEWER: Which he probably fails at, ultimately.
Brown: Yes.

INTERVIEWER: What fascinates me about the Jones family is that in spite of the horribleness of their background and their history, and all the things that have been going on throughout their life, they're a family. That's what pulls Gary back, tragically, into that milieu. The question of family and community is apparently very important to you. It's underneath everything you do, in your short stories and in the novels.
Brown: I'm concerned very much with family connections, relatives, and all that. That's like a nest you go back home to every night. You have these people around who are going to be with you all your life—the person you picked to marry, and your children. Your grandchildren are going to come from them, and you had the family that you came out of. And your mother had the family she came out of, and your father, on down the line. The Joneses are dysfunctional as a family, but still they're a unit. Fay takes it as long as she can, and then she goes. She's seen some of the others leave, too. Gary is young enough to remember Calvin. What happened to him and all. Putting all that in just illustrates how hopeless Gary's case is. I wanted him to have a chance. When you're writing something you never know how these things are going to turn out. When it came time to finish this novel, I wrote the ending of *Joe* about five different times.

INTERVIEWER: You rewrote the ending five times? Different outcomes?
Brown: Different outcomes. One was a happily-ever-after where everything was hunky-dory. But the question that I ultimately had to ask myself

was: Do the guilty always get punished in life, or do the innocent sometimes have to catch some stuff? And I said, in the real world they do, and if your fiction really imitates life, that's what you have to go with. I build my stories, and I try to be authentic in them. I sometimes get accused of being brutal and having a dark vision. That may be true. I don't know why my stuff is so dark. Except that I believe the whole process is just an attempt to pull the reader into the story, like I said a while ago. To make him forget that he's reading. Tragedy is inevitable in my stories, because of the circumstances people live in. I think my characters—most of them—know the difference between right and wrong. Certainly Wade knows the difference between right and wrong. So does Joe. But doing those things—that's where you come to grips with your characters, how they react in certain situations.

INTERVIEWER: Along with family, community is extremely important in your work. But the community is implied. It's interesting that you look at community from the points of view of those who are in fact, as you said in one of your short stories, living separate in the same house on badly eroded land, in a house of poor quality. I'm curious about that. Why do you choose to look at the issue of family and community from the broken side?
Brown: If Joe was a regular family guy he wouldn't have been involved in all this drinking and fighting and messing around with the police—all the things that he's done that have given him such a reputation and made every lawman around know him. He has a code of his own that he goes by. You have to respect him or fight him if you're going to tangle with him. I made his life the way it is to give the reader a sense early on of the brokenness of his life, and the amount of time he spends alone in that house listening to the tape player over and over again, watching junk on television that he doesn't even like, eating poorly, drinking way too much, smoking all these cigarettes, and all the carousing that he sometimes does. He has periods when he can do fine. He can go to work every day and go home and sleep every night. Then he has other times when he starts drinking and he gets in trouble. He starts running into people and making mistakes, and he has to start paying for all his mistakes again. Then he becomes partially involved with this kid, Gary. He becomes concerned about him and sees what the old man's doing to him, sees it the first day that he pays the kid off. He knows that the boy's old man, Wade, is going to take every penny the kid made that day. The way he looks at it is that there's no sense in paying him to work if Wade is going to take it

anyway. "It's too painful to watch and I don't want to have to watch it because I know what's going to happen." But a little later he thinks, "If he won't bring his old man back, maybe he'll have a chance." Things get a little better and he says, "Maybe I can sell him my truck. He'll have a ride," and all this. Then he begins to find out more: how the kid can't read, doesn't know what a church is, how ignorant he is of the world around him, the things that other boys around him take for granted.

INTERVIEWER: One reader has pointed out that another tragedy is that what Joe passes on in his initiation—such as it is—to Gary is the torch of some of his most destructive and worst habits, especially alcohol. I assume you would say, "That's the way it goes. That's the way things do tend to work themselves out." Nothing's wasted in this book, so you must have been keenly aware of the irony there.
Brown: Yes. Whatever kind of deal Gary is going to get out of Wade is going to be rotten. His father won't even defend him when some guy is beating him up. Even though he's in kind of rough hands, with Joe I feel like he's in better hands. There's hope towards the end that things are going to work out for him. But all these wheels have already been set in motion a long time ago.

INTERVIEWER: The rule of inevitability.
Brown: The rule of inevitability. It's got to drop off like ripe fruit in your hand, to be unexpected and inevitable at the same time. That's what Katherine Anne Porter said, and I believe that. Some readers have a problem accepting that life goes like this sometimes.

INTERVIEWER: I'm intrigued by the sheriff—that scene towards the end of *Joe*. The sheriff comes in as the voice of sanity and says, "You can't take your dog into somebody else's house and let them kill another dog. Joe, you just can't do things like this." Joe's wife tells him, "I can't have a social life because you'd go out and beat the guy up." And he says, "Me? Me, do that?" At that point in the novel, which is towards the beginning, you don't really know if in fact he's capable of it. But you find out yeah, he probably would do something like that. The sheriff's a guy who's been wild in the past and he's straightened around. You're not curious about a character like that? I think his story would be interesting.

Brown: He's the last voice of reason trying to speak to Joe. He's already witnessed Joe's descent into the place he got to when he had to fight with all the police officers uptown. He knows full well what is going to happen. He's got his ear on what's going on in the county. He knows Willie shot Joe. He knows what's coming. He says, "How long do you think you and Willie Russell can keep shooting at each other before one of you winds up dead?" Joe just laughs and says, "Huh, somebody ought to do the world a favor." That's what he means, too. The world would be better off if that son of a bitch was dead.

INTERVIEWER: He's right. But the sheriff knows something that Joe doesn't know about reality.
Brown: And the sheriff has to operate on the right side of the law, but Joe doesn't. There's nobody to take care of it but Joe. It just falls into his lap. If somebody doesn't take care of these people right now—Willie and Wade— this is going to happen again, and no telling how long it's been happening. They stole Gary's truck, Willie's beaten him up, now his dad's selling his little sister, took his money. How much more am I going to let him get away with? That's Joe's question.

INTERVIEWER: You still haven't answered my question about writing a novel from the point of view of these members of the community.
Brown: The novel I'm working on now is about a guy, Glen, getting out of the penitentiary after three years, and coming home. I was pretty sure that this novel was going to focus on him. But he gets met at the cemetery—his mother has died while he's in the pen—he gets met at the cemetery the first day he's home by the sheriff, a guy that he grew up with. And slowly the focus, as I wrote, began to slide over to Bobby, the sheriff, and his home life. Bobby is a really good man. He's that voice of reason in the book I'm working on now. But these two characters have something between them, and that is they both want the same woman. She has had Glen's illegitimate child before he went in, so the child is between three and four years old now. But in the three years he's been down, the sheriff has been out and she's been unattached. They haven't actually been lovers, but they've gotten to feeling very, very strongly about each other, and she's going to give Glen one chance to come back, claim this baby and give it a name. She's still unmarried. Bobby wants her. He's willing to take the baby too, give it his name, do everything.

All he wants is family. He wants them for his family. Glen doesn't really care if he ever has a family or not because he's very estranged from his own family, from his father, from things that have gone before. He has a lot of hatred. He blames a lot of people for the mistakes that he's made. The one thing that he's going to do when he comes home is take care of his enemies. He begins to do that as soon as he gets home.

INTERVIEWER: A lot of people who study the lives of policemen say that they have difficulty in their personal lives because their world vision gets skewed from what they're seeing all the time. In reading *On Fire*, I couldn't help but wonder if you think that all those years you spent on the Oxford Fire Department intensified that attention to the darker side. You talk in there about how mainly in your work you see people over and over again that have been out driving drunk, decapitated on bridges, young lives snuffed out, people burned to death from doing something totally stupid like driving while drunk, people who get drunk and burn the apartment down. Was it just a good source of material, or do you think in fact it shaped your view of the world?

Brown: What it showed me was that poverty causes many of these terrible tragedies, because the people who are on the lower end of the economic scale are the ones who have the lousy housing, who live in the firetraps. Why? Because the wiring is bad, because somebody's been careless, somebody's put a penny in the fuse box and there's a wire under the rug, or the smoke detector doesn't have a battery in it, or their child has never been told not to play with matches and catches the curtains on fire, then catches their pajamas on fire. Of course, it can happen to anybody. Some fellow can go out and have a car wreck in his big Cadillac. But so many times you may go from the biggest mansion in the city of Oxford that morning down to the most squalid shack on the other side of town that evening. You can figure which one's going to be the worst. It's because of the conditions that poor people live in. You get your eyes opened to something like that, and it makes you appreciate the life that you have, and the things that you've been taught, and your children. Even though they might get a little wild sometimes, at least they're not out selling drugs or robbing folks on the street. It also tends to make you appreciate family even more. Many of the things that I saw in the fire department were so bad, and the memories of them wouldn't let me sleep sometimes. All that stuff is what I write about—what I saw and the way it made me feel.

INTERVIEWER: Everybody who talks to Larry Brown hears that when he was twenty-nine he decided to start writing. But somehow there's got to be more to it. What happened? You'd been on the fire department seven years at this point. You were married. You had at least two or three of your children.

Brown: Right before I turned thirty I looked at my life and I said, "Okay, what are you going to do with it?" I think I just wanted to make something more out of myself than what I was. Being a firefighter was, and is, I still think, a very noble, honorable profession because it's in the business of helping people. But I said, "Isn't there something else you can do with your life that might be even better?" I said, "Well, what about writing?" As much as I loved to read, I wanted to know how people went into a room and sat down and created a book out of their imagination or memory or whatever—created this book where nothing had existed before, a tangible object you could pick up and hold in your hand. How did people do that? I decided, "All it's going to cost is a typewriter and paper, a very basic thing. I'm going to write a novel."

INTERVIEWER: It could have also cost your family life, your personal life, as you illustrate so well in some of your stories about writers.

Brown: For many years nobody understood what I was doing or why I was doing it. I'd had a project not too long before that where I was going to disassemble a '55 Chevrolet and put it back together. I had it up on blocks in my pasture. The whole thing lay in pieces and never got put back together. Somebody finally came and towed it away. Mary Annie probably thought writing was just another little whim like that. But a couple of years later I was still working hard at it. She began to see that I was dedicating myself to changing careers, to stopping the job as a firefighter to become a writer. I think the years that a person goes through learning to write are just like the years that a journeyman carpenter goes through, or a brick mason goes through, learning how to lay an even course. It's an acquired skill. I don't think people are born with talent. The reason I say that is because if you went out to the house and climbed up in the attic and looked at all those bad novels and stories that are up there gathering dust, you would say that Larry Brown has no talent. You would have to.

INTERVIEWER: That's interesting, because I know people who after twenty years think of themselves as aspiring writers and the stuff they're writing is still bad. I guess it's a question of learning from your mistakes. How did you identify the mistakes in the first place, to learn from them? Writing is so solitary. You don't have a steward over you saying, "You didn't tie that knot right. Here's how you do that."

Brown: One thing you have to do is lose all your sentimental feelings about your characters. You also have to get a certain amount of bullshit out of your system to tell what's genuine from what's fake. There are two ways you can go. You can be sentimental, or you can be hard-hearted. The perfect place to be is right in the middle. You walk a fine line between weeping over the stuff and turning a cold eye on it. You can't fool people. You have to be honest with them. I think that you go into a room and you believe in yourself. You must have this unshakable belief, no matter if you can prove it today or not, that you're going to make it. That's the only thing that kept me going. I told myself, "If I do this thing long enough, I will eventually learn how." It takes discipline to actually commit to sit down and do the work, to invent all these hundreds of stories and ideas that you come up with that don't even get finished, that get thrown away. It's mainly up to you. I don't think that I was born with any talent. I think it's more just a way I have of looking at the world that's different from how most people look at the world, but that people everywhere can identify with.

INTERVIEWER: You said you came to Ole Miss to take a writing course from Ellen Douglas. What did that teach you?

Brown: She told me, "I don't have any problem with the way you construct a sentence. It's your subject matter that you need to learn about—what the things are to write about." My first novel was about a man-eating grizzly bear in Yellowstone National Park. The next one was about a couple of guys who were going to raise a big patch of marijuana in Tennessee and sell it. The third novel was a supernatural novel. The fourth was a boxing novel. I don't know anything about boxing. I've watched a lot of it, but I never have done any of it. The fifth novel was about some guys who lived out in the woods around here, and it almost got published. Then I started writing *Joe* and *Dirty Work*, and I published both of them.

INTERVIEWER: You took six years to write *Joe*. How long did you take to write *Dirty Work*?

Brown: I wrote *Dirty Work* in two and a half years of very hard work. I didn't do anything else for those two and a half years.

INTERVIEWER: What started that?

Brown: I took six months off from writing in 1986 to build the house that I live in now. *Joe* was already underway, but I said, "Okay, I can't go drive nails for twelve hours and then write at night, too, so I'm just going to drop it for six months, get the house built and move in it. Then I'll start back writing again." During the time that the house was under construction, I got an idea about a guy whose face was disfigured from a rocket attack in Vietnam and he wouldn't come out of his room. That was all I had. It was just driving me crazy to get to work on it, but I couldn't until I had all the sheetrock hung, and the wallpaper and paint, trim, the cabinets, all the million things that go in a house. But the day that I had a table to put my typewriter on, and a chair to sit in—we hadn't even moved in yet—I sat down and started writing *Dirty Work*. That idea had grown and festered in those months and I just had to get it down. It turned out that I had to write it five different times and throw out six hundred pages. It went through five complete revisions.

INTERVIEWER: At what point did the two voices come in, of Walter and Braiden?

Brown: After the third draft, when I finally showed the manuscript to my editor, Shannon Ravenel. She wrote back and said, "Larry, the bad news is your novel starts on page 160." I said, "Oh, no. That's unacceptable. I'm just going to throw it away. I've put in too much work. I'm not going to go through all that." She wrote me a letter and said, "You have worked by yourself all this time. You haven't had any guidance, I understand all of that. But this is too good an idea for you to throw away. Just trust me and work on it with me. I'm going to help you." And she was right. We started working on it again. I started writing the fourth draft. We sent things back and forth. We'd argue sometimes. We'd have our disagreements. But in the process I discovered that she was right about all that stuff. She was the one who taught me so much about characters' histories, their relationships, their feelings, their memories, their childhoods, their concerns, and how characters had to be so well fleshed out.

INTERVIEWER: To what extent do you accept or are you comfortable with *Dirty Work*'s identification as a novel of the Vietnam era, and of you as a novelist of the Vietnam era?

Brown: The word *Vietnam* is never mentioned in that book. It's about the aftermath of the war more than the war itself. There aren't a whole lot of combat scenes. There's a little bit about the war in there. But it's mainly about what happens to people years and years on down the road. That's why it carries the dedication that it does: "This book is for Daddy, who knew what war does to men." He saw and went through so many terrible things. The guys that I met did too. I wanted to say something about the people who make these sacrifices for us, the veterans—the guys who we honor every Memorial Day. Sometimes what happens to them is not pretty. Many people's lives are not right, and are never going to be right. Those are the people I explore over and over. If you don't have problems in your characters' lives, then you don't have a story. The way to hook your reader is to give your character some trouble early on, and then find out what's going to happen, and sandbag him and put all this pressure on him and see how he's going to react when things really get tough.

INTERVIEWER: *Dirty Work* also seems to me to be a book that's about the question of how God works in this world. There's a real dialogue that's taking place at a philosophical and a spiritual level between Walter and Braiden throughout the book. Were you conscious of that as being one of the questions you wanted to address?

Brown: Certainly. I wanted to address what I felt God would say about Braiden, the situation that he's in, having lived for twenty years without arms or legs. He's reached a point where he just wants to die, but he has to persuade someone to do that for him. Jesus comes down and explains everything very straightforwardly to him: "I can't take your life. This guy over here, that's something else, but you're treading on shaky ground." It's not exactly suicide, but in a way it kind of is, too. But I also believe that God is very merciful and compassionate, and would not blame Braiden for wanting to leave, even though life is what he gave you—"all of us," that's what he says. That's very much true. Life is what he gave us. But some lives get to the point where they're unbearable, and Braiden's life has gotten to that point.

INTERVIEWER: Braiden says at one point about the question of suffering in the world, "God doesn't work like that. God doesn't visit suffering on the world. Things just get out of hand." So what do you think, philosophically? Is Braiden speaking for you?

Brown: I don't know if he's speaking for me. I've got a very deep faith. I'm not a compulsive churchgoer. I was for many, many years. I was raised in a church. I don't go like I used to, but I still have this faith. I believe that the world is a hard place for a lot of people, but there are also many, many good things about it. You hardly ever hear about the good things. I think in some ways I was trying to create a situation that most people would never encounter, but I wanted those people to know what Braiden had been going through and what a good human being he was, and what the loss of him was. We lost a schoolteacher, we lost some guy who was going to try and help other people with his life. He was really a kid, and then he lost everything that he had. The world's forgotten about him. All the medals have been pinned on and the TV's turned to another channel. He's still here, and he's going to be here unless somebody can do something for him.

INTERVIEWER: You've talked quite a bit about the struggle you went through to establish yourself as a writer. How do you feel about it now that you have published five books?
Brown: Many times it's still a complete shock to me to just see a finished book and say, "How did you ever manage to accomplish that?" But it's an accumulation of time. You spend every day doing it, and you spend enough days together in a row, then you've got a book. It's like building a house. It may be real hard—the days may be real hot or real cold when you're doing it—but after the house is finished, no matter how tired your muscles have been on all those other days, the memory of the work is something that goes away. You're left with the finished product.

On the Home Front: Larry Brown's Narrative Landscapes

Tom Rankin / 1995

From *Reckon: The Magazine of Southern Culture* (Fall 1995): 90–101. Used by permission.

Larry Brown, born in 1951 in Oxford, Mississippi, is the author of four books of fiction and a nonfiction account of his days as an Oxford firefighter. Primarily self-taught as a writer, Brown first published a short story, "Plant Growin' Problems," in *Easyriders* magazine in 1982. *Facing the Music*, a collection of short stories, was published in 1988, followed by *Dirty Work* (1989), *Big Bad Love* (1990), and *Joe* (1991). A stage adaptation of *Dirty Work* was produced at the Arena Stage in Washington, D.C., in 1994 and at the Dallas Theater Center earlier this year. Recipient of the Mississippi Institute of Arts and Letters Award for Literature in 1989 and the 1992 Southern Book Critics' Circle Award for Fiction, Brown published *On Fire: A Personal Account of Life and Death and Choices* in 1993. He is currently completing a new novel, *Father and Son*, to be published by Algonquin Books. With each book Larry Brown has moved readers with his sharp, clear, unflinching voice, telling stories of the aspirations, struggles, failures, and triumphs of Mississippi hill country working-class people.

The interview that follows has been edited from three separate conversations Larry and I had during the past year. The majority of the interview comes from one afternoon we spent on a pier that Larry built on his Tula, Mississippi, pond. Tula, a town of approximately 150 people in the southeast corner of Lafayette County, was Larry's first home. He lived there until he was three years old, moving with his family to Memphis in search of better opportunity. The Browns returned to Tula when Larry was fourteen. After two years in the Marines, he returned home, marrying Mary Annie Coleman within two years. Larry and Mary Annie were owners and operators of the Tula Grocery in the late 1980s. They now live with their children—Billy Ray,

Shane, and LeAnne—in a house they built in 1986, some five miles northwest
of Tula in Yocona. Across the gravel driveway lives Mary Annie's mother,
Esther Lee Coleman. Both homes overlook the fertile pastures that slope
toward the Yocona River bottom where an assortment of beef cows graze.

As we sat in well-worn lawn chairs on the pier at Tula, casting bass lures ran-
domly out into the greenish water and drinking beer, Larry talked about his
early life, the local influences on his writing, his habits of listening to old voices
from Tula and surrounding communities, and his evolving views of home.

Rankin: What do you remember about reading as a child and the importance
of it?

Brown: The thing I remember the most is a collection of classic literature my
mother had bought with a set of encyclopedias. She bought one of those little
ten-book sets, everything from Grimm's fairy tales to Greek mythology. I
remember reading all those books when I was pretty young—getting into all
kinds of stuff like Jack London, Herman Melville, Zane Grey, all kinds of
things, all this Greek mythology. I was big on Greek mythology when I was
pretty small and read a lot.

My mother was big on reading. She passed it on to all of us, and we picked
it up real early. . . . It was probably just by watching her that I came to it,
more than anything. I discovered just how much fun reading was.

My mother read some old trashy novels once in a while, because I can
remember one called *Leave Her to Heaven*, and there was some guy and
woman scantily clad on this beach and one of these big lurid covers. And I
know she read a lot of romance stuff, those little thin paperbacks you see. She
had boxes and boxes of stuff. She read the Bible a lot, too. She read a lot of
magazines. Whenever she was sitting down—if she wasn't cooking or ironing
or washing or something, taking care of us—when she was sitting down rest-
ing, she was reading something.

Rankin: What books were you reading then?

Brown: Back along in that time I read a lot of what I call boy-and-dog
stories, like James Street's *Good-Bye, My Lady* and Jim Kjelgaard books
about dogs, like *Big Red*. Books about hunting dogs, about labs, bird dogs,
and cat hounds. Fred Gipson's books, *Old Yeller, Savage Sam*. Anything that
was about hunting and dogs, I was really into that. And I liked, and still do
like, a lot of stuff about Westerns, about cowboys and Indians and all that.

Rankin: If you think of your childhood and try to think of a very influential book or some of the most influential books, does anything come to mind?
Brown: The Bible more than anything, I guess. I probably read most of that when I was young. I was raised in a church from an early age. I went to church every Sunday and prayer meeting on Wednesday night, Methodist Youth Fellowship on Sunday evenings, and all that. So I was introduced to it early and read a whole lot of it. Then sometimes I would come down to Mississippi in the summertimes and stay with grandmother, my mother's mother. . . . She had raised something like twelve kids . . . and they were all big on it, too. It was a family thing, you know. They were all big in the church, and I grew up in that.

Rankin: Is there a link between the structure of Bible stories and the way you structure some of your stories?
Brown: Well, I think all good fiction is moral fiction. Harry Crews said— maybe not necessarily written by moral men and women, but he said it's always about whoever kicked who when they were down and whoever reached down and gave them a hand to help them back up. It's always about the battle between good and evil. That's probably what most of my writing is on. I get kicked on sometimes because I use brutality and dark vision in my work, but I go back to Shakespeare. I say tragedy is the highest form of drama.

Rankin: What kinds of things did your father read?
Brown: He read the paper, that's about all he'd read. As far as reading a book or something, no, he didn't read books. But he liked to keep up with the news.

   I can remember my mother hiding different books and magazines from my dad. I'm not really clear what the reason was. I'm not sure if he thought reading was a useless pursuit or what. I can never remember him saying, "Don't be reading." Maybe he thought she spent too much time reading, or he didn't agree with what she was reading.

Rankin: You're a well-versed fan of movies. What role have films played in your storytelling?
Brown: I've got a couple of favorites I watch over and over again, and *Dr. Strangelove* is one of them. And I'm still crazy about *One Flew Over the Cuckoo's Nest*. I like that one. I saw *Shane* when I was probably about twelve or thirteen. I was a safety patrol boy, and they took us all out to the show one

Saturday morning. I watch *Shane*, and I still watch *Once Upon a Time in the West* about once a year. That's still one of my favorites. You know, I've got all these old ones that I still like. Some of those movies just can't be beat. *The Searchers* with John Wayne, that's one of my favorites. *Red River* is one of my favorites.

The first television I remember watching was one my grandmother had, a big, old cabinet about four feet high, but the picture tube was only about twelve inches in diameter and it was round. The whole thing was full of tubes; you had to turn it on and let it warm up. That's my earliest memory of any television. That was at my grandmother's house in Memphis, my father's mother. She lived on a street right behind our street. We moved to Memphis in 1954 when I was three, came back to Lafayette County in 1964.

Rankin: Do you remember being here before you moved to Memphis?
Brown: I have clear memories of all the trips we made down here. Coming down here was a regular thing because this is where my mother's mother lived, my grandmother Mattie Barlow. And she lived up here in this house, right up the road here, with my aunt, Aunt Ura, and Uncle J. B. She had lived with them, gosh, I don't know how many years. Her husband had been dead since the early '20s; he died when my mama was just a baby and she never did know him. It was always our favorite thing to do, to come down here and get to stay about a week, take a vacation and come down here.

Rankin: Why did your family move from Mississippi to Memphis in the first place?
Brown: I think it was probably because of the difficulty Daddy was having making a living sharecropping. He came out of World War II in '45. He didn't get out until it was all over because he went all the way until they surrendered. Then they cut him loose, and he came down here and they got married. My oldest brother was born in about '47. They lived in a little house down here at Potlockney, about seven or eight miles south of here, on a farm owned by a guy who wasn't any kin to me, but I've always called him Uncle Check. His name was Chester Stanford. Him and Daddy had been good friends all their life, and Daddy started sharecropping for him, but it wasn't long before they had four kids. My older sister came along, then I came along, and my little brother came along. There's not over about five years' difference between the oldest and the youngest of us. We all came along pretty

quick. And I think it was probably just a question of economics. I guess he had this job located, Fruehauf Trailer Company in Memphis. So we went up there in '54.

My mother worked too. She worked at several different places. She worked at a place called Katz Drugstore, which was over there on Lamar, or it used to be over there. And she worked at a place called Camp Electric Company, which was just about next door to Sun Records. She introduced my sister to Jerry Lee Lewis one day. He came in there to use their cigarette machine, to get a pack of cigarettes while they were cutting a record.

And just up the block is where I went all my six years of elementary school. I can drive through that area of Memphis now and it seems so tiny compared to how big I used to think it was. I had a paper route and used to get on my bicycle and go around and throw my papers. I kept a paper route for four or five years. I got one when I was about eight or nine and kept one until just about the time we left.

Rankin: With both your parents working, who took on the major responsibility of looking after the kids during the day?
Brown: I guess it was probably about equal between them. There were periods when Daddy didn't work, wouldn't be working, and he'd be there in the daytime to take care of us. I can remember him helping me. I was always building stuff, building stuff out of wood. He was always trying to help me, show me the right way to build something.

I can remember getting aggravated with him and wishing that he'd go on and leave me alone. I wanted to do it myself; I didn't want somebody to do it for me. I wanted to saw the stuff and get the nails and all. He'd always have to show me where I was going wrong. [My son] Shane, you know, you don't have to show him anything. He can build anything.

Rankin: Do you remember the first time you ever thought about writing? As a child and early teenager you were reading all these books, at that time did writing ever cross your mind?
Brown: The only thing I ever remember was some assignment we had in about the fifth or sixth grade to write about some weekend trip you took. I wrote about a trip down here to Mississippi, and that's been so long ago. That's probably the earliest attempt I can remember to write anything. But I never had any active desire to pursue that.

I was more interested in drawing. I drew a lot. I used to go to the Memphis Boys Club every Saturday without fail. . . . I spent a lot of time over at that Boys Club. Really good organization. They had so many things to involve you. They had gymnastics, they had wrestling. I was on the wrestling team and gymnastics team. They had pottery classes, art classes, and once in a while they had a big swap meet. You'd bring whatever you wanted to swap, anything from a doll up to a lawn mower and anything in between. You spent all day swapping stuff back and forth. We would carry all this junk up there and spend all day swapping and come home with another truckload of junk. But it was a lot of fun.

They had a father-and-son dinner once a year, and me and my daddy went to that. It was a pretty big deal. They had a huge Halloween celebration. They had a huge gym. They had all these grown volunteers. I guess some of these boys didn't really have much of a daddy to take care of them, and these guys were kind of like big brothers, came in and spent all their time. I'd spend a lot of time thinking about that, what a nice thing it was for those guys to do all that.

Rankin: Is there a day that you can recollect that you decided to write?
Brown: It was sometime during October of 1980. I know I was working at Comanche Pottery on my days off, working the regular shift at the fire department. And that's when the question kept occurring in my mind about giving it a try. There was not really any big fanfare about it. It was something I had been thinking about on my own for a long time. I guess I'd probably been kind of studying it for several months before I actually ever sat down and wrote the first word. And that was when I went and got [my wife] Mary Annie's typewriter back from my sister—a Smith-Corona portable—and sat down and started writing that first novel.

Rankin: Did you know what kind of story you wanted to tell? Did you have something you were interested in telling?
Brown: Not at that point. I was really naive. I was probably trying to write something I could sell there initially, without knowing that it took a lot of time to learn this and it's a very serious matter, and that you were trying to create a piece of art that would last. It was only by writing more and more that I got deeper involved with it and started really trying to study it with some kind of professional attitude as far as my vocabulary, spelling and

usage, grammar and all that. That's where the library started coming in, going to the library checking all these books out, essays and things like that, as well as trying to discover who the best contemporary writers were.

That probably didn't come along until about 1982, when Jo Haxton [Ellen Douglas] got me to reading what I'd call the right stuff, literature she taught out of the *Norton Anthology of Short Fiction*. You know, there are a lot of people in there that I'd never heard of. I'd never heard of Flannery O'Connor, I'd never heard of Tolstoy, Dostoevsky, Joseph Conrad, Ambrose Bierce. I didn't know any of those people. And so seeing all that for the first time . . . I think that's what the real eye-opener was. And also going to her book party—I think that party was in November of 1982, for *A Lifetime Burning*—and realizing that there was a bookstore in Oxford, which I didn't know.

There was this little bookstore [Square Books] upstairs to the left of Neilson's, up there on the second floor. I think that was the first time I'd ever been there. I can remember I had to take Shane with me, and he was only about two—a little bitty fellow just walking around in there—and I got to looking around and looking at the titles. I'd heard something about Raymond Carver and there were his books on the shelf. So I started going back to the bookstore and buying books. That was the first time I think I'd actually bought books. I'd always used the library before.

That whole thing was another step along the way. I would talk to Richard [Howorth, owner of Square Books] about contemporary writers, "Now, who's good?" And I'd go to Tobias Wolff. I got those Flannery O'Connor books. Just started reading more and more, and expanding my reading more and more, in an effort to help me with my own writing. I've said this over and over; I keep telling young writers that reading is just as important as writing. The two go hand in hand.

Rankin: Since you grew up and live in and around Oxford, I'm sure people frequently ask you about the legacy of Faulkner. When did you first read William Faulkner?

Brown: When I was in—I guess it was about the tenth grade, we all took shop together, agriculture, and worked in the woodworking shop and learned all this carpentry stuff. And Gary Coleman, a friend of mine, was running a board down through one of these joiner-planers one day, and somehow the guard on the thing got pushed back and he shoved two of his fingers into this blade. It took his fingernails off at the top of his fingers. So he had to go into the hospital and stay a while, and we all chipped in and bought him a present. It was a book called *Big Woods*. That was the first time I ever read Faulkner and probably wouldn't have started reading him then if it hadn't been for Gary sticking his fingers in that planer.

Rankin: What about the influence of stories, not written stories but stories from the oral tradition, from the talkers?

Brown: I grew up listening to all that. I grew up around a lot of old people, which I think is a big advantage. They tell such great stories. I used to talk to all these men up here at Tula who are all dead and gone now, been gone for years. They used to talk about World War I, which was something that nobody but them knew about. There was an old fellow that lived down the road here named Mr. Elmer Neal. Gosh, when I first met him he was really, really old. He had this old pink International Harvester pickup he would park up here on a hill. The starter didn't work on it or something. He'd just step on the running board and give a little push, step in there and turn the key on, pop the clutch, and let it roll down the hill. It would come to life every time. He'd go on home. He'd do the same thing out of his driveway. Those were the only two places he ever went. He went to his house and he went to the store.

He sat around on a Coke case and talked about World War I. And Uncle Ontis, this fellow I used to coon hunt with all those years when I was a boy, he talked about World War I. Once in a while if nobody was around Norman Clark up here at the store, he'd talk about World War II. And Daddy talked about World War II. All these grown men that I knew around here, they'd all been in World War II, every one of them.

Yeah, it was the old people, too, the way old people. Uncle Ont and Mr. Elmer Neal and all them as well as people like my Daddy and Paul Coleman, who we saw the other day, and Junebug Foster and Cordis and Autry and all those guys who were all about the same age. Dow Harwell. They had all been raised as boys together, and they all went to the war at about the same time. It was so different back then. I think back then you could be called for the service at any age, something like seventeen to thirty-five which accounted for just about every able-bodied man in the county.

Then there were other people later on that I knew that had been in Korea. Five and six years later, you know, people who were a little bit younger than my father, so I heard all that, too. And then the Vietnam War came along and people started going to that and coming back from that and talking about it. I had—I lost one friend in that. That was Darrell DePriest. He was killed around '68, something like that.

Rankin: Did people tend to talk about the war whether you asked about it or not? Was it just part of daily conversation?

Brown: Most of the time it would be like overhearing someone. You might be sitting around the store in a group of people. It would be the older people who would be doing the talking. Boys would just be listening, unless there were, like, hunting stories where everybody could talk about it, or fishing stories where everybody could talk about it.

I came from a big city down to a real small, rural community where everybody knew everybody real well, and the whole community gathered up at the store—mostly the men; course the women came in once in a while to get groceries. But there were a lot of people who stayed there a pretty good bit, especially the older fellows. They just sat around there, didn't have nothing else much to do. Or the farmers if it was raining and they couldn't get out in the field, they'd come up and sit around the store. So you'd hear all this talk, what it was like in the old days and how hard the Depression was and how broke everybody was and how hard it was to make a living.

It wasn't just the men's stories though, because my grandmother could tell good stories. Mattie Barlow, she could tell them. She was probably up in her late seventies by the time we moved down here. And people would just get together. I've heard Harry Crews talk about that, about the best stories—and Clyde Edgerton says the same thing—the best stories are not being told on the front porch where all the men are. The best stories are being told back in the kitchen where all the women are.

You can't hardly miss it because your uncles, your aunts, your grandparents, they all know about the same things and they all talk about these people you don't know and all these events that happened way back years ago. They talk about this tornado that hit here, in '35 I believe it was, really a terrible, terrible tornado. And we all knew people who had been involved in it and they were still alive, the ones who survived it anyway. There were all kinds of things to listen to. Back then they didn't turn on the television, they didn't put in a CD. They finished supper and got a glass of ice water and went on the front porch and sat there and talked. You just grow up hearing it.

Rankin: Do you think you paid more attention to the oral stories than to some others?

Brown: I think everybody liked to hear all that. You like to hear all that stuff your parents tell you about, what happened when you were little or what happened before you were born—those things that had to do with your family, your immediate family, your mother and father.

At one time my mother let me have a bunch of letters that Daddy had written when he was in Europe. He couldn't say where he was or what he was doing. If he did they'd excise that part, they'd censor it because nobody's supposed to be sending information back home. So he'd just kind of talk around. . . . It was really kind of vague in a way, but it was just neat to see these letters that had come across from Europe to her, to know that they were dating, going together. This was a long time before I ever was.

And to look at old pictures, too, was another thing. That was a big thing we did a lot because they had—and Mama still has—a ton, just a ton of old black-and-white photos that were taken with one of these old box cameras or something. They're all just teenagers, you know; they're coming up. This was before the war started, and they're young men and women really starting their lives. There are these old Indian motorcycles sitting near these old '39 Ford coupes. The roads are all dirt, but you can recognize the old Tula schoolhouse that used to be standing in that period. You can tell that picture was taken right here in front of my place on this road here, this gravel. And the cars are old. The buildings look the same. But just to know that you are in the same place that they were in when they were growing up is fascinating to me.

Rankin: How important is that continuity to you, to live near Tula as opposed to living somewhere else?

Brown: To me it's important. I think it's the main reason that I bought this place here, because I can remember fishing in this pond when I was fourteen, all those years back. And this is the place where I feel my roots are, more so than Potlockney, even though we lived there for three years. This is where my family's from. This cemetery up here is where all my kinfolks are buried, all the Barlows, everybody else is up here. They've been here a hundred years, I guess—a long, long time. So this is the place, even though I've lived in Yocona for twenty years and have a house there that I've lived in for eight years, I feel like this is the place where I'm from. Even though I was born in Oxford, this is where I feel like I'm home. Mama still lives here and some of my cousins, a couple of my aunts still live here. This is where I feel like I'm home.

I have never really tried to write anywhere else. I hear writers talk about not being able to write in the South. I know so many people who have left the South, become expatriated in some way, geographically or whatever, to distance themselves because they say they can't write about it here. They want to be someplace else—say, Wyoming—to write about the South. But to me it's important to be in it and to observe it every day, year-round, to take note of the weather and changes in plants and the seasons and all. To me that's just such an integral part of it. And to keep looking at the people. I really can't imagine doing it anywhere else.

All my writing, most of it, comes out of here. Of course, I do have things sometimes that are set in cities or like *Dirty Work* being set in that hospital. But so much of it goes back to the rural part, where they were raised, grew up, and went to school.

A long time ago I didn't know that I needed to write about home. I didn't know that you had to write about what you know. When I started writing I wrote a novel about Yellowstone National Park, and I've never been to it. . . . I think you really have to draw on your own experience to create from what you know best. That's just one of the things that you learn if you spend enough time writing.

Rankin: Where is Mary Annie's family originally from?
Brown: They actually lived at Tula a long time ago. I think when she was born they lived down the road, down here on a place where Junebug Foster lives now. But I think that shortly after she was born they bought that sixty acres over there and moved. Her mother didn't get married until kind of late in life. She was forty when Mary Annie was born, and I think that Mary Annie spent most of her growing-up period right over there.

As a matter of fact, her father used to work for my grandfather sawing logs with crosscut saws for fifty cents a day, along in the Depression. That's my daddy's daddy. Used to work for him. So there's a connection that goes back. I think her daddy and my daddy got in a fistfight down at Tula, drunk over a gambling debt or something. They used to be wild around here, have these gambling matches and they'd get to drinking and get in these fistfights. They'd all been good friends all their life, but they'd get in a fight and it would be over in five minutes. Wasn't nothing to it. I've heard all about that.

I've heard all these stories about what my daddy and all his friends, and her daddy and all his friends used to do. They used to be a bunch of hell-raisers. I guess that was after the war was over and they were all back home, and they hadn't all got settled and married yet.

Rankin: You ran the store at Tula for a few years. Did that influence your writing?

Brown: I actually got some material out of that store and not only from the time that I ran it, but times that I remember from before, when I was a boy, when Norman had it. Because as far back as I can remember—and I can remember Norman's father, Mr. Clark, who was a real old man when I first started going into the store on those summer vacations, I was probably seven or eight—but that was where the old store was and that building is gone now.

One of the main things that went on there was storytelling. People would sit around and talk. It was common back then. It's kind of sad in a way. It's not like that anymore and probably won't be again. People don't come to the store anymore and hang out, not in this community. They still gather at the store over there at north Tula and play cards. Down here at Paris they play dominos. One thing, I guess, is that so many of the old people who were around are gone now. They've simply died off. So many of them were already old when I first met them. The new generation doesn't really have the time to do that. They've all got jobs in town or they're working somewhere. They stop by in the evening maybe and get what they need from the store, but then they go on home. We've lots more now to occupy us than we used to have.

Rankin: You mentioned earlier about reading books about dogs, coon dogs and other hunting dogs. The whole thing about being outside, about hunting and fishing, how important is that to you?

Brown: To me, it was a major part of my life for a long time. The focus has shifted now from hunting to writing. But probably from the time I was fourteen until I married and raised a family, probably from 1964 until about the late '80s I was an avid hunter. When squirrel season opened, I was going to be sitting under a tree over there before daylight with my shotgun. And before deer season rolled around, I was going to get out in the woods scouting around and build my stand or make plans to go with some people who had some dogs, and go every day I was off. That was something that I pursued for a long, long time. It was a major influence on my growing up.

One of the things I wanted the most when we finally moved down here was to get a dog. That was one of the first things I did. You couldn't have a dog in Memphis, couldn't have one on the city street up there. Just out of the question.

So I missed out on that for so long, and I knew what all was going on down here. I knew that my cousins and my uncle went squirrel hunting and had squirrel dogs; fished, caught and dressed their fish and ate them and everything. So when I finally got turned loose, I pretty much went crazy. I got some coon dogs and I started going in the woods every night.

That's probably the major reason that I failed English my senior year, because I was out in the woods with my dogs every night instead of being at home studying. Another thing was that I didn't really care. I think my father dying when I was sixteen probably had a lot to do with my attitude. I think when that happened my world pretty much fell apart and changed. He was sitting at the breakfast table early one morning, I guess around six o'clock. He had to be at work at seven at Chambers. Me and my brother woke up, or I woke up, and there was nobody in the house. I asked my little brother, Darrel, where everybody was, and he said that Daddy had gotten sick and they had to take him to the hospital. It was only just a few moments until Mother and Knox Jr. and Joy all rode up in the car. She came in the house and said, "Boys, I got some mighty bad news for you. Daddy had a heart attack and died at six o'clock this morning." When that happened all kinds of things happened. You got this figure that's the head of your household, depend on him, look up to him, and in a flash he's gone. We were down here at the end of this road where mother lives now. So I think that's one thing that contributed to my delinquent attitude when I was in high school. I think the only reason I even passed the eleventh grade is because of a little old girl, my teacher, a first-year teacher just out of college, felt sorry for me because of the death. But I really didn't care.

I pretty much knew by that point—the war was real bad and I knew there was nothing going to keep me out of the war, so I didn't figure I had a hell of a lot to look forward to.

Rankin: What did you do after finishing high school?
Brown: I worked for nearly a year and a half, and I went and had my physical and got classified in the summer of 1969. You went and had your physical and you got classified, and then they put everybody's birthdays into the big

barrel, the lottery system, and drew them out. If you had a low number, say under 100, you could be pretty much assured you'd be on your way. If you had a high number, like 250, you were pretty much assured you weren't going to have to go that year. So in 1970 they drew them out. They drew them out in the fall and they drew mine out number 1. The lady at the draft board called my mother and she said, "Well, tell Larry he's got about two weeks to decide which branch he wants to go into. If he wants to go into the Navy, Air Force, or Marines he's got to contact them because the Army is going to draft him in two weeks." So I said I wanted to go in the Marines. I called the recruiter, and he came over to the house and signed me up.

Rankin: What did you know about the Marines?
Brown: Well, they sent me some literature. I knew all about Iwo Jima, all those Pacific battles they had with the Japanese. I didn't know the magnitude of them until I actually got into training and they started showing us the film where three thousand Marines were killed the first day at Iwo Jima, until I started talking to some of the old master sergeants who had been seventeen years old on those beaches and hearing firsthand what it was about. I didn't really have any idea of what they were going to do to us. I figured it would be tough, sure, but I didn't know it was going to be the nightmare that it turned out to be.

When I woke up down there the second morning, man, I would have given anything to be in some other place. There was no way out. There were ways out, but it would take a dishonorable discharge or something like that. So you had to pretty much make up your mind if you were going to stick it out or not. They sent a lot of them home.

They could just take a dislike to you. They could just say, "You're a shitbag. We're going to get rid of your ass." I couldn't do close-order drill. I'd come up there. We'd been walking in formation, rifle moving and everything. He'd come up there and write my name down, you know. They'd say,

"Where's Brown at?"

I'd say, "Here, sir."

"Well, the series gunnery sergeant told me to put you in a tube and launch you. Get you out of here."

And they kept scaring me with all that stuff, you know.

The only time I every really felt like crying was one evening, I guess. We had all these inspections every night. And we had these rifles, these M14s.

I had never had a gun like that in my hands. I had never had a gun that had that capability. It was that fine a piece of machinery. And once we got out to the range and saw what it could do, that you could hit a twelve-inch target at five hundred yards with iron sights, I said, "Damn, this is the finest gun I've ever had." I just loved everything about the way it looked and the way it felt. It was really heavy, about eleven pounds. It was just a superb piece of weaponry.

I cared so much about that gun, you know, tried to keep it clean and everything. And he came by—you always got a good DI and a bad DI and an intermediate DI, and they play all this psychological warfare stuff with you. The bad one was a guy that nobody liked, a total asshole. So we were all lined up there and they were doing inspection arms, where you lock the thing open and he looks into the chamber. He said it was dirty and he slapped that damn thing out of my hands. It hit the ground, hit the sights, the trigger guard, all that shit. And that's the only time I ever felt like trying to break. Just 'cause it hurt me that he had so little regard for *my* weapon that *I* had tried to keep so clean and care for like a baby that he would knock it down like that. But the Marine Corps had a million of them, and it was just rented to me for a while out of some armory that had 500,000 or so of them. That wasn't my gun.

Rankin: The hardscrabble, rural, working-class world you write about intrigues many readers.

Brown: You'd be surprised at some of the letters I get from people who are complete strangers to me who might be in Chicago, Detroit, California, Florida, wherever. I had a letter from a lady—I met her later on some-where—and she said that she had come from a poor, rural background, like really poor, rural background, but she had married this lawyer and she belonged to the country club and she spent a lot of her days reading by the pool. She had read *Joe*, and it caused her to realize that she had been pretty much ashamed of her upbringing and had tried to hide the fact of all that from her friends. All the friends she had now, the people who were in her group of doctors' wives, etc., all the ones at the country club. And she wanted me to know that really touched her and put her back in place with that other part of her life that she had left behind a long time ago.

I don't know. I come from a pretty, you'd have to say, pretty poor back-ground myself. My father was a sharecropper. It's not something that Joy, my sister, is particularly happy to hear me tell. But it's nothing that I'm ashamed of. Hell, if he'd been a ditchdigger, I wouldn't be ashamed of it, because I've dug plenty of ditches myself. I've sacked plenty of groceries. I've done just about any kind of manual labor that you could name when I was trying to keep my writing career going, because the simple fact the fire department—I just didn't make enough money at the fire department to feed my kids. Mary Annie worked too, worked all the time. When you got three kids, got a growing family, you got to feed them. That meant taking a part-time job no matter what it is.

But the main thing was that writing wasn't paying any money. I was doing it every night I had the chance, every minute I had the chance in my spare time, but it wasn't bringing any money. So it had to take a back seat to sacking groceries or working for the telephone answering service or running this store up here, which I did for seven days a week. It was just something that had to be done. I didn't have any problem with that. It was a necessary sacrifice that I had to make to learn to write.

Rankin: How important has Mary Annie been to your being able to write, being able to carry on?

Brown: She's always supported me. I think early on when I started she might have thought it was a whim like a lot of other whims I've had. Like my rabbit raising. I think at the time I started writing I had a '55 Chevrolet jacked up in the pasture about four feet off the ground. I had already taken the frame out from under it, completely dismantled it and all the brake shoes and the pads and the backing plates and everything else that was under it, and I was going to rebuild that car. Finally weeds started growing up under it, you know, and I'd gone to all this trouble to haul this damn thing from Eupora on a damn trailer and get it here. Completely dismantled this car, except for the body, except for the front fender. I had the two doors and the roof and the front seat and the back seat and the trunk, back fenders all in one place, up on the—it was a long crazy story. But I think she thought it was one of my whims like that car.

Then I think she saw how much I was working and she would let me go into a room, usually in our bedroom, and her and the kids would go in the front room and watch television or play games or read for a couple of hours and give me that time, trying to help me all she could. I think she said one time that the worst thing for her was to watch me go down to the mailbox and see if anything had come back or a rejection letter had come back. I kept stories out all the time. Whenever I had one ready, I'd mail it out. I'd have ten or twelve out at the same time. And she said the worst thing was to see me come back up the driveway with those manila envelopes under my armpits. You see them, you know you've been returned. And she says I'd sit down and read those rejection slips, and I'd get up and go back to my room and start writing again.

I think she also regretted the fact that I had to work all these part-time jobs when I could have spent that time writing, but there really wasn't any choice about that. We went into debt early when we got married and we had to just keep working and working and working. We were trying to save our money to build the house that we got now—that we finally got. So I think she just watched and watched and watched to see what would happen. I don't think anybody's been happier or more satisfied than she has.

Rankin: You recently published a piece of nonfiction titled "Billy Ray's Farm" about your oldest son. Can you talk about the origin of that essay and where it might be going?

Brown: The first thing that happened was that night the first calf died, just how bad it was. I was overcome by a feeling of helplessness because everything that could have possibly gone wrong went wrong. First, we couldn't catch the cow, like to never caught her. She didn't want to behave, she didn't want to let us get our hands on her. Just a poor dumb animal in pain is all it is. And then the flashlight wouldn't work and the mud was so deep you could barely walk. It was freezing cold, and then we got him halfway out and the thing jammed and had to lay there and watch it die. We tried as hard as we could to pull him with our hands and we just—just like I wrote, just like trying to pull a tree out of the ground.

I think it came out of a feeling of helplessness that his luck was just so damned bad. . . . One of them had already died on him the summer before, and it looked like everything was turning bad. I wanted to put down what all that felt like, and at the time I started it, it was just a few days after that happened because it was such an emotional thing. Then all this other stuff started to happen. I didn't know any of this was going to be coming, but as soon as something happened I'd go home to write it down. I think the day I had to pull that dead calf, if I'm not mistaken, I came home after all that all day long and wrote about twenty-one pages on it. I was putting it down just as fast as it happened. The writing, of course, naturally didn't take very long.

It was coming so straight and was so fresh, it was just pure emotion. More like I was transcribing exactly what it felt like.

Billy Ray asked me a while back when I was going to write more, and I said something else is going to have to happen. We got to have some more events to put down.

Rankin: Do you ever find yourself listening to Billy Ray's stories?

Brown: Oh, yeah, Billy Ray is a great storyteller. And he tells things that seem like would never happened to anybody else. Mary Annie, Shane, and LeAnne, we all like to listen to him. He has these crazy things happen to him. But I don't think that they're so crazy, it's just that he is a good observer of human nature. And he's able to imitate anybody after hearing them talk and watching their mannerisms one time. Then when he starts telling a story he's able to just—if you know this person, it's hilarious because he's duplicating them exactly. He's always meeting these people and coming home and telling us this wild stuff. He keeps us cracked up all the time.

Rankin: You've been working on a new novel for a while now. Can we talk about where the ideas for *Father and Son* come from?

Brown: Actually the idea started several years ago. It lay around out in my old office for—it's hard to say how long it did because I write things and I don't always date them and I don't remember when they first got under way—but I would say probably that the first scene I wrote for it was written maybe as long as three years ago, maybe longer. I had other things going on, and then I picked it up and it still looked good.

I needed to write another book after I finished *On Fire*, and I had a bigger chunk of that than I did of anything else, so I started working on it again.

Rankin: Where does the title come from?

Brown: Well, it's all different references to fathers and sons. That's one kind of theme that plays through different characters—how some sons treat fathers, how some fathers treat sons, and the different kinds of relationships that they all have. I've been trying to show that in different ways too. The title was something I didn't have for a long time. Sometimes you get them pretty quick, and sometimes they come later. A lot of writers just pull them out of text somewhere. I worried about it for a long time, then finally wrote a scene that had a scene with "father and son." I just thought it would be a good one. I think the title fits absolutely.

Rankin: Where do you see *Father and Son* taking place?

Brown: I see it set here, in a place that I remember from thirty years ago, like we were talking about. It's not really people I know at all. I don't think there's anybody in here who is based on anybody that I know. They're fictitious. The places are real, but in some instances the names have been altered. I don't want certain places to reflect real names. Most people are going to know where I'm talking about when I mention a certain town or a place in Lafayette County like Paris or Old Union. Some of those places are left real and intact because they're the places that I've got fixed in my head where events are happening.

Rankin: You've been working hard to end this novel. Talk some about the pressure you feel when you get toward the end.

Brown: I think the thing that makes something like this so hard to end is knowing that for some of them there's not going to be an easier way out— that some of them are going to have to pay the price, the human price. It's kind of like trying to decide who you got to let go. Because you get so attached to all of them, they just become like real folks. It's always like that. Whatever fate you hand them, if it's not a good fate, you got to live with it. And you always wonder if you've done the right thing. You can't really do anything but just keep working and working and working until there's nothing else you can possibly do to it. Send it to your editor.

Rankin: Where do your notions about fathers and sons come from?

Brown: It comes from the relationship with my father and his relationship with his father and my relationships with my sons. I've always regretted that they never were able to meet their grandfathers. Preston died when Billy Ray was just a baby. I'm sure he doesn't remember him; he couldn't have been over eleven or twelve months old when Preston died. And that's been something that's always been missing from their lives that I did have in mine, at least for a short while. I only knew one of them, but I remember him well.

I guess I'm just trying to explore. It's a case of a father who has a lot of love, but he's a father who has made a lot of mistakes and his son [Glen] has never forgiven him for those mistakes. He's blamed him always. He continues to blame him and a reconciliation is not possible. It would be if the son was willing, but the son is not willing to change his nature. That's the whole thing that I've been exploring. The other one is that Bobby has always been deprived of a father, never really had a father. He knows who his father's supposed to be, but he never really met him. Shot down in the war. So it's about the different ways that they grew up and how one had a father and turned out the way he did, the other one didn't have a father and turned out the way he did. And how lives take different shapes and how it's not always influences, it's also strength of an individual character to not follow those patterns—not to take the easy way and blame all your trouble on somebody else, but to go on and try to do the best you can. All these people got so many problems.

I'm just thinking harder and harder about it now than I have ever before. I said a while ago about how hard it's been, but the writing that has gone before has been relatively easy compared to what I'm going through now. It's hard to describe it. It's kind of like finishing a house, where you got all these little details and you got to make sure that there are no loose ends.

Rankin: We've been talking about how you remember your home place, say, thirty years ago and how those memories inform your writing, most recently of *Father and Son*. Now that we've looked back, let's look to the future briefly. What do you see for yourself thirty years from now?

Brown: Probably I'd have a place built at Tula by then and be spending more time over there than I would over here in Yocona. That's my eventual plan. In thirty years a lot of things will be changed. Billy Ray will be fifty years old by then, Shane and LeAnne will both be grown. And I'll be seventy-something. I just tend to think about moving back that way, from Yocona to Tula, gradually. Getting back over there. And that's probably where I'm going to stay when all the kids grow up and move off. We'll probably keep this place, too, just because of the house and all the land. I know Billy Ray's going to want to use this land eventually for something.

I've always kind of envisioned having a home over there one of these days. Growing up in Memphis for ten years and living by the Southern Railroad tracks, I really wanted to get back down here. I would visit Mississippi in the summers or come stay at my grandmother's and all that. Maybe that's why that land with the pond at Tula means so much to me. It's so peaceful and quiet. It means a lot to have a place like that. To a kid like me in Memphis, I felt like I was kind of imprisoned in that huge city for so long. There wasn't anything I could do about it. I was just a child. But I felt like this was my home, and finally I've got some land. I've got six acres and a pond. So it feels like it's all come around. I'm back where I ought to be after all this time.

Bard of the Bottoms

Jim Dees / 1996

From *Oxford Town* 162 (19–25 September 1996): 13–14. Used by permission.

"Sometimes there's a hard place you've got to go to."

—Larry Brown

Larry Brown knows there is evil in the hearts of men—and certain monkeys.

He remembers his Daddy telling him about a monkey turning on his trainer at the Mid-South Fair in Memphis.

"He said it was one time while he was up there working the rides, you know, picking up a little extra money," Brown says. "Said that damn monkey just snapped one day, and jumped on that trainer and shredded his hand with them damn teeth . . . Tore his damn hand up. Daddy said he never forgot that."

Larry Brown never forgot it either. It is an image that would tend to stick with you . . . a friendly monkey suddenly turning on you and avenging thousands of years of cages, Ronald Reagan movies, and organ grinders. One can only imagine the scene: Terrorized onlookers stampeding for the exits . . . the monkey chewing on a live human . . . flesh flying into the cotton candy . . . Could be a Larry Brown story.

"Monkey just turned on him, huh? No warning," I asked.

"No warning," Brown said. "Nope. Nope. Just a monkey out of the blue."

As Brown tells this, he looks far away and the furrows on his face show real empathy for those who had to deal with that particular monkey. He mentions another monkey moment.

"An old friend of mine out in the county used to have a monkey as a pet. I don't know if you can print this," he says with a wry smile, "but that was the horniest thing I'd ever seen. Humping the cage, and carryin' on with himself. Anyway, he'd get out of his cage and go sit up in a tree and scare people and be a nuisance. Scared the s— out of me. I thought he was a squirrel. Yeah, shore did."

Brown smiled and exhaled a plume of cigarette smoke.

"A damn monkey can be nasty," he says, shaking his head. "F—in' primate, sum-bitch."

All of which, of course, leads us to the monkey in question—and the question of evil.

A monkey sees action early on in Brown's hot new novel, *Father and Son*.

"Yeah, people have said, 'I betcha there's some big ole monkey in a dive somewhere down there in Marshall County that Larry went to,'" he says. "But actually, there used to be this guy that came down to the fire station— brother-in-law of one of my old Fire Department boys—and he had this big ole hairy monkey. 'Bout two feet tall—had a big ole long tail.

"That sonofagun, I's just terrified of him, man. He would just run crazy all over that fire station. He'd just come in and they'd turn him loose and I'd squeeze up in my damn chair. I was scared of him, and that's where the monkey [in *Father and Son*] came from."

That's the unfortunate irony for Larry Brown, because so many of the incredible incidents that inhabit and shape his fine fiction actually happened. He is the walking embodiment of the write-what-you-know school. When you talk to him he has his character's transmission fluid under his nails.

Thus Yankee book reviewers can be excused if they find the characters too redneck, or "overdone." Truth is stranger than fiction in Gonzopatawpha. Brown intimately knows his setting and his faithfully realized characters. On a short drive around the county, he can point to real places where he has set his fiction.

"That's where Fay started walking," he will say, pointing to a small, dusty road and referring to his last novel, *Joe*.

"That's where Glen caught the bass."

Then, cryptically, pointing to a beer joint, "That's where the monkey bit it."

More than one reviewer has pointed out that in the hands of a less talented writer some of his characters and plots would come off as bad Southern stereotypes or parody. Brown's skill, crafty nuance, and unerring ear for dialogue keep his tales from drifting into "hillbilly overkill."

And yet, his fictional world is real. Ask him about it and he seems to relish telling the origins of his tales, like an enthusiast magician graciously showing a pupil his tricks.

"I like to make sure everything's real," he says. "Like, that scene where Glen is handcuffed but still manages to pull the shotgun on Bobby? I got my pump down one day and I said, 'Now could I do this if I was handcuffed?' and I got one of the kids to tie my wrists together to see if I could work that pump slide and fire it."

And I said, "Yeah, it could be done."

What about Glen, who shot his own brother in a childhood accident and tried repeatedly to repent by jumping off the family barn?

"The whole germ of that story," he says, "was something that a friend of mine told me probably twenty years ago. About an old man who had just died. But when he was a boy, his parents would catch him up on the roof of the barn trying to jump off and have to make him climb down.

"He had gone into the kitchen one morning, with this ole shotgun—always hung above the door—always unloaded—and his little brother was eating breakfast. He didn't know it but his Daddy had got up during the night—something had gotten after his chickens—and he went out there to see about it. Loaded the shotgun. Went out there to see about it; came back in. And that one time, he didn't unload it.

"And that was the morning he took it down, cocked it, and held it up to his brother's head and said, 'Go out there and feed them chickens.' And his brother said, 'I will when I get done eating.' And he said, 'Naw, I said go on and feed 'em now.' And he said, 'I told you I'll go when I finish eating my breakfast . . .'

"And he pulled the trigger.

"Now he was an old man when he died and this had happened when he was a child, so you're talking about a really old, old, story, but it always stuck with me."

With the publication of *Father and Son*, Brown seems to have a hit on his hands. The "buzz" is positive and some of the early reviews are raves: *Kirkus, Publisher's Weekly, Newsday, Village Voice*. His publisher is adding more cities to his book tour. Brown will undoubtedly garner new fans with this book. In fact, *Father and Son* may be the introduction to Larry Brown for some new readers and they should brace themselves. In Brown's writing, the portrayals and language are unflinching and the subject matter is (monkeys aside) raw.

The *New York Times* said *Father and Son* is a "blue collar tragedy that is the work of a writer absolutely confident in his voice." This confidence is born out of Brown's years of watching his world and having the integrity to call 'em like he bleeds 'em. He hasn't hop-scotched the globe searching for stories like many authors, preferring instead to work hard tending his family and fiction in Yocona.

As he told *Reckon* Magazine last year, "I know so many people who have left the South . . . They want to be someplace else to write about [it]. But to me it's important to be in it and to observe it every day, year round, to take note of the weather and changes in plants and the seasons and all. I really can't imagine doing it anywhere else."

Aside from the characters, the uninitiated reader will experience a bleakness and bitterness beyond his own. Glen Davis has a chip on his shoulder the size of a monkey. He murders, rapes and plunders over the course of this raging, profane novel. As the *Village Voice* said, "Glen's a natural disaster. He commits the physical and psychic damage of a white-trash hurricane."

Which brings us back to the question of evil. Most reviewers marvel at the malfeasance in Brown's work.

"I'll be the first one to admit that it's dark," Brown says.

Still, it is Larry Brown's hard-won literary craftsmanship (he is basically self-taught, having taken only one writing course) which redeems much of the bleakness and gothic decay and elevates it into the art of high tragedy. Happy endings aren't his specialty. Many of his characters pay the ultimate price, or "they sacrifice for somebody else."

So, having wrestled his art from real life and rendered a fictional world of hurt and mayhem that is utterly believable, just where does the author stand on the sin question? Is he for it or agin it?

Evil has a central role in *Father and Son* as it does in all of Larry Brown's work. It's North Mississippi evil. Evil in our own backyards. It is raw naked drunken peckerwood evil that drives a rebuilt truck and hates out of habit. It has a purity that's almost admirable.

Does Brown take the pessimistic view? Is the race doomed in the face of the savage impulses of our disenfranchised or drunken miscreants? Do the low-lifes have the upper hand?

"Do you believe evil is more powerful than good?" I ask.

"No, I don't. I don't," he answers quickly.

He looks out the window of the farmhouse where we're seated, some ten miles from Oxford. The window looks out onto a pasture and beyond that, there's another pasture and beyond that, the Big Woods. The big, bad woods of Larry Brown's native soil.

"I think it takes a lot sometimes to stand up to evil," he continues. "Like I say, 'The Allies had to stand up to Hitler,' you know, and that's true evil in the world. You have to face up to it and fight it sometimes, yeah. Sure do.

I certainly believe that evil exists; very much so, in a physical presence in the world. Sure do."

He lights a cigarette.

"Yep."

"But more often than not, you feel like the fellows in the white hats prevail?"

"Yeah. I feel like that. I feel like they do. I sure do. I believe that."

One can only imagine the horrors Larry Brown witnessed in his fireman days. Likewise, in his writing career, he has chosen to venture into the darkness in search of his poetry. In light of all the pain and flames shooting through his fact and fiction, it's a relief to know he still sees hope on the horizon.

Barry Hannah, Brad Watson, and Larry Brown: The Radio Session

Barry Hannah, Brad Watson, and Larry Brown / 1997

From *Authors: The Radio Sessions* (Oxford, MS: Hyena Productions, 1997). The session was recorded on June 4, 1997. Transcript by Jay Watson. Used by permission.

BH: Well, this is Barry Hannah. I'm here with my friends Larry Brown, the famous novelist, and Brad Watson, the debut genius of *Last Days of the Dog-Men*. And I'm trying to struggle to play my part in such fine company here in Oxford, Mississippi, where we have a new mayor [audience laughter] and the magnolias are bigger than yours [more laughter], and the children are just heavenly blessings each and all. I'm the author of *Airships, Ray, Geronimo Rex*, lately *High Lonesome*, and it's a good time to be writin' and talkin' here on the porch, boys.

[musical interlude]

. . . And then there's always some guy who's like almost an assassin, but he loves you.
LB: Some psycho, yeah.
BH: And he came to the reading, and then he writes. Or he's with the most horrible band in the world, and they've dedicated their lives to you. And he sends this hideous CD, and you're supposed to support his life and everything he believes. And it's just awful.
LB: Or a demo tape he's cut for you.
BH: And you wish you had better fans. You doubt your whole craft, if you're inviting these people. You know what I'm talking about, Brad?
LB: Exactly. Exactly. Although I do get some pretty good music sometimes.
BH: Yeah, sometimes.
LB: I was up in Minneapolis-St. Paul last fall, and some boy came over to the hotel and interviewed me, and then he gave me this tape, or he sent it later. And the name of the band was Aunt Beanie's First Prize Beets. [Audience

124

laughter.] And these guys had some good music on there, man, I ain't kidding. I've been getting some good stuff—this ole cowboy out in Montana, his name's Bruce Delaney, and he used to play with Lefty Frizzell a long time ago, back when the [Vietnam] war was going on, and he had long hair, and it was unpopular to be in the place he was at, and all this kind of stuff. And he just sent me—the last record he cut he cut at Pearl, Mississippi, about four years ago. And he's just been sending me his music for a good while. He just wrote me and said, "Your books have gotten me down the road a lot of times." And the last couple he sent, he's got a few that are just really killers. He's got one called "Waltz of the Angel," and he's played it on his steel, you know, this National Steel, and he's got another one called "I'll Never Be Free," and this guy's really good, really good.

BW: I've only had one CD given to me, and it was a local band in Tuscaloosa called Pain. I asked them if they'd heard Barry's story, you know, "Constant Pain."

BH: Well, you know, that was just the most vicious coincidence. I wrote this story, "Constant Pain in Tuscaloosa." And *Airships* came out, and I got this threatening note from a black guy who had been in the bar behind me. It said, "I'm on your trail. I'm gonna get you. Look over your shoulder." I didn't know what the hell I'd done or that he had ever read any. But apparently he just read the title or something. Anyway, within a month, Mr. Alabama, who was a weightlifter, was in the Tuscaloosa news, and his name was Constant Pain—

BW: I remember that. *Baaaad* looking guy, too.

BH: —his lifting, his stage name. And I can't believe he got a hold of the story title. Can you imagine the weightlifting champion of Alabama reading Knopf books?

LB: Good gosh.

[musical interlude]

BH: Did somebody have to tell you—because I know that you told me that "Facing the Music" was the big breakthrough piece for you—did you have a religious feeling, a special ecstasy, or did somebody have to convince you that that was good stuff?

LB: Well, Richard Howorth is the one who probably helped me the most with it of anybody. I think I wrote that story in 1985 and sent it out steadily for two years, and it was rejected over and over and over.

BH: In its current form?

LB: Yeah.

BW: The title story in *Facing the Music*?

LB: Yeah. They would admit at *Esquire* that it was good, but they couldn't publish it. "But you will publish it," you know, "Take heart in that, you will publish it." Well that didn't do me no good. So I finally carried the story to him one day and said, "Why don't you just tell me what's wrong with this story?" And so he sat down and read it and said there ain't a damn thing wrong with it. He said, "You might need to revise a word here or there, just a few, not much." He said, "But I'll try to help you publish it."

BH: Richard Howorth, the owner of Square Books.

LB: Yeah, the owner of Square Books. And Richard Ford tried to help me publish it. Richard Ford submitted it to *TriQuarterly* himself in I think 1976 or so. No, not that late. A few years after I'd written it, yeah.

BH: You mean '86.

LB: '86, yeah. And they wouldn't take it either. So finally after I had exhausted just about every other place I could exhaust, I sent it down to the *Mississippi Review*, and they accepted it immediately.

BH: That's become a really special magazine, hasn't it? They're doing a piece, a couple, of mine. I'm real proud to have that in the state.

LB: They have really done some good stuff.

BH: *Georgia Review* also is very strong. I mean, it's better than *New Yorker* to me.

LB: Yeah, they did a whole complete issue on Rick Bass.

BH: It's more various, more risky. I'm winding up asking a lot of questions, but there's a false impression that writers ever meet in this town, or much at all. We don't, and I just have wanted these things, so I've got one more. It seems to me that there are too many novels out now that are merely adequate, and we're at an impasse in American fiction. The great exception would be Brown's *Father and Son*, which needed to be written. I'm thinking that many of those novels should have been short stories. I don't think that they carry as novels and I think the public knows it. They're shunning almost all of them except the big thrillers. And it's a down time now, because the short story market has never, not lately, been very massive. And you have to put them in the *Mississippi Review*. It's either *Esquire* or *Mississippi Review*, right?

LB: You've got no choices.

BH: Or *Southern Review*. And you're going to have a few hundred readers, right?
BW: Yeah.
LB: Yeah.
BH: So it's a troubling and kind of discouraging time, but I don't see many novels that need to have been written nowadays. I don't think it's a great age. I think there are a lot of them that are adequate, and they're between covers, and they look like novels. And there's not much wrong with them, they just don't stir you.
BW: Are you thinking mostly of the shorter novels, that are kind of like long short stories?
BH: I'm thinking of four-hundred-page novels too. It's a stretch of writing, I think it's almost dying of competency, I really do—the American novel.
BW: You mean they're boringly competent? They're boringly, technically competent?
BH: They're boringly competent, and they have really the ideas of a short story, no more than the ideas of a short story. And we're kind of caught in a place where you don't have a huge format for the short story. That's why I love it when a book like Brad's breaks through.
LB: Yeah.
BH: *Facing the Music* broke through. *Airships* broke through for me. This is so—it's rare and lucky.
BW: You know, I could've written the title story ["Last Days of the Dog-Men"] as a novel. I could've written it as a short novel. I could've stretched out several of the sections in that story and made them into chapters, or expanded other parts of it. But it didn't seem as if it would have the same energy.
BH: Right.
BW: And it didn't have the same appeal for me. And I had been writing short stories, so there wasn't a whole lot of incentive to do that form, even though I knew that, as far as marketability goes, and even a career goes—
BH: Right, everybody's going to tell you to write *the* novel. And that way the novel becomes an artificial thing. You don't get the sense it needed to have been written.
LB: Yeah, that's what your publisher wants you to do.
BH: And a writer's due about every two or three years: clank! clank! It doesn't have that great burn on it like *The Stranger* had. Camus, you know—God knows, I just tremble when I put it down.

BW: Yeah, well there's a short novel that has a whole world. Length doesn't mean a thing in a case like that.

BH: Right, it's just that literacy is really not very interesting to me.

BW: (Laughs.)

BH: It used to be interesting, but when a novel is merely literate, I have very little interest in it anymore.

BW: I saw your comment recently where you said that you were a lot more interested these days in the short story than the novel, then you said, "Well, of course I'm writing a novel myself now, so . . ."

BH: Right.

BW: But the novel, are you still working on that novel? And if you are, do you feel like it ought to be a novel, or do you feel like you're just kind of letting it go, that it's a story you're letting go?

BH: Well, that's the trouble. I can't write unless I'm committed with a pretty deep fire. Daily. Otherwise I feel like just a banker, or somebody getting to work. And I just won't write like that. It's never been good. And I've also wasted a lot of time projecting novels that I believed in only with my head. I should've been writing stories. You know, like songs. Writing the shorter stuff and not wasting the time on this American convention. So, it's hard for me to—I think that big stories are going to happen to all of us if we are lucky, and just to kind of wait for them to happen and have the book worth writing because it just had to be written. I think that novels should be things of necessity. Absolute necessity.

LB: Yeah, novels take so long to write. God, they take years and years and years, and all those nights and days. It's a big commitment of time.

BH: Do you ever feel artificial? Did you feel artificial when you were writing *Father and Son* at all?

LB: I was afraid that it was made way too melodramatic, that it was too much like a damn soap opera.

BH: But that wasn't how it was greeted by the critics . . . and by me.

LB: Not at all. Not at all. I worried that it was too heavy, too dark, all this— well you have all these doubts. I do, working on anything. "This is no good," you know. But you just never know till you get to the end what you've got to do to go back and revise and try and tie all the loose ends together and make it all make sense. When you're dealing with that many words, you know, that manuscript was 534 pages long. That was the biggest thing that I'd ever written. And I did like three drafts, so that's like 1,700 pages I typed through my typewriter, because I've still got a typewriter, I don't have a computer. That's just the way I work. I just put them in a three-ring binder and just constantly revise and rewrite and retype, and it's just a big incredible mess until it all gets over with. (Laughs.)

BW: Well, that novel was a revisiting of your earlier reading of the Greek mythology, probably, you know.

LB: I guess so. I guess probably so.

BH: It's got Grecian overtones: stark tragedy, simple revenge, elemental, ugly, and beautiful feelings.

BW: Irony, irony within the tragedy there.

LB: Basic desires. Things of the heart. But no, I never thought it would do anything like what it did. I just didn't expect much to come of it.

BH: Do you ever think in terms of a whole special language such as Kurt Vonnegut invented to be a best-seller? My publisher, Seymour Lawrence, stood by him when he was selling nothing. And then he changed his style to that of the eighth-grade reader. He just busted up paragraphs, single lines, elemental style. And he became a best-seller. You ever think about refashioning your whole mode for a newer, more intelligent or differently intelligent public, Larry? Or are you just committed to hanging in with what you got?

LB: I'm pretty much committed just to hanging in with what I got, because it took me so long to discover that what I had to write about were just these people out in the country that I grew up with, or knew, or my family or relatives or whatever people I've lived with most of my life or lived around—that that's the only thing I know. I don't know about Yellowstone National Park.

BW: (Laughs.)

LB: I don't know about a lot of other things I tried to write and failed at early on. What I know is rural Lafayette County, Mississippi. That's my whole deal.

BH: Do you feel strange when you move out of the county? Like for a Memphis story? I mean, you lived there briefly as a child. Does it not feel good to write a Memphis story to you?

LB: I don't know, my stuff just seems to keep harking back to the same place, which is always close to farms and rivers and woods and cotton fields and all.

BH: You really love it, don't you?

LB: Yeah, all that kind of stuff. And that's what's right down the road at Yocona there. You leave the house and in two minutes you're cruising beside

a river or a big cottonfield or something like that. A big territory, vast woods
and ridges, hardwood timber and all that.

BW: What about fiction about firefighting, Larry?

LB: I actually started writing a piece one time about that, but I think I only
had like ten pages on it when I quit. It felt like something that might be a
novel or a novella, you know. But I never did finish it. And I've got all kinds
of things at home that I've started like that and never have finished. I've got
I think thirteen stories in my notebook right now in partial stages of comple-
tion. Some of them are up to thirty pages. But I just never have found the
time, doesn't seem like, to finish them. I get started working on another novel
again, or I get asked to do an article for somebody or an essay for somebody.
I turn down most of the stuff that I get asked to do, I really do. Because I
want to write what I want to write.

BW: You should. I guess you would have to.

LB: I want to write fiction. I did read a piece in Chicago Saturday about
[Mississippi musician] Charlie Jacobs's funeral. Or Sunday. I wrote it
Wednesday and Thursday and then went ahead and read it. It was only about
ten pages. Just what he was like, what he was all about, what the funeral
was like.

BH: He was a wonderful saxman who died in New Orleans, drug overdose
apparently.

LB: Back in April. About the middle of April.

BH: In April. We all went over to his funeral, and he was with a group called
The Tangents, who were just a great boogie Delta band. And it was very sad.
He was not even forty, was he?

LB: He was thirty-nine.

BH: Thirty-nine. Had a daughter who was just all to pieces at the funeral.
The funeral was out on the levee about forty miles from the church, in an old
personal graveyard, where they sang some tunes.

LB: Overlooking a big cottonfield.

BH: Overlooking a cottonfield.

LB: They were planting cotton that afternoon. All those tractors were
rolling.

[musical interlude]

BH: What keeps you from writing the most? I'd like to hear that from
you—the stuff I've never asked. Because I don't ever have real blocks,

but I sure go for weeks without an idea. What's the most harmful to your writing?

LB: Probably drinking.

BH: Drinking?

LB: Mmm-hmm. Probably drinking and just hanging out with my friends and staying up too late and playing my guitar for four or five hours instead of being there working. Goofing off. 'Cause anything is easier to do than that, than to go in there and sit down and work. Anything is easier than doing that.

BW: That's right.

BH: Well, reading and writing letters works on me like that now, since I quit drinking.

LB: Yeah, that too.

BH: Every time I need to be working I go in and write for no damn reason, just write a friend. Or read— "Oh here, *this* book's gonna be it!"

LB: (Laughs.) I do that too.

BH: I need to be a little smarter before I start, I need to know a little—but then it occurred to me as I'm counting my books, that writing itself is harmful. [BW and LB laugh.] You know, I mean that reading is harmful.

BW: What do you mean?

BH: You stay the constant grad student. You're always filtering other people's lives. You're not, you're forgetting who you are. Because I'm very influenced, very. If somebody says, "I believe there is a God and that he is in Jackson, he's the vice-mayor" —

BW: As God would be—

BH: —and it was a decent story—

BW: Where else are you gonna find Him?

BH: Right—I'd think about it a while. I mean, I find reading can be like booze. It's just as insidious as TV.

BW: Well, yeah, if you just think of it as a time consumer.

BH: Yeah.

BW: For me it's been jobs, though.

BH: Jobs kill you.

BW: Yeah, jobs kill you. And teaching.

BH: Newspapers, huh?

BW: Newspaper writing. You know I'd get home from that just really so tense that then that'd have a combination: all I'd want to do is drink, and I'd drink whiskey, and I'd get off at ten or eleven o'clock at night and I was just so wired that all I'd want to do is to have about four or five drinks just because it was driving me nuts.

BH: You quit the firehouse, Larry. You were a captain, had your future pretty good assured. I assume they'd have a good pension, health and all that.

LB: Oh yeah, if I'd have stayed I could have been retired by now

BH: And I went to the party, when you were scared. You said, "I've quit, I'm a writer." Are you very glad now?

LB: Yeah.

BH: Did you write better? Or were you too scared to write well at first? When you quit everything else?

BW: That's a good question.

LB: I think I was probably kind of scared for a while, but it only lasted about two weeks, something like that.

BW: (Laughs.)

LB: I got over it.

BH: First bills start coming in, maybe?

LB: I got over it, and I said, "This is my life now."

BH: Do you respond to financial pressure positively or negatively?

LB: Positively. Very much so.

BH: I do too. I work as if it's homework. I always wrote better against deadlines.

LB: Oh absolutely. Yes, yes, very much so.

BH: I think it's always been a myth—if somebody takes like twenty years for a novel it's almost always no good. They always assume that it's so packed with genius it can't be released. But it always works that the longer you take on something the sorrier it gets, it seems to me. It almost never improves.

LB: The worst thing to have is a vague deadline: "Well, you know, next year sometime." That tends to get you lazy, and you don't work like you ought to. Or for me anyway.

BH: You do better when it's not open-ended.

LB: Right, when you know you've got to deliver by December 31. That tends to make you get focused.

[musical interlude]

BH: Brad survived modernism. The thing that was wrong with Alabama was that his colleagues were trying really hard to be postmodern, with Borges and

Alain Robbe-Grillet and, oh, a little bit of Donald Barthelme thrown in. But Brad always had a basic story. That was the difference. And "Mr. Lonely" is absurd, and the family throwing beets at each other is absurdist, but it was also a good story. You cared about the folks in it. And his work was singular that way when I saw him. I thought that he was clearly the best around at Alabama.

LB: What year was that?

BH: That was twenty years ago.

LB: Twenty years ago.

BH: Yeah. I was proud that he was from Starkville, Mississippi. You say that you were sort of saved by modernism. You were writing pulp adventure. About a hundred stories.

LB: Pulp adventure crap, mostly. (Laughs.)

BH: Yeah, but it's still a legend. It's still a legend. Nobody I know would be rejected over ten times without folding up. Really, I don't know many people who'd take it, can take it. But you read Faulkner, Flannery O'Connor, and it was kind of a conversion.

LB: Yeah.

BH: You said, "Well, hell, I wanted to say this all along. I wanted to be on this team."

LB: Right.

BH: And you almost instantly got better, it seems, right? Didn't you almost instantly publish?

LB: Yeah, Ellen Douglas was the one who turned it around for me, by taking her course at Ole Miss in '82. She's the one who showed me this is what's worth writing, this stuff. And before I had been doing all this horror, science fiction, junk, folks killing each other for the fun of it and all that jazz.

BW: The infamous grizzly story that I read you talking about?

LB: Yeah, the novel, the first novel I wrote. I'd never been to Yellowstone National Park and wrote a novel about a man-eating bear in Yellowstone National Park. That kind of junk.

BH: Capote thought—who didn't go to college—thought it's bad to go to college for a writer, that you take away your most creative times in that schedule, and taking a lot of things that could be irrelevant to your craft. Well, it was good for me. I didn't know anything, and it helped shape me. But do you think school has anything to do with writing?

BW: If I hadn't gone I probably wouldn't have read any good books. I just wasn't exposed to it anywhere else. Larry was in a university town, but I wasn't. And this is kind of a close town. If you want to write, then you start running into people who can point you in the right direction, but that really wasn't happening to me in Meridian. They were pointing me to other things. (Laughs.) Illicit substances, and things like that. But I didn't, so it was good for me, too. Of course, you do waste a lot of time, but I was exposed to a lot of things I wouldn't have been otherwise. As far as the M.F.A. goes, I think the quicker you can get through it the better, if you're going to do that. You don't have to do it. A lot of good writers haven't done that. But if you choose to do that, if for some reason you want the time in a place where there are a lot of people trying to do the same thing, then that's fine. But go ahead and get in there and do it and get out.

BH: Do you think college teaches you too much moderation, too much classicism? Could it possibly paralyze you? I think there are too many writers anyway, so I'm not worried about it one way or the other. But there are folks whose perfectionism—you're taught the very best, you're taught excellent stories that could diminish your own talent. It is possible to spend your life as a reader and a perfectionist, which is nothing at all like a writer. And there was that tendency in every graduate school I ever was involved in. The big readers often had such a criterion for themselves that they couldn't perform. They couldn't come close to it.

BW: I didn't have that problem because whenever I'd read three or four chapters of something that really turned me on I'd have to put it down and go write. It always made me want to go write. More than likely I wouldn't finish the book. It'd be more likely than it would to just keep reading and ignore my writing time. So I have to make myself read more than I do, so the well doesn't dry up.

LB: That happens to me too. Reading something really good inspires me to go try to write something good of my own.

BW: You get excited about writing again.

LB: Sure.

BH: It doesn't kill you, obviously, not to be bookish when you grow up. Because nobody ever read me stories, and I think we had the Bible and a few inspirational tracts my mother wanted in the house. I don't think Larry came out of a bookish house, but you were a voracious reader, right? Even in the Marines?

LB: Yeah.

BH: Where'd you get it? Why literature anyway? Why aren't you a millionaire cotton guy or something?

BW: (Laughs.)

LB: I think my mother pushed me toward it more than anybody else, from the actual act of seeing her read when I was a child, and just picking it up on my own, and then also because she made sure every one of us had a library card and used it regularly. And so I just developed this love of reading early on. And then I got into all kinds of things on my own, like Greek mythology. I was crazy about that stuff when I was a kid. And then I got to reading all these books about boys and dogs, Jim Kjelgaard. And James Street, *Good-Bye, My Lady*. And all these hunting stories with boys. I was big on that when I was a kid. And then just Westerns, and then just a little of everything, man. I read just about anything I could get my hands on, really did. And it continued up through my adolescent years, and I went in the service and stayed in the library all the time, whatever naval base I was on or Marine Corps base I was on, I'd go check out books. And just kept on reading and then about age twenty-nine I had been wrestling with this question for so long. What does it take for somebody to learn how to write a book? So I went into my room one day and sat down and started writing a novel. That was in 1982.

BH: That's when I came to Oxford.

LB: It's when you came to Oxford.

BH: So you hadn't been writing long at all when I met you first.

LB: No, not even two years. Not even two years. I had published one short story in *Easyriders* motorcycle magazine, of all places.

BH: It came out while I was here. I remember that. It's about the sheriff finding out somebody's marijuana patch.

LB: Yeah. (Laughs.)

BW: I would have given anything to have published a story in *Easyriders* magazine! I would have considered myself a success.

BH: And *Twilight Zone* magazine.

LB: Yeah. I was just publishing wherever I could. And then I finally got to trying to write some more literary things and finally had some stuff taken at the *Mississippi Review*.

BW: You stopped making money then, didn't you? (Laughs.)

LB: (Laughs.)

BH: Right, that's the thing, see, you go from *Easyriders*, *Hustler*, to *Twilight Zone*, and then you get real, and you get no money. [All laugh.] Did that tell you anything? I'm a little tired of being a critical success, myself. [Audience laughter.] I've got all the damn fame I can eat.
LB: The *Easyriders* story I know paid $375, and the *Mississippi Review* paid $30.
BW: (Laughs.)
BH: Right, you knew you'd made it to the postmodernist crowd.
BW: I was desperately trying to write those little jokes for *Reader's Digest* when I was in college.
LB: I tried that too, yeah.
BW: And what was it, 300 words and $3,000, or something amazing like that. Those were my first rejections, from *Reader's Digest* joke columns. [Audience laughter.] Talking about inauspicious beginnings.
    My mother made us go to the library too. You know, there was a weekly reader type club where you would go in, and there was a great old library in Meridian—it's now the museum, the art museum there—and the stacks were real close together and tight and a real musty smelling place. It was great to hang out in. But somewhere along the line I turned into a juvenile delinquent, somewhere around thirteen or fourteen years old, and I stopped reading. I didn't really read at all during adolescence.
LB: I know that the old library at Ole Miss, before they did the big renovation, I'd be out there for just like hours, prowling the stacks, looking for books. I mean, I'd go down and hit that card file and find out what floor and aisle a book was on, a rare book that was hard to find, like some of Harry [Crews]'s early stuff or some of Jack London's early stuff. I mean, they had a copy of *Martin Eden* that was published in 1910 I checked out one time.
BH: No kidding.
LB: Still sitting there with all that dust on it.
BH: Right. Well the real rippers is what got me into lit—Jack London. I didn't know that Poe was refined when I read him. I read him for the horror, to be terrified. I had no idea that he was Europeanized or fancy. I thought it was just good stuff. I devoured that right along with the Jack London—you know, Jack, "To Build a Fire" is as good as it got to me. Then one boy came from out of town, and—I thought I was pretty smart—he stood up and recited from memory, "The Wreck of the Hesperus." I said, "Well, you smart-ass son of a bitch." [BW and LB laugh.] It's always some ringer comes in from Union,

Mississippi. So my stock went down, and I was blown away that a man would spend the time, or had the room in his head, to recall these lines, of "The Wreck of the Hesperus," without missing a breath. And I was kind of enamored at the same time about why it would be worth it. Why would it be worth it to remember poetry?

It was gradual. I wanted, really, to just write rippers about wolves almost getting you, and rich babes in need—

BW: Of you!

BH: —of me at fifteen. Big chance, you know, circling the Dairy Queen, where they wait just for teenage losers to help out. [Audience laughter.] But we'd seen James Dean. Hell, that's one thing good about Mississippi, you were so stupid that everything was possible. Elvis didn't shock me that much. He made it, it wasn't that big a deal. Take a guitar and go in there and, you know, lay it down. One thing good about ignorance is that you don't know what you can't do. So you just go ahead and have a shot at it, you know?

LB: That's true.

BW: Yeah, you head out to Hollywood and become a movie star.

BH: Absolutely, like in the books.

[musical interlude]

BH: I'm not hurt by critics that much. Sometimes they're—they seem to be such exceptional human beings. [Audience laughter.] One guy in Britain actually wished that I would have bad days, for having the British version of *Airships*, which was hugely applauded over here. Something got to him, and it was just so crude, or so viciously un-British or something, that he wished bad days on me. This is fun for me.

BW: Did you have a critic one time who said at the end of his review, "In all seriousness, this man is dangerous, and we need to make sure that he is contained," or something like that? I seem to remember one review that said something like that.

BH: Hunter Thompson said that I shouldn't be allowed near students. [Audience laughter.] But this is a badge of honor, especially from Thompson. I like—Sven Birkerts, one of the best critics, says that I write maybe some of the most interesting sentences being written. Now this one, I like it but it hurts too. But he's right, I am more interested in the sentence, and what you can do in the paragraph, than I am in the continuing narrative. I think

Larry's more interested in that continuing narrative. I like to see words play up against each other. Not superficially or intellectually or in an Irish, easy way. So that hurts, but it's also—I'm proud of it. I like to develop from the sentences.

LB: Well, you've always written some of the most interesting sentences that I've ever seen.

BH: I'd hate to be contained or just understood as a guy who wrote decent sentences. Uh, that's not much. But on the other hand I try to get as much as possible out of a line. It must be the old musician in me. The thing that makes me the proudest is when a musician likes my work.

LB: Yeah, me too.

BH: More than other readers. I would like to be in the tradition of Little Richard, Elvis, our great Delta bluesmen, that kind of crying from the heart, when there's nobody but just you and maybe your woman, who doesn't like you now. [Laughter.] And there's not much else, even if you've got a Grand Cherokee Jeep, which I just bought my wife.

BW: (Laughs.)

LB: (Laughs.) What, that red one out there?

BH: And she's a good-looking blonde and all. But you've got the blues, and it's your daydreams and your blues, and your loneliness and howling, from Elvis, Little Richard, Jerry Lee Lewis, B.B. King, and all the great cats from Clarksdale and Greenville. I grew up with these dudes. Bobby "Blue" Bland, "Do You Know Who's on the Radio?" So I lived to see the blacks join up with whites. And the white preachers railing against them. So it's kind of a hard won thing, I go back to a '57 Chevy and listening to a bad little radio, when it was dangerous. And that's my idea of art.

BW: Do you think that maybe there's something in that, in your appreciation for musicians and the blues and that sort of thing, there's a connection between the way a blues song tells a story and some of your stories tell a story? Something like, say, "Ride, Fly, Penetrate, Loiter," which is sort of a blues song on the page: do you think that that's a way to appreciate your stories that some people might overlook?

BH: Yeah. Because you know I'm a loser at what I wanted to do most, and that was music. I wanted to be the white Miles Davis. And then Jimi Hendrix meant a lot to me. I just didn't have the goods—or I made the Jackson Symphony, but now you're only like Mars distance from Miles Davis. So I was like a B-minus trumpet player and it just killed me. It was worse than not being the school quarterback. So yeah, I loved that music so much, I think there is a musical quality in it. Also I'm Scots-Irish like everybody in the South, almost, and there's a huge musical portion that you just have it at birth. You can get it in so many—you even get it through white churches. I mean, "Amazing Grace" is a wonderful tune. I just learned this year it was written by a slave owner who converted. They sang it at my dad's funeral. That kind of music just stays with you deeper than any, that church music and then later the blues.

BW: But the blues, also you see that in something like Larry's story, "Samaritans," one of my favorite stories in the first collection. If that's not a blues song, I don't know what is.

LB: (Laughs.)

BH: It's a blues song. It reads like a long poem.

BW: Yeah. You know that closing line, what is it? "You sure are a dumb son of a bitch"?

LB: "Boy you a dumb sumbitch." [Audience laughter.]

[musical interlude]

BH: I'm not interested in fiction of a "let's pretend" variety anymore much. I don't like the stuff, imagined fantasies, as I used to. Severely exaggerated. I think I've just come around to the fact that history has given me enough exaggeration, and I don't have to evoke original and fantastic shapes.

BW: Well I'm interested because I've got this good story of being a garbage-man out there that I've written some on and never have made anything out of. But how much does memory change or shape or arrange things? I mean, you are a fiction writer, you've been a fiction writer for a long time. Your imagination shapes and changes things. What do you—you take a memory, say, of your uncle from the story "Uncle High Lonesome," and what do you, what transforms, when you're basically going back and you're trying to treat the true emotional experience that you had and get it onto the page? What's different from the way you might approach that now from the way you might approach it thirty years ago?

BH: I just know more interesting things about people than I did when I was younger. I had to make them up more.

BW: Oh. So you think you have a broader understanding, a deeper under-standing—

BH: Or just been hanging around long enough.

BW: Yeah.

BH: And also with my uncle I learned things late that were kind of more delicious after he died. It's always fun to learn some huge "X" about somebody once they're put down. Or to—I find I can write better about my own teenage-hood now than ever.

BW: I guess so, now you don't have to worry about it anymore.

BH: Because I know what I was doing. It had no shape. Now I can kind of see it as a story, almost just like handed out by God, you know? 'Cause you got that time distance.

LB: Right, yeah.

BW: Larry, your models, how real are your models for characters like Joe and Wade, folks like that?

LB: Some people are based on actual characters, like Joe, but some people like Glen Davis are just totally figments of the imagination. The whole germ of the story about *Father and Son* was a story that a friend of mine told me probably twenty-something years ago about this old man who had died. And I didn't know the old man, but he told me this story that his daddy had told him. See, when he was a little boy about ten or eleven years old, he went into the kitchen one morning and took this shotgun down off these two horseshoes where it used to hang over the back door, and cocked it, and stuck it to his brother's head and said, "Go out there and feed them chickens." And it was the rule in the house that the gun was always unloaded. It was always unloaded. Everybody knew the gun was unloaded. But the boy didn't know it, but his daddy had gotten up during the night before—he'd heard something out there, a fox, a coon or something after his chickens—and he had loaded this shotgun, gone out there to see about it, and didn't shoot it, carried it back in, and I guess he was just sleepy and just hung it back up there. And his little brother said, "I'll go feed 'em in a minute," he was sitting there chopping up his eggs, eating breakfast. And he said, "No, I said go feed 'em now," and he said, "Well, you better put up Daddy's gun." And he pulled the trigger, just thought it was gonna click, and blew his little brother's head off. And thereafter that they would catch him up on the roof of the barn, getting ready to jump, because he killed his little brother. And it took maybe a minute for him to tell me that, but it all stuck in my mind. And all that eventually worked its way out in the way of explaining why Glen was, in a large part, the way he was.

BW: Well that's interesting to me because, you know, you talk about an iceberg theory—the way you treat that in the book is as a submerged fact, you know, behind, that becomes a motive or a reason for a lot of different things in the book, but it takes up very little space on the page. But it's real powerful when you read it, you work up to it right.

LB: That's one of the best things that my editor, Shannon Ravenel, has taught me about fiction and creating characters, is that people have got to have reasons in fiction for doing what they do. In real life you don't know why somebody goes out and pulls a nine-millimeter and robs a local gas station. He's got a reason for doing it, but it don't come out in the newspaper. But you've got to explore all these things and find out, if you're going to write about serious fictional characters, why they do the things that they do. You've got to find out what drives them.

BH: Do you believe in original evil in a guy like Glen? Country folks, I used to laugh at them, like these people around my uncle's, they always think, "Those Vardamans over there, they'll steal from you." I mean, there's like five generations of Vardamans, and you know they're all thieves? Same thing in Georgia, right? People are understood by their birthrights.

LB: I think those genes get passed down.

BH: And it's, I used to laugh at that but it's true, it is true.

LB: I do, I believe they do get passed down.

BH: Or they say, "Oh those Smiths, well they're just sorry," you know? [BW and LB laugh.] And it's true. I mean, one of them might be a banker, but he's sorry. As this trait that goes through. [Audience laughter.]

BW: He's spent his lifetime trying to overcome Smithdom.

BH: Right, right. It's always the guy on TV, like he's killed five people, and they say, "Well, he fell in with the wrong crowd."

BW: "He's running with the wrong crowd."

BH: You know? And the guy comes on, "Now I made some mistakes," you know? [Audience laughter.] "But I am running for mayor of Chicago." I mean, it's always—notice that the "crowd" is always there, that they fall in? Hell, they're *it*. Like Hitler fell in with the wrong crowd, baby, you know?

LB: Blame it on them.

BH: He was fine, he was going to be an artist—fell in with the wrong crowd.

[musical interlude]

BH: Brad, your stories have been pointed out as perfect, ear-perfect language, and I believe that's true. But Brown himself has written poetry, the only one of us to have had poems in his books of stories. So this man likes the country tune and the poem too, don't you?

LB: Oh yeah, sure.

BH: I mean, you're not immune to it.

LB: Sure, yeah. I love a great song, man. Oh yeah.

BH: What is your ideal poet? I learn a lot from poets, more actually than from—

BW: You put poetry in your work. I mean, your narrators will spontaneously combust into poetry sometimes.

LB: To me, I guess my favorite one is probably [Charles] Bukowski, just because the language of his poetry is so simple, but they, like the best of poems they're also stories.

BH: Yes, they are.

BW: Narrative poems.

BH: Dick Hugo was like that too.

LB: They tell something.

BW: I think that's one reason I like Hugo's poems.

BH: Hugo's are great stories.

BW: And Bukowski's stuff too, because they are stories.

BH: Right.

LB: But there's a lot of other ones that I admire greatly. You know, Donald Justice, Mark Strand—

BH: Do you like the way Bukowski takes the obvious and just simply does it better? About being hung over, or meeting a whore.

BW: Or being perverse?

LB: I think he just works so hard at it, just works so damn hard at it.

BH: He works hard.

LB: Every day, he must have worked every day, to have produced what he produced.

BH: Oh, you mean you like just the volume.

LB: Well, not just the volume but just the quality of it, too. And all the short stories and things that he did. I mean, it's just such a large body of work that he accomplished.

BH: You don't mind the unchanging attitude? I don't, but the kind of, half-lit at the racetrack . . .

LB: No, that doesn't bother me. He's writing about living, living in L.A. and going to the racetrack. Meeting these drunk women. (Laughs.)

BW: It's just amazing that the guy can get that much pathos out of a situation where a guy's in love with a mannequin. I can't imagine approaching a story where a guy's in love with a mannequin and achieving pathos. I can see it being absurd but not caring about the poor guy.

BH: He'll also, like Brown does at his best, he will report really abased thoughts that men of pride shouldn't admit, but do. This is poetry to me.

BW: That's true.

BH: Somebody will just say something, and I'm like that but I would never dare tell anybody. He would just blurt it. And then you feel at home. You feel, my God, he had the guts to say that.

BW: But he says it with a lot of grace, too.

BH: He says it with grace.

BW: You can say it without grace or you can say it with grace, but Larry's characters do it with grace, they achieve that.

BH: But he's a lot more misanthropic than you are, Brown.

BW: Well that's true.

BH: You tend to like your folks.

LB: Yeah I do, I do. I care about 'em. I do care about 'em, even the worst ones.

BW: He was a misanthrope, he was entirely a misanthrope.

BH: You can't imagine Bukowski in Yoknapatawpha County or in Lafayette County.

BW: I could see him pissing on Faulkner's grave.

BH: He would, it wouldn't be mean enough for him. Or he'd find something lousy at James' Grocery, though. Some guy who had pretensions and a Saab, he'd go after that. But some people can't do with beauty and nature. You take L.A. out—he loved L.A. because he could hate it so much. You know, he didn't have a subject. Those of us who've had L.A. experiences know where he is sometimes, too.

LB: I like the land that I live in. I have no problem being identified as a southern writer, because I think a lot of people I hear from identify with my work whether they live in Michigan or L.A. or New York City or wherever. Not because the stories are so much based in the South but because they're about the relationships between people, no matter where they live. And I think they can identify with that even if it's rural Michigan. I think some of my stories could be set just someplace outside town. I hear from all kinds of people, too, and I get all kinds of different things from them. It's just amazing how much stuff comes into the house.

BH: None of us have the sophisticated, or at least the theology that Flannery O'Connor had. She's a master. I sometimes almost wish I was Catholic. She puts these hard-shells, Protestant folks, though all the trials, and thought that life was meaningful that way. We've had, most of us have done without theology. Am I generalizing? Isn't it kind of true?

BW: Well, it's chaotic if it's there.

BH: If God comes it's a flash—in my work. It's a flash, it is not theological, and it tends to be temporary and instinctual reception of heavenly or religious things. I don't find that much religion in Brown's work. There's no attack on the church, but the folks don't spiritualize too much. They don't pray much do they, Larry?

BW: Well, a lot of them are in despair.

LB: Mmm-hmm.

BH: They're kind of secular humanists.

BW: Well, you take *Joe*, where Wade is the embodiment of despair and Joe himself is pretty damn near it.

BH: But Wade nor Joe [is] looking for spiritual enrichment.

BW: They're not looking for it, no. It's not a discourse on it.

BH: The heroes of Brown's books are spiritual in their own code. Like this guy who—Joe poisons trees for a big concern and he's not too happy with his job. But that's what's here, that's what you do.

LB: That's what's happening.

BH: You poison trees for Weyerhaeuser, you know. But you still like him because he's got a code and he's got honor. He's almost a duellist, the old-fashioned duellist. Don't mess with me or my kind or my love. I think that's why people respond positively to Brown. There's some old good virtues in there that haven't been outworn.

BW: There's a line I remember from that book where he looks out—you know, he's looking at the forest—and it's sort of darkly beautiful, a little oppressively beautiful, and it says, "He hated to be the one to kill it." But it's his job.

BH: To make a living.

BW: That's what he's gotta do, and so he's going to go ahead and do it, 'cause you gotta do it. But he's not happy about it.

LB: Yeah, all that comes from seeing how much of this damn state has been tore up by the logging industry, man. When I was eighteen years old, I could go anywhere in Lafayette County I wanted to, kill a sack full of squirrels, shoot me a deer. There was no posted signs, nobody'd say anything to you about getting on their land. But all that stuff has changed enormously since I was eighteen years old. I'm forty-five now.

BH: You're the only one of us that has actually picked cotton.

LB: Yeah, I picked it.

BH: Did that make you a better writer?

LB: No, I think it just—well, when I was fourteen I had to do that kind of stuff, you know—

BW: Makes him the worst typist, probably.

LB: —chop it for four dollars a day. But that was the only way we had to make any money. I mean, as a kid four dollars a day was a lot of money. But it took a price to get it. (Laughs.)

BH: One thing that fascinates me about this whole Flannery O'Connor thing that she said herself was she couldn't understand why they kept calling her a master of the grotesque. And I get the same charge. It's as if I'm deliberately inventing eccentrics. I'm not being disingenuous, but I have never started out in a story to write about, deliberately, weirdness. They call me postmodern. I'm baffled by that—I think *people* are postmodern. They're just strange.

BW: (Laughs.)

BH: When you get to the bottom of folks they're very strange. And Bukowski admits it. And your folks with their dogs admit it, the guy who pushed his partner off the cliff. They're very curious, and I am reviewed often as if I am— "Oh, here's Hannah with a house of wax again. Come on in." [Audience laughter.] "Yep, he's beating—you know there's this guy in here who likes bees too much." And it's like *Freaks*, like I've got a traveling freak show. I have never seen anything myself except as an accurate portrayer of obsessions. I didn't have to have Flannery O'Connor's obsessives—

BW: To do what you do.

BH: No, I was writing long the way I was. I didn't even know about Flannery O'Connor till I was twenty-five in grad school, last year in grad school. I was at Bennington talking to some students one time, and there was a lady, kind of a middle-aged lady, I was talking about Larry Brown and Mark Richard, and this lady said, "Brown makes me uncomfortable. He frightens me. These people act like folks from the fifties." And basically what she meant was guys in pickup trucks who have a six-pack. I mean, come on, get real, they do this in Pennsylvania. This is life, baby, from the steel mills. Men haven't changed from the fifties that much. What is it, that they're supposed to be alert to organic vegetables more?

BW: (Laughs.)

BH: What's changed? I mean, they're no fins, basically. They're no fins. And the music's worse! That's the change from the fifties. I don't get the fear. Because how come I can read a book about vicious lesbians and enjoy it and not feel threatened? I don't get this "Everything's got to be temperature-controlled." I think that people are just disturbed by human behavior.

The Rough South of Larry Brown

Larry Brown, Mary Annie Brown, and

Leona Barlow Brown / 1999

From *The Rough South of Larry Brown*, dir. Gary Hawkins (High Point, NC: DownHome Entertainment, 2005). From conversations taped 1997–1999. Transcript edited by Jay Watson. Used by permission.

MAB: I met him on the first night he came home from the Marines. I did. The first night he came home from the Marines I met him. I was friends with his cousin, and so she wanted to go see him when he came home, so we went over there, went over to his mother's trailer and he was—had his duffel bag and he was pulling out all these cigarettes and clothes and throwing them there on the couch and I thought to myself, why don't you just empty your bag? I know what you're doing is saving your underwear. And he finally admitted after we started going together, that's what he was doing. Saving his underwear. Didn't want to pull 'em out. Wonder how many underwear I've washed in twenty-five years? (Laughs.)

LB: She thought I was a smartass the first time she met me, 'cause she came along—me and Dan Hipp were going to town one afternoon in my mama's car and I hit this wet curve and said, "Hold on, Hip," and we spun out of control. Spun in a ditch. I landed in his lap and blew out two of the tires. And they come along to help me and I'd done called the wrecker and she thought I was getting smart with her daddy. And I said, "It won't do any good to pull it 'cause two of the tires are blown, the wrecker's on the way, but thank you anyway," all that. She claims I got smart with her daddy, so that's where I first met her. She was about fifteen then.

MAB: I don't remember that.

LB: Then I saw her the day after I got out of the service and she was with my cousin. They came over to my house to see me. Over at my mama's house. And she had grown up and changed a lot by then. And we started dating. Had our first date on New Year's Eve 1973. 1972. 1973, right!

MAB: I remember I was sitting on the swing of my mother's house when he gave me the engagement ring. And then he went and bought a trailer. He went and bought it and I never did see it till after they brought it out here and set it up. And then when we got married it was so hot that day. I cried. I woke up at three o'clock in the morning the day before I got married and started crying and cried until I walked down the aisle. I was nineteen. I was nineteen. He was . . . twenty-two? Twenty-three?

LB: Actually she proposed to me. Something like, "Are you ready to get married," or something like that. That was at, in her daddy's living room, right over here . . . 'cross the trailer. (Laughs.) Yeah. She wouldn't want me telling that, would she? She's probably told some shit on me, though. (Laughs.)

MAB: And we got married August 17th of '74. Yeah, '74. He worked at the stove factory when we were dating. And then he got on with the fire department. Why? It was a job opening in Oxford, didn't want to go anywhere else. He didn't have a college education, he didn't want to work at the factory. I guess the . . . wanting to help people. Maybe.

LB: It looked like it might be a pretty exciting job to have, too. Something that would be pretty interesting, to learn all this stuff about how to be a firefighter and go put out fires and do all that kind of stuff. I'd just had two years in the Marines. I was ready for something like that.

MAB: I never worried about Larry. Never. I don't think I ever worried about him once. Not even when they had the big fire at the carpet place. Knowing that he was there, I never did worry about him. I trusted him.

Your life was controlled by on-duty/off-duty. If it was Christmas and he was on duty then Santa Claus came the day before, or three o'clock in the morning so we could have Christmas before he left to be at work at seven. Everything revolved around the fire department.

LB: There was *always* the fire department. Every third day there was always the fire department to go to. That was just regular clockwork.

MAB: A shift, B shift, C shift. Then he worked twenty-four on, forty-eight off. So he worked part-time jobs, on his off days: bricklaying, carpentry work, cleaning carpets, answering the phone. He worked for a surveyor before. He ran a little country store. He did it all. He had to. Had too many babies to feed, too many bills to pay.

LB: It goes by so fast, man. When you grow up you don't really think about that. And then you get married and start raising kids, and I'd get to asking myself, where am I going to be ten years down the road? Are you still going to be doing the same thing you're doing now or are you going to try to do something better with your life?

MAB: Fire department, babies, get up, go to bed, go to work the next morning.

LB: Because I didn't feel like I was doing a whole lot with it. I had a pretty good job, being a firefighter, but I worked all these shit jobs too, man, where I was sacking groceries, cutting pulpwood and hauling hay, painting houses, building chain link fences for Sears & Roebuck, all that crap. And I worked for seven days a week and I did that for years. And I said man, ain't there something else you can try to do?

MAB: Larry always had these whims, right? When he was always gonna do this, gonna do that. And he picks me up from work one day and I said, "You're late, where've you been?" and he says, "I've gone to Joy's to get your typewriter. I'm going to start writing." And I said, "Oh yeah, well, okay" and he goes and I had this old-timey desk, he sets everything up and he just goes into it and he writes constantly, every day, all the time. When he's not at the fire department.

LB: I was just . . . I think I was just curious if I could do it. If I could sit down and write a book. And so I sat down and wrote the book, but I was so naive you know, I thought that I'd mail it off to New York City and they'd mail me back a check and I found out it don't work that way. (Laughs.) Not for most people it doesn't. Once in a while somebody slips through the cracks.

MAB: So it was like, work at the fire department twenty-four hours day, go to a part-time job, come home and put himself in his writing room and set there until he couldn't stand it any longer and had to go to bed. We never saw him. (To LB:) Right?

LB (to MAB): That was pretty much it.

MAB: I mean, I didn't marry Larry the writer. That came years later.

LB: She didn't marry a writer.

MAB: I didn't. This was thrown at me. I didn't ask for it.

LB (to MAB): You didn't ask for it, did you?

MAB (to LB): I didn't ask for it.

LB: You're not born with it. Nobody's born with it. That's just something you develop, just like—I compare it to a bricklayer who goes and studies with a journeyman for five years. To learn how to lay those courses. And the reason I say that is because if you could've seen all the early stuff that I wrote, like the first five novels I wrote, and about a hundred short stories, you would *have* to say that I have no talent. You wouldn't have any other choice, to say that. It was just that bad. So I think it's something you just develop, according to how bad you want to—you know, if you're willing to hurt enough you can have it.

(To interviewer): This is a list that began in 1982 and this runs up until 1999. And this is a document or a record of the titles of all these stories, the magazines they were sent to and when they were sent out. And each one that has a line drawn through is a rejection. Now just about *all* this stuff, *all* this stuff was rejected. You can see there was about five or six stories out of all these pages.

MAB: Those were hard. To see him work so hard, and then those slips come in. They'd be just little short sentences like, "Well we're sorry, but not this time. Try us again." Things like that.

LB: Here's one called "Old Frank and Jesus" that was never taken. It was sent out over and over and over. Here it was sent to the *Paris Review*. Here it was sent to the *Carolina Quarterly*. Rejected. Same with so many of these short stories. Just rejected. There's where "Old Frank and Jesus" was rejected by the *Georgia Review* in '84. "Old Frank and Jesus" rejected, *Antaeus*, November '84. "Old Frank and Jesus" rejected by the *Antioch Review*, July '85. "Old Frank and Jesus" rejected by the *Michigan Quarterly*, May 10, '85. "Old Frank and Jesus" rejected by *Ploughshares*, May '85. (Laughs.) And it got so repetitious I just started putting down the initials, "OFAJ," "Old Frank and Jesus," *Texas Review*. (Laughs.)

MAB: He was so determined to make it he would stay right there with it all the time. He might come in and sit down and eat with us. To this day he usually doesn't eat with us, because if he's writing, leave him alone, let him write. He'll eat when he gets hungry. So we've always done everything without him around because he was always writing.

But when Larry writes, that's when he's the happiest. But when he's not writing he's so depressed that you don't like to be around him. (Long pause.) You can't stand it.

LB: I just kept going, and I just kept collecting those rejection slips and just figured out about after two years, well, it's the kind of thing you got to be in for the long haul. Keep on going.

[A short conversation between Brown and his mother, Leona Barlow Brown, in her okra patch]

LB: I don't know how anybody could eat this much okra. I just don't.

Leona Brown: I think they . . .

LB: I love it as much as anybody, but boy, this is a lot of okra.

Leona Brown: Too much.

LB: I don't know what they'd do with *this* much.

Leona Brown: No, this was planted too thick.

LB: They ought to thin a little of this out maybe.

Leona Brown: Uh huh.

LB: I can't figure how he got it to grow this tall.

Leona Brown: I don't know. Just keeps getting taller and taller, looks like.

(To interviewer): I always just put a little bit in at a time and flour 'em, get 'em completely covered. Make sure my grease is hot. It's going to pop.

When we lived in Memphis we were just a short distance from the library up there, so as soon as they all started school they got their library cards. And we went once a week and got books. And everybody read. All my children. And we still do.

LB: She was really the one who turned me on to reading. I mean I think I started reading way before I went to school. Grimm's fairy tales, *Moby-Dick*, Jack London, loved all that stuff. One of the best things she did for us was bought us a set of encyclopedias, those Brittanicas? When I was like ten or something. Then I just kept reading. Even when I was in the Marine Corps that was one of my favorite things to do. Whatever base I was on I went to the library, man, and got me some books. Yeah. Sure did. So it's just something that I've done all my life, and that's what brought me to writing finally. I finally got to wondering how a person could go into a room and sit down and write a book where nothing had existed before.

Leona Brown: When they were children, they stayed at home. They were not allowed to roam around anywhere while I was at work, or their daddy, and that was good pastime for them. Kept them from fighting a good bit, too, all four of them like that. (Laughs.) But that was when they learned to read. They realized what you could learn, what you could memorize and keep within yourself. What you read. You know, you don't ever forget when you see the printed word. You may hear something and it goes in one ear and out the other, but when you read it, you've got it. It stays with you. That's the way *I* feel about it.

LB: I wrote that, that inscription [the dedication to *Dirty Work*]. It says, "For Daddy, who knew what war does to men." And I got the first copy after it was finished and I carried it over to her, and I wrote in there, "And for Mama who got me to read." He had such a hard time in the war. He was in the infantry for four years. And he was lucky. He was only wounded one time. But he went all the way to Berlin. And a long time ago we had a piece of pink granite that he chipped out of Hitler's actual fireplace with his bayonet.

I'd see him read a newspaper once in a while, you know, catch the news, but as far as opening a magazine or a book, never saw him do that. Never saw him do that. And I don't believe that he *thought* very much of reading. And I *might* even go so far as to say that he thought it was, you know not too good a thing to be doing.

I read a lot of westerns at one point. Then I got to going to the bookstore, and I got to discovering people like—well, I discovered Flannery O'Connor in a short story class, but then I got to buying books by people like Raymond Carver, Tobias Wolff. Really started reading a whole lot more short stories, 'cause that's what I wanted to write too, was short stories. I mean the first thing I wrote was a novel, but I really got to wanting to learn how to write short stories.

I had probably written, I don't know, forty or fifty stories I guess, and nothing had sold, you know, nothing had flown. And so I was trying to do different things with language. I was really impressed along about that time with Donald Barthelme's work. His stories, the way he told things. And I was trying to do something that Barthelme hadn't done.

"Boy and Dog": I was working then in the kitchen in the house that's across from our house of my mother-in-law's house. I'd go in every night. I had a few hours and try and write a story, and I started this one and was inspired by seeing this dog walk out into the road one day in front of this Mustang cutting about sixty down the by-pass. And the dog—it was just incredible to me that the dog could not see something that big and that fast coming. And just walked straight into it and of course it was killed instantly. And so then another thing started happening—what if that dog had belonged to some kid that loved the dog a whole lot and the kid was, you know, kind of unruly? What would he do? I got to looking it over after I'd written the first page and I said you know, I bet I can do something a little different here and just stack these lines, one under the other. And put five words in each sentence and make it look like a poem but really be a short story. So it was really just an experiment in form.

When I write the first line, that's when I want it to start happening, boom, from the get-go. That's what I try to do, is to get my reader involved really deeply, and hook him, and essentially make him forget that he's reading. We hear a yelp and a thud.

[The following comments accompany the dramatization of "Boy and Dog":]

LB: Man, I almost killed one going to town the other day, a little ol' beagle with a red collar. I mean I hadn't had nothing to drink or nothing. I just came so close to killing him, but you know, he just hit the road at the wrong angle and I went over into the other lane and a damn curve too. Wasn't nothing coming, thank God, but man, I'll do just about anything to keep from hitting a dog, man.

I think one reason I love them so much is because I was denied having one until I was about fourteen years old because I lived in Memphis, and you couldn't have a dog up there, you know. My parents wouldn't let me have a dog. So the first thing I did when I moved to Mississippi was get me a bunch of dogs. And I've had 'em ever since.

They've got such great personalities. They're like people. I mean, they know stuff like jealousy and anger and fear and humiliation and all kinds of things.

Yeah, those wrecks . . . those wrecks were always the worst, man. I got to hating those worse than the fires. I had gotten to the point where I could deal with fire fairly well 'cause I'd been around enough of them. But the car wrecks. No two are ever the same. They don't follow any pattern. There are so many different—so many forces involved. There's speed, weight of a vehicle, and human behavior—no way to predict what you're ever going to see when you get to one of those.

The thing that always bothered me the most was children, you know. Children being involved, you know? That's what used to really tear me up. Which you didn't see a whole lot, but you did see it some.

["Boy and Dog" is] one of the few instances that I've put something about the fire department into fiction. You get a bunch of boys—firemen, firefighters are the *craziest* group of individuals I have ever met in my life, without fail. Don't matter if they're in Portland, Oregon, or El Paso, Texas, they're all just alike.

[Here the dramatization of "Boy and Dog" ends and the "conversation" resumes.]

LB: I got to the point where finally I was making a little money off my writing. I didn't have to work a part-time job on my days off at the fire department. All I had to worry about was pulling ten shifts a month up there at work and the rest of the time I could write, and that's what I wanted to do was write.

MAB: I was an only child. My mother and father had me when she was forty. I remember thinking it was lonely.

LB: Mine had four to divide their attention between. But I know she had to do a lot of hard-ass work, man. She used to run these cows around this place with a stick. And I think I can remember her driving the tractor up and down—this used to be a cotton patch in front where our hay field is now—but I know she'd get on that tractor and drive it just like a man when she was fourteen years old, sure.

MAB: I was raised as a boy, just about, where Daddy had two tractors and we farmed and he was on one and I was on the other all summer long. In the morning you got up early, you went to the field, you did what had to be done, and you'd come home and you'd be so tired you'd eat your dinner and go to bed. I remember at holidays thinking it was lonely. One reason I enjoy going up to Larry's mother's for holidays, 'cause all of Larry's brothers and sisters and their kids and—it's a lot of fun. Loud. Stories being told on one another. Larry doesn't stay in the family room much, in the house with us much.

LB: I think the less trouble going on in my personal life the better my work is and the easier it is to do my work. [It] doesn't really bother me to spend these long periods of time by myself. That may just be part of my personal nature.

MAB: His routine now is to get up about six or seven o'clock at night, drink his coffee, mess out in the yard for a while, go to Tula, come back, mess around in the house a little bit, and as we're getting ready to shut our day down, he's starting his day. And he'll write all night long. That's just the way it is, I don't know why.

He was never around the kids that much. I mean, he did help raise LeAnne more than he did the boys, because LeAnne was born premature, hole in her heart. But I'm the one that's in charge of the kids. He likes to be off at Tula and I like to be home with the kids and that's the way it's been all our married life. Larry's always wanted a place over there to write, to go to, peace and quiet, his own little place. As we all said, Larry's always been in his own little world. Well that's Larry's little world at Tula.

LB: This is at Tula, this is where my parents are from, my mother and daddy, and all my ancestors clean back to the ones who got killed in the Civil War are buried up here. And this is really the place I came back to when I was about thirteen, when I was brought back from Memphis. And my mother just lives a mile away up the road over here. But to me, this is where I come when I want to be in a quiet place and a relaxed place and just get away from everything that I do the rest of my life.

We've talked about getting a house in town. We've talked about building a house in Tula—in addition to the little one I'm building—but we haven't made up our minds yet. We don't know yet what's going to happen.

MAB: We'll move to Tula.

LB: We might, we might not, I don't know, we might have a house in town, too. I've always kind of wanted to have a house in town.

MAB: But you always wanted to go back to Tula.

LB: I'm going to have that place in Tula.

MAB: But it's not like a house.

LB: Well . . .

MAB (to interviewer): Maybe he just don't want *us* over there.

LB: No, it's not that. I just don't know if I'm ready to *move* over there full time or not.

I do a lot of work over [t]here, a lot of manual labor over [t]here, like cutting down these trees that the pine beetles have killed, and just trying to clear it on up. What I'm eventually working my way back around to is getting cleared enough to where I can re-fence it all again and keep some of my cows over [t]here. I've got a pretty good barn up on the hill there. Just don't have a residence over [t]here yet.

All my kinfolks, my daddy and my baby, are buried over at Tula and that's, that's where I'll be buried eventually.

MAB: I didn't care that he was writing. I knew where he was. He was right there in that bedroom, with the lights on, with me trying to sleep and little bitty baby in the baby bed next to us, with him, you know, at his typewriter, typing. So I knew where he was. I could sleep. But when he's not there, I wondered where he was, what he was doing. He was usually out, at a bar.

LB: There's so much material in there.

MAB: Yeah, that's what he says.

LB: But that's what I've been around and what I'm still around, it's one of the things that I know best.

MAB: I'm sure that's where most of his stories come from, sitting in a bar. The slimier the better, you know.

LB: The way I do, I kind of, I go to a bar for a while, then when I leave that bar, I don't go back no more. I just kind of move around.

In the case of Opal's [a bar in Oxford] it got be the damn level of the humanity coming in the damn place was too bad to put up with. I mean it got to where they were having shootings and stabbings. Some dude walked in there one day, somebody'd whipped him the night before and he brought in a damn 30.30 and let off a round right through the middle of the damn bar there. And it just got to be too damn rough for me. I mean when I go out I'm not looking for no damn trouble, or somebody to stick a knife in my face. I want to have a few drinks, you know, and have a good time. All this fighting bullshit, that's. . . . So I started at Opal's, then I went to Ireland's, where some more of my stories are set and a lot of the stuff in *On Fire* is set, and then I went to City Grocery, and I'm still at City Grocery now. So it's just like a natural thing for me, to put a place, to put a story in a bar, because that's where I spend so much of my life at, is in a bar. Because that's where I hang out with my friends, you know.

MAB: He loves his friends. Friends are *very, very* important to Larry.

LB: Most of the time I stay by myself, in that room back there, writing.

[The following comments accompany the dramatization of "Wild Thing":]

LB: I don't plan ahead for things. All you got to have is a character and a place and a situation—what's going on—then introduce another character into it and have these two people interact and then find out all this other stuff has been going on in the past. To me it's really fascinating to find out what they're going to do next. What *are* they going to do next? And then they do something totally unexpected that you did not see coming and then you know, okay, bang, that's what's going on here. That's the payoff for me.

That sex, that's what starts all the trouble. Between people—or maybe not always starts it, but it sure adds fuel to the fire. Yeah, the worse you can make it on your characters, I think, the better it is. You know, sandbag 'em and load them up with this stuff. And I try to start with trouble on the first page. Trouble on the first page.

MAB: Just because he writes women characters, that doesn't mean it's me. Or any part of the family. His characters are not always us. The only thing

I remember thinking that the refrigerator [in "Wild Thing"] was full of diet Coke cans.

LB: Yeah, I put those in. . .

MAB: That was me, but that's about it. You know, people shouldn't think. . . . Now I *did* have one person ask me did Larry abuse me.

LB: He did, didn't he?

MAB: Yeah. No, Larry would never lay a hand on me. When it's nonfiction like *On Fire*, those stories, yeah, that's fine, that's our life, but the stuff that he—the novels and the short stories he writes, that's not us.

LB: I think when you can't do anything else for your characters, when you can't help them anymore, then you know it's over. When you've done all you can do for them.

[Here the dramatization of "Wild Thing" ends and the general "conversation" resumes.]

MAB: I watched him burn a whole novel one day, page by page. Stood right out there at that burning barrel and pitched one page in at a time. He just came out of his room and said, "This is no good." He just didn't think he had it.

LB: I was real impatient when I was trying to come up and publish and I thought I ought to have it a lot sooner than what came. And I just didn't understand that I hadn't put enough time in yet. I'm talking about, say, four or five or six years in and still wasn't enough time. I thought at that time that it *was* enough time. It turned out that eight years is what it took to publish my first book. And this matter of patience, you just have to keep writing, even if you're not selling anything, publishing anything, keep writing and just believing that you eventually will. That's what always kept me going, just knowing that if I spent enough time at it I'd eventually learn how.

In the old days when I first started, I thought you wrote it and sent it off, but then I learned by reading people like Raymond Carver that to polish is the thing, you know, to work on each individual sentence, and try to get each word good as you can make it, and to use understatement more than over-statement. These things are learned very gradually. On your own.

The rough draft is the hardest thing to write—for me it is—that's the hard place I have to go each day when I sit down. Then the other part when you go back and revise, that's when you learn more about what the story's about, where you see where you've overwritten something. That's why it takes me so long to write a book, because I just revise and revise and revise. I'll retype a whole page to change one letter if that letter has to be changed, 'cause I don't have a computer, I still have a typewriter. I keep my novels in a three-ring binder, where I can sit there with my red pencil and work on my sentences. And when I'm doing that, when I'm doing revision, I can stay with it eight, ten hours, but I can't stay with the first draft over two, three hours. That's too hard.

I got my first book contract which was *Facing the Music*, which appeared in 1988, had good reviews, good blurbs, and I was working at the fire department. There was *always* the fire department, every third day there was always the fire department to go to, that was just regular clockwork. And that eventually got to be too much of a chore. You know I finally got to where I could make a living, and so I quit, I quit my job, and I've been away from there now ten years.

Sometimes it's hard for me to go in places, like when I ran in there to get those cigarettes last night, you know, before we left? I like to not got out of there, you know, people just coming up and wanting to talk. Some boy owned some bookstore over somewhere and told me how many of my books he sold and I'm proud to hear it and all but I knew y'all were waiting in the car and all and I wanted to get back out, get my cigarettes and go. So sometimes it's harder for me to hang out than it is the normal person. Just because of the people who have read my books.

MAB: It's like, you know, they try to be friends with him, then, "Oh, by the way, will you read a story of mine?" Or "Will you help me, will you call your publisher for me?" Or people just wanting to say, "I saw Larry," or "I had drinks with Larry," or, "Bought Larry a drink," or. . . . It's easier for Larry to say no to family than to friends. I don't know why. For a while there we were second place, they were first place. And that just don't wash with me.

LB: Yeah, if I'm home working, you know, I'm not out messing around or sitting uptown until the bars close or something like that. And I just get so much more done. And I've known this, it's no secret. Sometimes I just let it get away from me. Maybe I just get tired, I don't know.

MAB: Where Larry and I had our problems was me at home saying, "Okay, Larry, you've got to take the garbage out, Larry, the sink needs fixing, Larry, the yard needs mowing, we need to pay this bill." I'm bringing him back to reality. He goes uptown, everybody's stroking his ego, telling him how great he is, how they loved his words that he'd written down or how proud they were of him. I think that got to Larry, thinking that, "Okay, maybe I am just a little better than Larry the husband, Larry the father."

LB: Fame is something you don't want no part of. If you can stay away from it, I think it's best just to stay away from it. It's not what you thought it was, and there's too much stuff that happens that interferes with your work.

MAB: When we were first married, and for several years, we didn't have enough money for him to buy anything to drink. So he couldn't drink. But the more Larry was published and people recognizing him, it was hard. I think he struggled.

LB: I believe it's part hereditary too. I know my daddy was bad to drink and my granddaddy was bad to drink, and I hate to say this, but it looks like my boys are pretty bad to drink already, you know. And I hate that, but there ain't really nothing I can do about it and I'm not no good example 'cause they've grown up seeing me drink all their life. I ain't been a good role model.

MAB: There's things that Larry's done that he should not have been allowed to get away with. But because he was a writer, he got away with it. Larry and a friend of his had been drinking just about all day and they were really wasted at this bar uptown. And I went up there to get him and I was trying to talk him into coming home, and there was a band playing, just a few people in there. So I asked the bartender to cut him off. He looks at me and he says, "Who are you to ask me to cut Larry Brown off?" I said, "Well, being married to him for so many years gives me the right." And he said, "Well, I'm not cutting him off." "Cut him off." "No."

I said okay, if he leaves here tonight and he hurts someone or he hurts himself, I'll own your butt and this bar's butt by the time I'm through. There's no reason not to cut him off. I went downstairs, told Larry he could have at it and walked out the door. Left him there.

We were poor but I had a very loving home life. If my mother and I went somewhere, before the day was out my father was there. Because he wanted to be around us. And that's where Larry, I think that's where Larry and I have our problems, because I don't understand why you wouldn't want to be there.

LB: It's the focus, it's my work, it's my daily job, that I go to like other people go to their jobs. And my hours are erratic and I don't get paid but, you know, a couple times a year, something like that, and I spend all this time by myself, but that's just what it takes. That's the nature of the thing.

[The following comments accompany the dramatization of "Samaritans":]

LB: I wrote that one . . . this bar I used to go into on the west side of town called Opal's. I wrote it probably about 1985. Think I wrote it the same year I wrote "Facing the Music." And just what if a kid walked into a bar one day, wanted to buy cigarettes and wasn't old enough, that's where the whole thing started. And what would happen, would they sell them to him or would they send him on his way? And so it just went from there. And I just lifted the whole place in my mind. Because I remember when I'd go out there after getting off one of my jobs, and it'd be so damn hot outside you just couldn't stand to be out in it. And step in that cool darkness there, man, that air conditioning hits you, and they got cold beer, so it was a logical place for my character to be hanging out and all he needed was a reason, and I came up with that. He said, "My wife left me to live with somebody else," and that's where it all started, right there. He don't even want to fool with it, you know, but he just kind of feels bad for them, you know, looked like the kid hadn't always had enough to eat, gym shorts way too big for him.

It's the kind of a thing where you think one thing's going on, then you read a little more and you find out, you know, something totally different's going on. That's why I like to read that story, 'cause the audience starts laughing at first—they think it's funny you know—then later on, about three-fourths of the way they find out it ain't funny worth a shit.

[Here the dramatization of "Samaritans" ends and the general "conversation" resumes.]

LB: There's a fine line I think you have to walk between hard-heartedness on this side and sentimentality on this side. You know, you can't go off into either one of those ditches. So you gotta try to go down the middle of the road without leaning. And you really can't shade things. I mean you can't say, "Aww, how bad this is," you know, without sounding sentimental, and you can't blow this terrible thing off, you know, to veer into hard-heartedness. You've got to try to just lay it out straight the way it is, and let the reader form his or her own opinion about it. You know, you can't be influenced either way. And that's why, you know that's why I get whatever negative things I get said about my work. It usually refers to how brutal it is, and I say well that's fine. It's okay for you to call it brutal, but just admit by God that it's honest.

MAB: He has a lot of morals. He does. His mother taught him that. If I had his fault, it would be a fault that I would want. He trusts everyone. Where I don't. I'm very protective of my family. If I become your friend I'll be your friend for life. I like a person for what a person—how the person acts toward me. Not what he's done with his career, because everybody's different. Not everyone can be a writer or a filmmaker or anything like that. You just have to be a nice person.

All I saw first was Larry. And the words came later. Just met Larry, fell totally in love with him, his wild side, 'cause I was so different from him. (Laughs.) And it's always been what Larry's wanted, Larry got. Always. But the kids say whatever I want, I get. Larry always gives me everything I want.

I think down deep he knew that he had to turn it around, that it was not the way that he needed to go, it was a life that he didn't want to lead. And he finally got his priorities in order. They left him for a while but he got 'em back. And now he seems happier than he's ever seemed in his life.

LB: I wasted so much damn time, man, sitting on a bar stool. God, that's what kept me from working. I mean, I should've been finished with this book a long time ago. But I just can't do both of them at the same time. It's just counterproductive for me. And not good for me, either.

MAB: And if it changes tomorrow or tonight, then I've had the most wonderful last year and so many months in my life.

LB (to MAB): Those are the roses I gave you, huh? Well, they're really pretty. They're still pretty after almost a week. Kind of starting to get the fade on 'em a little bit, ain't they?

Interviewer: What are they for?

LB: Twenty-four years of . . . bliss. (Laughs.) Started to say "hell." (More laughter from LB.)

MAB: Oh, well, *I* was supposed to have said that.

LB: You'd have been pissed if I'd have said that, though.

MAB: Well, you did say it.

LB: Well, just in a joking way.

MAB: Well . . .

Billy Ray. He's tall, red-headed, and the funniest person you'll ever meet on earth, and that's what I tell everyone. He's the good old country boy who likes to have a beer or two, but family's very important to Billy Ray. I tell him all the time I hope he has nine girls. Because he's so rough with LeAnne. So bossy with LeAnne. I hope he has nine girls 'cause it'll straighten him out. I depend upon Billy Ray. I have for years depended on Billy Ray.

Shane is an avid sports fan. Loves sports of all kinds. Hopes to be a baseball coach when he gets older. Loves to party like his daddy. Always becoming friends with everybody he meets, very outgoing. And everybody will say Shane's my favorite. Billy Ray will say it in a heartbeat. That Shane's my favorite. And I've ruined him and I've spoiled him and he won't be worth anything. Because he'll hit the real world one day and he'll fall flat on his face, because of me. But I don't think so. Shane's too determined.

LeAnne. She has been something from the day she was born. She's very headstrong, and at the age now where she and I do not get along too well at times, because I want to protect her. She doesn't want to be protected. She reminds me of me, but she has more guts than I ever had, or ever will have. At seventeen she's got more guts than I'll ever have.

Larry, he may not say it but I raised these kids. For him to write, to stay out in his room. And he's still got his writing, and now I'm losing what I worked for, by them growing up and going on. That's why I look forward to grandkids. Larry says I look forward to it too much. Well, you know. Your kids grow up, you're ready to look at them again as little babies. That's why I've got those two rocking chairs on my front porch. I'm ready. One for him, one for me.

LB: There's only so many books I can write in my life. You know, I'm going to die at a certain age. I don't know what that age is, but while I'm alive I want to write as much as I can. And I want it to be good. I figure if my health continues and all I probably still got twenty more years of writing in me. That'd be good. To be writing at sixty-eight, that'd be nice. I'd be relaxing by then. Sure. Yeah, but I hope my books survive. You know, I hope that they're still being read after I'm gone. That's probably about the most you can hope for. Is for them to stay in print. Like Faulkner and Flannery O'Connor, people like that, you know. I don't know if my stuff comes up to that high a level or not, because it is so high, but only time will tell. Only time will tell.

The Rough Road of Larry Brown: Smith and Wesson Meets Smith and Corona

Jim Dees / 2000

From *Oxford Town* (23–29 March 2000): 12–13. Used by permission.

It should come as no surprise to anyone who has read the low-down Bubba Realism fiction of Larry Brown—including his latest, and perhaps darkest novel, *Fay*—that as an eighteen-year-old faced with 1-A military status during the Vietnam War, Brown signed up with the U.S. Marine Corps.

"That's how we bought beer back then," he says, noting one of the few bright spots of his two-year military career. "Go across the river and show 'em your draft card."

Also unsurprising is that his specialty in the Marine Corps, the area in which he was trained, was plumbing. A metaphorical foreshadowing, it seems, of his later fictional plumbing of human depths.

"Marine recruiter signed me up in Tula in November of 1970," Brown says, lighting a cigarette while driving the backroads recently.

"I ended up spending Christmas in boot camp at Parris Island. It was a stupid-ass thing to do. We picked up seventy-five, graduated thirty-two," he says, furrowing his lined brow and flicking an ash. "Sent the rest of 'em on home. People would like, cut their throat to get out of there."

Brown said his checkered military service ("I was a sh—bird, man. I just barely scraped by") came to a close when he was brought up on charges while stationed in Philadelphia, Pennsylvania regarding a barroom brawl.

"These Turkish sailors would come in the Marine bar and hit on our women. They couldn't speak but, like, two words of English—that was 'beer' and 'whiskey'—was all they could say. But what they got me for was I got in a fistfight with a bunch of Puerto Rican sailors. The damn fight was over with I reckon and we's all standing out there. All these sailor boys come running by, and somebody said something I don't know what it was. But one of 'em just reached out—great big ole tall guy—and hit me right in the damn nose just as square and hard as he could hit me, man. Almost knocked me down."

The bucolic tranquility of Brown's native Lafayette County rolls by in a perfect juxtaposition with his harrowing tale.

"We chased 'em over to their damn barracks and was screaming for 'em to come out and fight. Called 'em chickens-it motherf—ers, all that.

"They later hung two of 'em for possession of marijuana. Our Admiral said 'No, no, no, you can't hang these people on American soil.' They said okay. Backed their damn boat out into the Delaware River and ran 'em up the damn yard arm and hung 'em out there. Came back in and redocked. Big stink over it."

Big stinks and hard knocks have been fellow travelers on Brown's rough road, even from the earliest years.

"I loved my dad a whole lot but he was hard to get along with. He drank so damn much and everything, that's what broke us up to start with. Mama just left Daddy, we just left him in Memphis. But there was always trouble before that, I mean all my life. Like my earliest memory is like fear, man, fear. His whole problem was four years in the infantry in World War II. But he came from a broken home too. My grandaddy drank. It just gets passed on down the line," Brown says, lighting another cigarette.

Following his Marine stint, Brown came back to Lafayette County in 1972, moving in with his mother and collecting unemployment for a couple of months before going to work in the Chambers stove factory on Old Taylor Road.

"I went around and asked the Chief (Bill Whitehead) about getting on with the Fire Department. He told me I'd have to get a haircut. It was pretty long."

About this time, his cousin introduced him to a pretty girl with auburn hair, Mary Annie, and they married in 1974. Three children followed.

Of his early firefighting days Brown says: "I was scared every day for five years. The scariest thing, though, is driving that fire truck to a fire for the first time. Your legs are shaking on the gas and the clutch. The lights are going, the siren is going, and you're running red lights and people are getting out of the way and your just hope you can get it down the street, thinking 'What the f—k do I do now?'"

Between shifts and stolen weekend moments, what Brown did was write.

"I started writing in October of 1980. One night, I ran into Barry Hannah at Dino's, when it was still on the Square. I introduced myself to him. Then

I went to see him a couple of times when he lived over on Johnson. Barry told me that Ellen Douglas was teaching a good writing class on campus and that I should go see her. I went to see her and told her I wanted to take her writing class.

"She said, 'Well, what have you written?' I told her, three novels and about eighty short stories.

She said, 'Yeah, you can come to the class.'"

At the time, Brown had only been published once and that was a short story in *Easyriders* magazine.

"I was naive when I started. I didn't even know you were supposed to double-space. That first novel I wrote was 327 pages, single spaced."

After a semester of Douglas's class, Brown found himself writing when he could between his regular fire department job and the myriad part-time jobs he took to feed three children.

"Hauling hay, or painting somebody's house, I built chain link fences for Sears and Roebuck for awhile. Cut timber . . .

"One of my last projects before I started writing full-time was disassembling a '55 Chevrolet that I hauled up from Eupora on a damn trailer; two-door hard top. Took the sumbitch completely apart, jacked it up with these trailer jacks, jacked the whole damn thing up off the frame, took the whole thing completely apart. Completely dismantled the car and was going to put it back together. I never did get the damn thing back together. It sat out in the yard on them jacks for a couple of years. Somebody finally come hauled it off. So when I told Mary Annie I was going to start writing she said okay. But I'm sure she thought it was going to be about like that '55 Chevy."

More like a Mercedes. In the summer of 1985 Brown wrote three of the stories that would form the basis of his first book, the acclaimed *Facing the Music*. After over one hundred short stories and thirty rejection letters, Brown had a book contract.

Pay attention all you writing students. The central image that formed the inspiration for the title story of Brown's debut effort hit him in a vision while sitting at an Oxford red light.

"I was sitting at the damn red light on, uh, Jackson Avenue, gon make a right hand turn onto Ninth, right there, at the Post Office.

"I saw this guy with his toes up in front of him, watching TV. Had his socks up there you know and the TV was framed between his socks ya know? And he's watching TV. Watching Ray Milland, *Lost Weekend*, his wife's over there in the corner crying. So I wondered what the problem was. So I thought about it for a couple of weeks and I sat down and starting writing the story. When I wrote that story I knew I had turned the corner. I knew by then I had enough objectivity for my own work to know that it was good. I knew it worked but it took me two years to sell it. It was having something really crucial going on between two people but having it be low-key, but with all this tension underneath it. Didn't take that long to write it but I couldn't sell it."

Brown said his second book, the Vietnam novel, *Dirty Work*, was based on stories he heard back in his Marine bar in Philadelphia. Some of the plot information came from fellow soldiers attached to the Naval hospital who would tell war stories over beers.

"They told me what happened when you got captured. Said the Vietnamese would kill our guys, cut their penises off and leave them there in the jungle with their penises in their mouths. I saw a lot of pictures of that."

And yet, as with *Facing the Music*, the central image that sparked *Dirty Work* came from Brown's imagination.

"I got the idea for it when I was building my house in '86. All I had was like a guy, his face was messed up. He lived with his mama and he wouldn't come out of his room. That's all I had. It was just an image, it just kind of festered."

Brown said his publisher told him the novel actually started on page 160, that he could throw out all those pages and start over.

"It took a week for the reality to set in but I realized she was right. So I started over . . . twice more. I ended up throwing out 600 pages all together. Threw out 1,200 out of *Fay*."

From 1983 to 1990, Brown wrote the stories that would become *Big Bad Love*. Once again it was an image from his Marine days that found its way into his fiction ten years later.

"In 1972 we had this job where we went down into the bottoms of ships in the Delaware River and chipped tar aloose from oil tankers. Three-foot thick tar, and put up in carbo-barrels and haul it up out of there. We'd get off—this was in New Jersey—and go to this bar and have a couple of beers before we'd go back to the base. We're sitting there and I looked out the window and here come these people running down the street. Just running, man. They had this little ole girl, she was about four or five years old, had on this long white dress on. And her little legs, man, were going so fast trying to keep up with them. I said, man what is so wrong in their lives that they hauling that kid down the street this way? Raining.

"That really disturbed me to see that. Some stuff you see it just burns its image into you and you know you're going to use it sometime in your fiction somewhere, you don't know where. Then a perfect place pops up."

Brown finds a perfect place to pull over and we quietly share a smoke and a beer. He tells me his work *On Fire* and novels *Joe, Father and Son*, and now, *Fay*, garnered the Artists' Achievement Award last weekend bestowed by Governor Ronnie Musgrove. One of Brown's co-honorees at the event was the great Mississippi bluesman, Charlie Musselwhite. The ceremony also included a reunion with Ellen Douglas, Brown's first teacher. A giant slide show was presented showing Brown at various stages of his life—fishing, drinking, and ruefully contemplating the rough roads with what pal Jonathan Miles has described as an "achy, worried look."

Brown's precise rendering of peckerwood mayhem has even caught the attention of Japanese scholars who now teach Larry Brown in their fiction classes. One, Masaru Inoue, a Faulkner authority currently in Oxford on a year-long sabbatical from Yokohama University, says this: "I find a parallel between *Dirty Work* and *Soldiers' Pay*; *Joe* and the Snopes trilogy. By writing *Joe*, Larry struck a 'vein of gold.' In it he depicted 'Snopeses' in the new age, and it is not the imitation of Faulkner, but his own."

Such acclaim may fall on a deaf typewriter, however, and unfaze the Bubba of Bleak.

"It's just impossible for me to write a happy ending," Brown says. "Happy endings have escaped me so far. It just has never come together for me like that."

WUNC-FM Radio Interview

Keith Weston / 2002

From North Carolina Public Radio's *The State of Things*, WUNC-FM, Chapel Hill (April 2002). Transcript by Jay Watson. Used by permission.

LB: I'd always loved to read, and I wondered if it was possible for a person to teach himself how to write. And so in October, twenty-one years ago this month, I sat down and started writing a novel. But I didn't really know that there was a long apprenticeship period that you had to go through. I should have known better but I didn't. And so I just kind of kept going. The first thing I wrote was a novel during about seven months, and of course I thought I was going to send it off to New York City and they were going to send me a check back for a million bucks, but it didn't quite happen that way. (Laughs.)

KW: I understand that one of your first pieces of fiction actually was in, what, *Easyriders*?
LB: Mmm-hmm. Yeah, that was the first piece I published, in April of 1982, in *Easyriders*.

KW: But you've gone now from *Easyriders* to winning, this year, the Thomas Wolfe award from UNC. So how does one go from *Easyriders* to the Thomas Wolfe award, is what I want to know.
LB: (Laughs.) Well, you just have to write a lot and keep believing in yourself, and be in for the long haul. It requires writing a lot of things and throwing them away, but that's just part of the normal process.

KW: Did you read a lot as a kid?
LB: Oh yeah, prodigiously. I've read all my life, it's always been one of my main pleasures in life, reading.

KW: What were some of your favorite books as a kid?
LB: Oh, I read a lot of stuff like Greek mythology. I was into Greek mythology big time. Westerns, boy-and-dog stories like the books by Jim Kjelgaard,

Old Yeller by Fred Gipson, *Savage Sam*, *Stormy* [sic] by Will James. Just all kind of things. Outdoor things, a lot of times.

KW: Most of your writing has centered around your hometown or around your region.
LB: I just write about the place I live in. I talk about what's in the weather and the seasons changing over the land, the same land that I've been riding around on since I was eighteen years old, and how I never seem to tire of that and I never run out of things to write. I just get 'em out of my life experiences. I wanted to write a book one time about the boys who fought in Vietnam and who lost limbs or were maimed real badly, and I took some actual Marines, disabled Marines that I met when I was stationed at Marine Barracks, Philadelphia, in 1971 and 1972, and used them as models. And the other stuff like *Joe*, I took the job I used to have where I deadened timber in the summer and planted pine trees in the winter, and had them doing that job. So I take stuff from my own experience but then I use my imagination to create fiction with it.

KW: In your past you've done many other things as well. You were a fireman for a while, and you wrote a memoir about your experiences as a fireman. Can you tell us a little bit about that?
LB: That book evolved starting I guess in 1989. I just came back to the station one day and wrote down what we'd done that day. And started kind of keeping a journal. And then after I kept working on this thing, I began to pull up all the other things that we'd done in years past, and I began to discover that there was a whole wealth of material there to write about, nonfiction, that I never had even used before.

KW: That became *On Fire*.
LB: *On Fire*, which was published in '94, I believe.

KW: Now, you were just recently in Toronto, where one of your books has been made into a film. Or at least where a screening for one of your books, *Big Bad Love*. What was that like?
LB: I think it's good. I was there for just about the whole production last fall in Oxford and Holly Springs and Red Banks, Mississippi, and Collierville, Tennessee.

KW: That's where it was filmed.

LB: That's where it was filmed. I was there I guess for probably about half the shooting. I was actually doing the editing on *Billy Ray's Farm* at the same time, trying to get that finished, 'cause you're always under a deadline to get your manuscript in. But it was produced for five million bucks, it was an independent film, it was directed by Arliss Howard, and he stars. He plays Leon Barlow, and his wife, Debra Winger, plays Marilyn. And we also have Michael Parks, Paul LeMat—

KW: Is that Michael Parks of *Then Came Bronson*?

LB: That's him.

KW: Oh, man. Wow!

LB: (Laughs.) And Rosanna Arquette and Angie Dickinson.

KW: That's quite a cast.

LB: Yeah, it was a good cast, it sure was.

KW: Now I understand that when you were in Toronto, this was about the time of the unfortunate terrorist attacks in New York, and you took a bus from Toronto into New York, and you were there about the time that the tragedy happened with the firemen. How did that make you feel as previously a fireman yourself?

LB: It was terrible. It makes me sick every time I think about it. I got there on Saturday night, after riding the bus, and of course I was downtown there, at the Port Authority terminal, and the posters we've all been seeing on TV were just stuck up everywhere. New York was really strangely—not deserted, but the traffic was not near as heavy as what it usually is. The night we were there, we went down the Hudson River, and we started seeing these enormous tents that had been set up, like a two-story tent. And they were full of nothing but powdered concrete that they had hauled out of there. They had to dump that stuff somewhere and so they dumped it down by the Hudson River, just mountains and mountains of concrete. And of course you could see across the river there where all the lights were set up for the rescue operation in that empty space where they used to be standing. And then when we flew out Monday, the pilot came out and introduced himself, and he shook hands with everybody on the plane, and he said, "I've got a wife and four children that I'm going to be home with tonight, and we're going to have a safe flight to Chicago, and y'all go ahead and board whenever you'd like to." Never had seen anything like that before.

When I got home from New York that night—it was the following Monday—Sid Evans called me from *Men's Journal*. He had published one of the essays in here, about the coyote that came to kill my baby goats one by one, and he asked me if I could possibly write five hundred words before two p.m. the next day, when they were going to close the December issue. And I told him I'd try. So I went to my room and wrote down five hundred words about just what it felt like to fly past the remains of the towers and think about all the firefighters who were buried underneath that and what it took for them to do what they did, to go up when everybody else was coming down.

KW: Your latest work, *Billy Ray's Farm*, it's kind of part memoir, it has a lot of other elements in it. How do you describe it when someone asks you, "What's your latest book about?"
LB: I'd say it's just a collection of different essays that involve things about writers, about musicians I've known and about life on the farm there, and mostly just living in the country.

KW: Is there something you would like to read to us from this latest?
LB: Sure, I can read something for you.
    [Brown reads five paragraphs from the essay, "Billy Ray's Farm."]

KW: Your language is so precise and full I feel like I'm there already. I can really picture it from that description.
LB: (Laughs.) Thank you.

KW: Tell me about the real Billy Ray's farm.
LB: It's about sixty-two acres that belongs to my mother-in-law. We built our house there in 1986, and Billy Ray lives on the other side of the house with her, which we remodeled and had air-conditioning and carpet and all that put in before they got married last year.

KW: Now that's your son?
LB: Billy Ray, my oldest son. I've got two other children. But he still lives there, and he's got about, oh I guess thirty or forty brood cows, couple of bulls, and

he farms for a living. That's what he does. He works for some people on the other side of town, he mainly plants and harvests, and in his part-time he works on his own farm. And he's going real good, he's had a lot of success with it since a lot of the stuff that I wrote for this book.

KW: I don't think I've ever heard a bull described as an intelligent monarch before.
LB: (Laughs.) Some of those bulls are pretty amazing, some of those that run about three hundred thousand bucks apiece.

KW: You'd almost have to be a monarch to afford one.
LB: (Laughing.) Yeah, you would.

KW: Can I borrow the book for just a moment?
LB: Sure.

KW: You have a question here in the prologue that if you're gonna go through an interview you have to be asked. So I'm gonna go ahead and ask, just to see what your response is, to see if you give me the same lines as from the prologue here. So what is it about Oxford that produces writers?
LB: (Laughs.) That's a good question, and I never have been able to come up with an adequate answer for it. I know the town is full of young people who are working in bars or waiting tables and going to school and trying to write, but it wasn't like that when I was trying to come up. I think the only writers we had in town were Willie Morris, Barry Hannah, and Jo Haxton (Ellen Douglas), the lady I studied with. But now it's like the town's full of them, with more coming all the time.

KW: So is there a writer on every corner almost like a church on every corner?
LB: Just about, just about. And more and more people are living there now who have actually begun to publish their books.

KW: Well, Larry Brown, thank you very much. We wish you the best with *Billy Ray's Farm*, and thanks for coming in today.
LB: Thank you for having me here.

Pulling Rabbits out of a Hat:
An Interview with Larry Brown
Charles Blanchard / 2003

From *Oxford Town* 526 (11–17 September 2003): 16–17. Used by permission.

Larry Brown's new novel, *The Rabbit Factory*, is an image of several different characters in and around North Mississippi and Memphis. The strongest quality of the novel is its scattered narrative structure, which switches from one character to another with great frequency through the course of the novel. The characters' stories are thinly connected, but all share the same charm that permeates the novel. Readers are treated to a tilt-a-whirl of emotions and imagery, ranging from laugh-out-loud comedy, to the brooding tragedy typical of Brown's work. The plot and characters reflect the shifting tone with elements just as diverse: a navy ship colliding with a whale, orphaning its calf; a one-legged dog-sitter experiencing drunkenness for the first time; an aging man who can't figure out how to hold on to his much younger wife; and a tiny dog who gets stranded on the roof of a house. For readers who may have been turned off by the tragedy of Brown's previous works, this novel is a chance to give him another try. *The Rabbit Factory* is simultaneously as entertaining as a book can get, as true to life as a walk down to the local bar, and as filled with marvels and oddities as the late night storytelling over any campfire. Larry was gracious enough to offer a few minutes of his time.

OT: Do you think that there are still new stories left to tell for southern literature?
LB: Yeah. One of the best things that I've read here lately is *The Clearing*, the Tim Gautreaux novel set in 1927 down in Louisiana. It's a fascinating book about a bunch of guys clearing this whole bottom full of all these big trees, sawing it all up and everything, with these brothers in WWI. I think there's still plenty of fascinating stuff being written about the South. Of course, the characters in the South always get caricatured, like the crazy sister, or the drunk in the family. So, sure, stuff in the South still gets made fun of sometimes, but I think there's still plenty of serious stuff, good stuff coming out about it.

OT: What have you tried to do in your work to avoid the retelling of the same old stories?

LB: What I'm trying to do every time is do something different. I don't think you want to keep doing the same thing over and over. This novel is more comic than anything I've done before, I believe. It's got more humor built into it. It's not as grim in places as some of the other stuff I've done. In some places, it's grimmer.

OT: Do you have any predictions about the future of southern literature?

LB: I think it'll be okay. It's in pretty good hands. There are a lot of good young writers out there, already publishing books, and there's more coming up all the time. That's not something that I'm really worried about. That's one of the best things is discovering new, exciting young writers who are coming up, people like Brad Watson. He had a book out called *The Heaven of Mercury*. That's one of the best novels I've read in quite a while too. He studied with Barry Hannah. He's from Meridian, and he's down in Florida teaching now.

OT: How much of what you write comes from your own life, and what kind of balance do you strike between observation and creation?

LB: Well, when you're writing fiction you just pull up stuff. That is, Stephen King said once that all your human experience—your memory, everything you ever heard or saw, everything anyone ever told you about, all of that stuff—is like a well, and you drop down into that well every day for your fiction. Then something pops up that you need; it could just be a glimpse. I can give you an example. Back when I was still working on *The Rabbit Factory*, I was riding by this preacher's house one night and these weird looking dogs ran out. I was writing all this stuff about the character Eric and his daddy and all the dogs he had, and these dogs looked like they might have been a mix between a pit bull and a Dachshund. I said, "Damn, I'm gonna use that." So, stuff just pops up everywhere, and I just lift that stuff and use it. Some of the places that I write about exist, and some of the places don't exist. Some places I just make up totally out of my imagination, but as far as what the characters do, that's not usually autobiographical.

OT: How did you go about writing an animal character?

LB: Well, I figured that I would have to use a point of view for the dog, just like I used a point of view for a person, except that the dog could not articulate what he was thinking. I could only use images. For example, he didn't know the name of a squirrel, but he knew that it ran up those things he raised his leg and relieved himself on, which were trees. So, I just kind of rolled it out that way without trying to go over the edge and make the dog actually be able to think. But who knows what goes through the brains of animals? Anyone who's been around dogs knows that they have all kinds of human qualities. They have jealousy, fear, and anger. All kinds of emotions live in dogs, just like they do in people. They're just not able to articulate what they feel except through their actions: either love towards you, or growling at somebody they don't like. They're able to communicate, but not on the same level that we are. Also, I wanted to say something about the relationship that people have with animals, and how animals affect people's lives some times. The whole thing with the characters Arthur and Helen started because he wanted to catch a cat for her, and she didn't even want the damn cat! (Laughs.)

OT: Some authors say that characters and stories take on lives of their own, independent of the author. While others say the opposite, that they rule their story rigorously. Into which of these camps, if either, do you fall?

LB: People do it different ways. Me, I'm of the camp that just follows 'em around and sees what they do next, because you can't ever tell what you're going to do next. That's why I never use an outline. I've never written an outline for a novel, because I want to find out what the story is day by day. If you think about it, what happens to the reader is the same thing that happens to the writer, except in a much more condensed form. It's not six hours here, and fourteen hours there. It's a couple of days of reading the book, which is very different thing than putting it together. You have to make it appear seamless, as if it were all written at one swoop, the way it's going to be read, but then you get things wrong and you have to change them. I cut my third or fourth draft from 652 pages to 513 in six weeks, and that was the book. It was finished.

OT: What were you trying to do with the narrative structure of this novel?

LB: I wanted characters who had, in some cases, very tenuous connections. I wanted to have their stories go along parallel, side by side, in roughly the same time frame. Some characters were closer related than others were. Eric, Arthur, and Helen were more closely related than Wayne and Anjalee. Wayne and Anjalee got together at the very first of the novel, and then they didn't see each other any more until the very end of the novel. Whereas Arthur, Helen, and Eric had all this stuff going on in the meantime, and then Miss Muffet was stepping in and out once in a while. Domino was stepping in with his story going on as well. It was kind of like a juggling act, and I wanted it in a hundred segments—not chapters, but segments—and that's just the way I tried to put it all together. I had these charts going of how many sections each character had, and I was trying to even it out. But you keep going on, and you meet more characters, like Merlot. When I met Merlot, I didn't think he was going to turn into such a major character, or Penelope. Their story got to be really important to me, as all the stories did. So it's just an effort to keep all that stuff rolling at the same time. The hardest thing was trying to tie it all up at the ending and give everything resolution. It started with the kid. I knew it had to end with the kid. That's the way I tried to do it. It took me fifteen months to write it.

OT: What do you think the structure of this novel does for the reader?
LB: Hopefully it gives 'em some emotional punch in the belly, some closure at the end of it, and a satisfying ending. I sometimes get criticized for the dark stuff, the tragedy in my books, but I can't do anything about that. In real life, it doesn't always end up happily ever after.

OT: One scene in the novel that involved the characters Merlot and Penelope was related twice from two different points of view. Why did you choose that particular scene?
LB: Because I wanted the reader to see that what he was seeing on her face was not even close to what was really going through her head. She was thinking about the kid she gave up for adoption, how badly she wanted to find him, and he was worried about Candy. The reader doesn't even know at that point who Candy is, and he's spending all this time worried about her. All that stuff, when you get into character's heads is just a way of getting to know the characters better, giving them history, families, and backgrounds. You've got to come to a limit where you dig deeper in some than you do in others, because you've got to end it at some point. You can't just go on forever. I had a lot of stuff about Wayne that didn't get into the finished book. It changed from the first version.

OT: Is it painful for you to have to cut material about your characters?
LB: Well, sometimes it is painful, but you're just trying to do the best thing that you can to make the book a little shorter, make it read a little faster. I'm used to doing that, though. I've done that on every book that I've written. About the only thing that wasn't really extensively edited was *Joe*, and I pretty much published it the way I turned it in.

OT: How do you make sure that the local flavor of your novels reads as well to those not from this area as it does to locals?
LB: You've got to talk about the weather, the temperature, rain, storms, growing things, plants, birds, animals, the seasons, and all that kind of stuff. I don't think people have any problems identifying with it, because I have so many fans up North and on the West Coast.

OT: Do you have a favorite among all your works?
LB: I don't guess so. For a long time, I said *Dirty Work* was my favorite, but it's been a long time now since I wrote that book. I guess I probably like my most recent one the best, usually.

OT: Who would you say are some of the writers that have influenced your work?
LB: Flannery O'Connor, William Faulkner, Raymond Carver, Charles Bukowski, Harry Crews, and Cormac McCarthy. They've been the biggest influences on me.

OT: Have artists in other media, such as music or film, influenced you?
LB: I'm really into music. I'm going to see Alejandro Escovedo in Austin. He played in Oxford a few times, and played the Double Decker show a few years back. I'm going to see one of the guys in Robert Earl Keen's band, Bill Whitbeck, the guy who plays bass. I get to see people everywhere I go. I run into a lot of musicians in my work.

OT: How does the business side of writing affect the art?
LB: It probably gets harder all the time for unpublished writers to publish their first book. You can hardly do anything now without an agent, and I hear from a lot of young writers who are having great difficulty getting agents and

getting publishers to look at their books. The business end doesn't really affect the writing of a book, though; it's the marketing that it affects. It's hard to say what makes a book successful. Sometimes a book hits, and sometimes it doesn't. There's so much stuff out there, that they really have to make a push. I've been doing interviews, and I'm going to all these cities to do all this promotion and everything. But that's what it takes; you've got to get out there, get on the road, go to the bookstores, sign books, and let people see and hear about your book. Then you hope that it gets some kind of buzz going where people will get out to the stores and buy it.

OT: What advice do you have for aspiring writers?

LB: You have to develop a thick skin for rejection, and you have to just keep on going. Everybody's got an apprenticeship period, and nobody can tell you how long it's going to last. For me, it was seven years. For Harry Crews, it was ten years. For Faulkner, it was about five years. It's different lengths for different people, and if you quit, nobody's ever going to hear from you. So, you have to write all this stuff and throw it away and fail and fail and fail and keep going, until you finally succeed. That's the only thing that's going to solve it, make you feel right, if you really want it. But it's tough, and it's lonely, and you've got to spend a lot of time in a room by yourself.

OT: When you boil it down to its core, what is a writer?

LB: Somebody who tries to re-create human life on the page, as accurately as possible, in fiction. You're putting on an illusion. You're making the person forget that he's reading. If you can pull that off, then you've succeeded.

OT: Who's your favorite character from *The Rabbit Factory?*

LB: I like Miss Muffet a lot, and I like Eric a lot. I like Arthur a lot, and I even like Domino. I kind of like all of them, I guess. (Laughs.) I guess I've probably got more hope for Eric than anybody. I wanted Anjalee and Wayne to be happy. I was trying to bring probably a few more happy endings into this book than some of the other stuff I've done.

OT: What's next for you?

LB: I've got to start writing another novel. I've got two started. I've got one that I'm calling *A Miracle of Catfish,* and I've got another one that I'm calling

The Indonesian Subterranean Termite Soldier Blues. It's a first person novel set in Oxford. It's about this guy who's got an independent termite office and a sixty-five-year-old nymphomaniac mother. I've got a lot of stuff set up on the Square, and I've also got some fictional places down on Jackson Avenue. I've got a new two-book deal with my publisher. They bought both of these; I showed ninety pages of one, and fifty pages of the other. I'm due to deliver the first draft of one of them roughly within a year from this month. So, I'll spend most of the winter working on this new novel.

An Interview with Larry Brown

Marc Fitten and Lawrence Hetrick / 2003

This interview was conducted for the *Chattahoochee Review* but was never published there. Used by permission.

CR: So after nine books is there anything you feel you've learned about writing that makes it easier? Is the writing any easier? Are there differences that you notice when you start a story or novel today that you didn't notice back in the eighties?

Brown: Yeah, I think I've learned that characters, finally, are not all good or all bad. If I could go back and rewrite some of my books I might do them a little bit different, because I found out that everybody's got good and bad parts of them. And just because you're going to make a character a bad man, it doesn't mean he doesn't have some redeeming qualities about him too. But I don't know if the writing gets any easier.

My revision process has gotten a lot easier, just since I got a computer three years ago. I used to write everything on an electric typewriter. And the last novel I wrote on my typewriter was *Fay*, which wound up being 883 pages for the final draft . . . but I had about 1,200 more pages that I threw out. So, the computer saves me all that retyping, basically. That's what was so time consuming, you know, to write a page and then take your red pencil and change it and then retype that page, and then if it still needed some more changes—which it usually did—I'd usually go through about five or six drafts on everything. So, the writing doesn't get any easier, but the revisioning process does.

I spent about fifteen months on *The Rabbit Factory*, and turned in 642 pages, and then I took my editor's suggestions and revised it down to 513 in six weeks, and they took it and published it like that.

CR: Speaking of editors, isn't this your first book away from Algonquin? How is that different? Why move?

Brown: Well, I had done fourteen years with them and eight books, and I turned in 270 pages of this new book hoping for an advance, and they wouldn't give me one. And I felt like they ought to have, as long as I'd been with them and as much work as I'd produced, but they wanted to see the whole first draft. And I was about broke; I really was. I'd had one of my boys in college for five years, and I'd been maintaining two complete separate households, and I had to borrow money from my agent to make it through the first draft. Then, when I turned it in, they still had all these questions. There were all these e-mails that went back and forth for a week: Hey, you gonna fix this? Hey, you gonna fix that? Why are all these animals in here? What's all this about? So after about a week, I just got fed up and I told my agent, "You tell them to make an offer today. I'm tired of the bullshit." So, they did, and I turned it down. It wasn't enough for me to seriously even consider taking it. So then, my agent had an auction in New York and there were seven publishers who got in on it and it got down to be between Houghton Mifflin, Knopf, and Free Press. Free Press just made up their mind that they were going to have it at whatever cost, and that was good for me. So, it's been different. It's been good. I like my editor. This is the first time I've had a male editor to work with on something this size, and they sent me out around the country earlier this year meeting with booksellers. I went to San Francisco, Ann Arbor, Cincinnati, and New York. As far as the book tour, it doesn't seem any different from Algonquin. You still just go to the same places and see the same people. The reviews have been good. We're supposed to get one in the *New York Times* before long, but we don't know who's doing it.

CR: Let me ask you about your prose style. It's always been clean, sharp, and simple. I would like to know how you do that? How do you write prose that seems sparse and yet has the punches that it does? It's just your style, you know? It was in *Big Bad Love*; it was in *Joe*; and it's here in *The Rabbit Factory*. It's wholly unpretentious. I wonder how the fact that you're a self-taught writer has affected your style. Is your style different from something you might have picked up in a writing program had you gone? Do you even think you'd be accepted into a writing program?

Brown: I took two writing courses. I took one in 1982, under Ellen Douglas. I wasn't a student. I wasn't enrolled or anything, but I asked her if I could get into the class. She said there were a couple of places left in the class and asked what I'd written. I said, "Well I've written four novels and about eighty short stories." She said, "Yeah, you can come to the class." As far as my style and whatever, I guess it comes from revision—just revision. I just continue to work on my sentences. I keep poring over them and over them and over them, to try and make sure this is nothing that sticks out, nothing that doesn't need to be in the story. The main thing I'm trying to do is make the reader forget that he's reading. I'm trying to pull off this illusion where you get drawn so deep into the story that you're not aware of the passage of time or things that are going on outside.

CR: How long does it take you to write a story or a novel?
Brown: Well, fifteen months for *The Rabbit Factory*, thirty-eight months for *Fay*. I don't really write short stories much anymore because there's just not any money in them, and this is my only source of income, unless I'm teaching somewhere, which I don't do very much of. The last teaching gig I had was in Montana in '99. I had the Kittredge chair for one semester, and taught two classes—short story and nonfiction. I had about thirty-six students and that took my time seven days a week. I don't have time to write when I'm teaching, so that's the only reason I don't like to teach. I do like working with young people because I understand what they're going through. They're going through the same things that I went through. And all it is, all you can tell them, is that every writer has an apprenticeship period, but nobody can tell you how long it's going to last. You got to write X number of words. I mean, somebody like William Faulkner's—his was five years. Harry Crews's was about ten years. Mine was seven years. You just have to keep operating on blind faith. Because if you stop, the world's never going to hear from you. If you put six years in and then quit, it's just wasted time unless you go on and succeed and publish. Not every kid has the determination and the discipline to sit down and write a bunch of novels that he or she knows are not going to be published. But that's what it takes, to write stuff and throw it away—to keep failing and keep going at it.

CR: How much writing have you failed at then?
Brown: I've failed at five novels. I burned one of them. I've written about 130 short stories whereas I've only published about twenty-five of them, probably. A bunch of essays. I don't know how many essays I've written.

CR: All right. Well let me ask you about the new book, *The Rabbit Factory*. It's a great comedic novel. Shakespearean I think my editor said. It seems like snapshots of different kinds of relationships—some successful, others not.

Brown: My whole idea was a series of characters that are sometimes only ten-uously connected, but they all had some connection, however faint it was, and to try and keep all the stories going parallel. Of course, in some of them, like Arthur, Eric, and Helen, the connection was very strong, also between Miss Muffet and the little dog, and Wayne and Anjalee. This book actually began as a short story in 1994. Pretty much the first five or six chapters are how I wrote them back then. It got to be too big for a short story and I just dropped it for a while, until about three years ago, I guess. Then, I picked it back up, still liked the way it looked, and I thought I was going to turn it into a novella. I started working on it again and these new characters—Domino, Miss Muffet, the little dog, and all that came along—before long I had way over a hundred pages and knew I had a novel. So, I just kept on going. Then, people cropped up that I thought would be minor characters like Merlot, and they turned into major characters, and he ran into Penelope and that devel-oped another major relationship.

I had it from the get go to try to have a hundred segments and keep it bal-anced where they all got about the same amount of time on the page. What I finally had to do was have these little charts to go with them to tell how many scenes they had, how many chapters they had, and to try to kind of balance it that way. I wanted it to be so that you could take any one of the stories of the individual characters and they would stand on their own, alone, without the other links that were in there. Like if you could take just the scenes of Miss Muffet and the dog and have them stand on their own. That's what I was try-ing to pull off.

CR: Someone who read this book said to me that it reminded him of John Grisham on crank. Do you think people might react to the subtlety of the book wrongly? Do you think they might perceive it as not being heavy or deep enough? Not that it matters, I'm just wondering.

Brown: The reviews keep comparing it to those movies by Robert Altman—*Nashville* and *Short Cuts*. But, everywhere I'm going people are saying, "Well, it's not as dark as the other stuff you wrote." I think I was consciously trying to have more happy endings, if I could. It also seems like the kind of thing that offered up more chances for comedy than some of the stuff I'd done pre-viously. Like my characters' names. That's just for the fun of it. Mr. Merlot, Mr. Hamburger, and I have the little dog, and putting the relationship between animals and people was something else I hadn't done. I also wanted to say something about that, because there are so many people whose lives are enriched by animals.

CR: That's actually one of my questions because I wanted to ask you about those animals. What was with the whales?

Brown: Man, that just kind of came out of left field. I was wondering if there had ever been an instance when a Navy ship hit a whale. So, I have a friend who runs a steak house in town and he was over by the house, and he says "Well, I don't know if it's ever happened or not," and I said, "Well, do you think it would happen? Could it be a possibility? Would a whale's sonar help her avoid a collision like that?" And he said, "Well, maybe, but what if she was sick and running a fever and her sonar was impaired?" And I said, "Hmmm. OK. I think I'll try that."

One of the reviews said that some of the stuff leans toward the far side of what is believable, but that it was easy to give me a long leash because of the compassion I had for my characters.

CR: Well it turned out pretty good. Seemed plausible to me. Whales get colds, right?

Brown: I knew for sure that any time Navy ships hit something they got to stop and have an investigation. Because Admiral Nimitz, he hit the docks one time on a big ship he was driving, but it didn't ruin his career. This other poor sap that surfaced the submarine and killed those people, which wasn't really his fault because they let a bunch of civilians in the bridge with him. I mean, what are the chances of that? Out in the middle of the ocean and having a collision . . . from the bottom to the surface. It's weird stuff.

CR: And how did you end up taking the novel out to sea, anyway? It started out in downtown Memphis.

Brown: Just kind of the way it arrived. I was trying to jump around from place to place, from scene to scene, from character to character, and have these different locations, and have them just barely cross paths. For example, in the book, Arthur is in the same coffee shop with Frankie for just a few minutes. That was their only connection. I was kind of using one thing to spring to another, to spring from one person to another. Mr. Hamburger and the little dog introduced Miss Muffet.

CR: Tell me about Memphis.

Brown: Well, I lived there when I was a kid. My daddy took us up there in '54 'cause he couldn't make a living sharecropping with four kids. I lived there until '64. I was educated in Memphis city schools and then went back to Mississippi when I was thirteen or fourteen. I always had relatives up there, so I've always spent a lot of time up there. I remember the Peabody Hotel back when I went and got inducted, back in 1970. When I went for my physical—classified 1-A. Back then, it was run down—an old, shabby, poorly lit, wormy, old hotel, but that's where they put us up. Later, a bunch of businessmen who wanted to revitalize downtown Memphis bought it and fixed it up, and it's a real showcase now. The hotel is in the book. All I had to do was go back up there a couple of times and check that I had everything right about the lobby. It just seemed like a good place to do it. I also needed the bar and some hotel rooms.

CR: Anjalee and Eric—the clear outsiders in this novel—where did you get their story?

Brown: I met a girl in a strip club one time who sat down at our table and talked to us. She told me her grandmother was from Toccopola—which is in the next county over from where I live. That's where William Faulkner's brother crashed William's airplane and killed himself accidentally, back in the thirties. William never forgave himself for letting his brother borrow the plane. It's also true that Elvis once played there, at the Toccopola high school, a long time ago, before he became famous. One of my friends, one of my older friends, over at the fire department saw him play. It must have been '54 or '55. So, I just lifted all that stuff and put it in there. I mean, I take stuff from life. I always remember something Stephen King said. He said that for a writer, all your human experiences are like a well that you draw on every day, that's everything that you remember, everything you've ever seen, and anything that anybody's ever told you about. You just pull it from that well and use it for your fiction. That's pretty much what I do too, what I believe.

CR: You're coming back to Georgia next week for the Flannery O'Connor conference. How much has her work really influenced you? And I guess she's not the only one. There's Harry Crews also, I think. Was he a mentor? Do you know him? Have the two of you been in a room together? I imagine that's a story in itself.

Brown: He wrote a blurb for my first book. Of course, I'd been reading his books for years and years because he'd written a lot about struggling to publish and staying on speed for weeks at a time to stay up and work, and to get the writing done. I always admired his essays greatly. I thought he was one of the best essayists that we have in our country, especially a book like *A Childhood*. Terrible things happened to him. And, well, I finally met him. He invited me down to the University of Florida to give a reading, years ago. I went down there and stayed with him for a couple of days and he had a big party for me. We got to be friends. I haven't heard anything from him in a while. I don't know how he's doing these days. But he was a big influence on me.

Flannery O'Connor now, I got onto her when I took that first writing course in 1982 with Ellen Douglas. She just taught out of *The Norton Anthology of Short Fiction*, but that was the first time I'd ever been exposed to Flannery O'Connor and Joseph Conrad. I mean I had read stuff as a kid like Jack London, *Moby-Dick*, *The Iliad*, *The Odyssey*, and William Faulkner, without really knowing that I was getting a background in literature. I didn't have any aspirations of writing back then. I was just a kid who loved to read and read anything I could get my hands on. By the time I got to be grown, I had read a pretty good bit of literature.

CR: Was there a thing in Mississippi where if you lived there and grew up there you just had to read Faulkner?

Brown: That happened because a friend of mine in shop class one day stuck two of his fingers in a joint planer and cut both of his fingernails off and was in the hospital for a while where they tried to do some skin grafts, and a bunch of us chipped in to buy him some books to read while he was recovering. One of the books we bought him was *Big Woods*. It had "The Bear" in it. It had those hunting stories in there. That's where I got on fire. Then I started on the short story anthologies and it was only later that I started reading the novels—*The Sound and the Fury, Sanctuary*, and all that stuff like that.

CR: So, how did you respond to O'Connor when you read it? Was she anything special?

Brown: She blew my mind because I read "A Good Man Is Hard to Find." First thing I thought was, how in the hell did a lady write this story? Something that shocking and real and scary. And then, of course, I got her whole collection and all the letters and everything. They're great because they talk about this nice young man named Madison Jones who comes over and feeds peacocks with her. Then I got to meet Madison later on and got to talking to him about all that stuff. It's really interesting to go back in time and see all that stuff.

CR: What I think is great about her is that you have this invalid spinster living with her mother, yet living this life through her writing that is more real and gutsier than most people ever do or are capable of living.
Brown: That's true, that's true. To read her letters and see all the things she says about the craft of writing is enormously beneficial to somebody like me who was trying to learn how to write. To hear her say: well, whether I write anything or not, I'm going to sit down for three hours anyway. Just sit there. That's the first thing you got to do. You got to be there! Whether you're going to get it or not. If you ain't there, you sure ain't going to get it. So, it helped me develop good working habits.

CR: So, do you generally work all night?
Brown: Yeah. I've holed up now on a Hank Williams script. I started on it full time just this January 6. I had it up to 120 pages in February, lost the whole thing in my computer, and had to start over on page one. I thought I was going to get it done in ninety days, so I set aside ninety days. But the ninety days went by and I wasn't halfway through.

What they asked me to do was take it from 1937 when he was fourteen to the first few days of '53 when he was dead and buried, and everything in between. So, what I did was follow Colin Escott's book. I had all these other books. I had Jerry Rivers's book, Chet Flippo's book, Roger Williams's book, all this other stuff, but Colin's was the main novel. His had a whole lot of direct quotes, things that were actually said, and I was able to go to some of those CDs and hear exactly what was said at the mike at the Grand Ole Opry, say, on September 22, 1951, between Red Foley and Hank. In some cases I had to just make it up. I didn't know what all was said between him and Lefty Frizzell or between him and Audrey. I didn't know a lot of things that went on, so I just had to try to make it all up for them.

I stayed on it just about every night for eight months. It was the most intensive period of work that I've had in a long time, including finishing *The Rabbit Factory*. I didn't work as hard on this novel as I've been working on

this screenplay. I was really trying to get it done and turn in my draft before
I began this book tour. I really didn't quite make it. I had to go to Austin, but
then I had eight more days off and I told myself that I needed every one of
those eight days to go and revise and everything. My first draft, I turned in
548 pages. That's what I come up with. There will be two more drafts and
we'll size it down from there. It's only supposed to be 120, ideally. I
told him it'd be more than 120 pages, right off the bat. If I only devote ten
pages to each year for sixteen years, that's 160 minimum. So now it's up to
them. It's really the producer's job to tell the writer what he wants.

CR: How did you get this project?
Brown: Billy Bob Thornton and Ben Myron were having lunch in L.A. one
day and it was something that Thornton had been wanting to do for years.
They were talking about who they might hire to write it and my name came
up. They called my agent and she called me and asked me if I'd be interested,
and I said yeah. That was about two years ago.

   Thornton holds the rights on my book *Joe*. He's trying to get his money
together to shoot it. That's a script that I did write. I was working with
another producer named Mark Rosenberg on that, and I had been out to
Austin and done two drafts. That was back in '92. I saw him for three days
while he was working on production for another movie called *Flesh and Bone*.
Then I went to Lynchburg, Virginia to start teaching that fall and Clyde
Edgerton called me one morning and says, "What's that guy's name you're
working for on that *Joe* movie?" I said, "Mark Rosenberg." He said, "Well his
obituary is in the *New York Times* this morning." The day before he had been
on the set and he either choked to death on a piece of food or just dropped
dead from a heart attack. I went ahead and delivered the third draft to his wife
at the time, Paula Weinstein. It never did get made, but Thornton's got some
money together—hoping to shoot it for two million. A million more than he
had for *Sling Blade*. So, I'm hoping it'll eventually come off. He'd play the lead.

CR: He'd play Joe? Billy Bob Thornton? That would be so cool. Could I ride
along in the truck with him?
Brown: I hope so. I hope it comes off. These movie deals, you can never tell.
It took seven years to shoot *Big Bad Love*. Arliss Howard had a script in '94,
but he didn't have any money. Then he finally found five million bucks and
shot the movie.

CR: I saw that on cable the other day. Were you satisfied at how that turned out?

Brown: Sure. It was fine. I was there for most of the production. They gave me a small part. I had a small role. We got a great soundtrack out of it. We had a bunch of North Mississippi blues players: R. L. Burnside, Junior Kimbrough, and Tom Waits had a couple of songs. I was happy with how it turned out. It didn't get a wide distribution for it. You know, I got stuck in Toronto after a showing there on September 10, 2001. The next morning everything happened. I stayed there all week and wound up catching a Greyhound to New York City. Then, I got a flight out of LaGuardia two days later. The weirdest thing about it was that the second day after it happened, I was out walking around in Toronto, kind of depressed, I guess everybody was, and I was hunting a liquor store when this fine gritty dust started falling out of the sky. And everybody just stopped and started looking at it. And I know damn well it was all that powdered concrete that blew up and went to the jet stream, because I'd never seen anything like that fall out of the sky before.

CR: Wow. So, what are you reading right now?

Brown: I just finished yesterday reading Edgerton's new book *Lunch at the Piccadilly* and I've also started [James Lee Burke's] *Last Car to Elysian Fields*. I haven't had much time to read anything much this year because I've been writing so much.

That Secret Code

Orman Day / 2004

The interview was conducted by mail; Brown's responses to Day's questions are included in a letter dated June 17, 2004. An edited and slightly abridged version of the interview material was incorporated into "That Secret Code," a forum on working-class literature that also drew on conversations with writers Dan Chaon, John McNally, and Susan Straight. "That Secret Code" was published online in *Third Coast* after Brown's death. Original interview material used by permission.

Orman Day: What kind of work did your parents do?

Larry Brown: My mother worked at Camp Electric Company in Memphis when I was a kid, next to Sun Studios. Jerry Lee Lewis used to come in there and get cigarettes from the machine. Later she worked at Katz Drugstore, over on Lamar. Much later, when we moved back to Mississippi, she worked at Sears for a long time, then the North Mississippi Retardation Center, running the switchboard. My father took us away from Mississippi in 1954 because he couldn't make it sharecropping. He worked at Fruehauf Trailer Company for a long time. Then he painted houses some, and worked at the Mid-South Fair. When we moved back here, he worked at a stove factory in Oxford until he died suddenly early one morning in 1968.

Day: Was money a major concern?

Brown: Yes. Always. We were very poor.

Day: How did you earn money growing up?

Brown: The first job I ever had was chopping cotton for four dollars a day, from six to six. Hour for lunch. Later I picked it for two cents a pound. I started working in a grocery store when I was about fourteen or fifteen. I got a job at the stove factory where my father had worked as soon as I got out of high school, before I joined the Marines in 1969.

Day: Were you surrounded by books growing up?

Brown: Yes I was. There were always books in our houses, of which we had many because we moved so much. We always had library cards and went to the library frequently, strictly with my mother. She was the influence on reading and instilled a love of it very early. I read all kinds of things when I was a child: westerns, Greek mythology, Norse mythology, horror stories, books about boys and dogs, short stories of all kinds, history, even *Moby-Dick*. Read Hemingway when I was in junior high school and I'd never heard of him. I would read just about anything I could get my hands on and it never occurred to me that I might write until I was twenty-nine.

Day: Back then what were your favorite books about the working class?
Brown: If you mean stuff like *Of Mice and Men*, then yes, I liked that stuff a lot. But of course back then I didn't identify it as that. When I was a boy, I liked stuff about boys and dogs, so I read some of Faulkner's hunting stories, Jim Kjelgaard, Fred Gipson, Wilson Rawls, MacKinlay Kantor, James Street. Anything that had hunting was good, or animals. But I liked other stuff, too. Twain. Bierce. Poe. O. Henry. Saki. Welty. Just lots of stuff. I read widely. I loved reading. I liked going to other places in books.

Day: Was culture part of your upbringing?
Brown: Not much that I remember. I belonged to the Boys Club and we had art classes, drawing, pottery. I never saw a real play that I can remember as a child. We had music, though. Even my daddy liked Hank Williams, and we listened to Marty Robbins, Elvis Presley. We had no art in the house. I liked to draw and did it pretty well, but quit. I tried to learn to play the violin, but I'm left-handed and they tried to force me to play it right-handed, so I never had a chance on that. I finally taught myself a little guitar by stringing one backwards about twenty-three years ago. Now that I'm grown I buy good left-handed ones. But I don't remember much culture in my early life besides *The Lawrence Welk Show* on Saturday nights. Books were about it. Nobody in my family had ever even gone to college until my cousin went in the late '60s.

Day: When did you first start writing and why did you start?
Brown: That question's got a lot of answers. I was about to turn thirty. I wanted to do something else with my life. I'd had a question burning inside me for a long time: how did a person learn how to write? I've told this over and over. I got my wife's typewriter and sat down and started writing a novel in October of 1980 and then went through seven years of apprenticeship, wrote five novels and enough short stories to make about thirteen collections

(if they had been any good). Writing got to be what I wanted to do with my life, but for a long time I couldn't make any money on it. I had to keep on working my job and part-time jobs and taking care of my children and wife. By the time I left the fire department I was vastly dissatisfied with it. I was lucky I found something else to do. Else I would've had to stay there until my thirty was up. Which wouldn't have happened until now, this year. I've been on my own for twelve years and haven't regretted it too much. Only a few times. Usually when I was broke or halfway through something like *Fay* and convinced it was no good and would never work.

Day: Was it always assumed you would go to college?
Brown: No, just the reverse. I fully expected to be drafted and go to Vietnam and be shredded. As it turned out, I volunteered and served all my time stateside. I wouldn't have gone to college anyway, even if the war hadn't been going on, because all I wanted to do once I got out of school was get a job and buy a car, and that's exactly what I did. Both my brothers got college deferments, but I had to send money home the whole time I was in the Marines to help my mother keep my little brother in college so he wouldn't wind up in the shit I was already in. Basically I had no desire for any more education, and probably had little ambition. My father died when I was sixteen and I was lost for quite a while. The world changed suddenly on me in an unthinkable way.

Day: What kind of working-class jobs have you had over the years? What did you learn from those jobs, especially from your coworkers?
Brown: Orman, that's a long one. Grocery store sacker, house painter, hay hauler, pulpwood cutter-and-hand-loader, fence builder, bricklayer's helper, carpenter, carpet cleaner man, truck driver, forklift driver, dock worker, fire-fighter, pine tree planter, timber deadener, surveyor's helper, plumber, answering service employee. Kind of hard to say what I learned from my coworkers. I guess the main thing I learned was that I didn't want to work with my back for the rest of my life and wanted to use my mind instead. I didn't want to remain poor. I wanted my children to have better opportunities than what I had. I wanted to work for myself. I saw people work their whole lives in factories, standing on concrete forty hours a week, and I didn't want that life. I wanted more than that from life. I thought I could find it in writing. And I did. I have great sympathy for the good people of the working class. They

have a hard time making ends meet, even when they work very hard and the fat cats in this country just keep getting fatter and not paying their fair share of income tax because the government allows it to be that way and gets rid of American jobs and gives them to foreigners. There's much injustice. The little man is kept down by the big man, and it's always been that way, and it always will probably. The factory worker can't find anything better, or figures he has no right to hope for anything better since that's what his daddy did and what all the people around him do. I was exactly of that mindset, but I changed over the years. Education is the only answer. For those that want it, I mean. I consider myself a working-class person who lucked out. I'm exploring some of this in the novel I'm working on now. I have a main character who works in that same stove factory.

Day: What did you learn from your time in the Marines?
Brown: Um. Gee. Let's see. They were without a doubt some of the meanest and scariest sumbitches I have ever met. Killers. Yes. And they trained you to be like them. We got picked up as seventy-five recruits and graduated thirty-three. It was good for me. It gave me some discipline and let me know I could do things a lot of people couldn't do, because if you kept fucking up you were out of there. It was the first time I ever saw any reverse discrimination. This black sergeant looked at my admission papers the first night I was there and said: "You look like a backwoods motherfucker. Get yo ass to the back of the line." I didn't understand why he was talking to me like that and told him I hadn't said shit to him. When I bowed up on him, he got kind of mad and threw my application on the floor. Another sergeant, a jovial Hispanic guy, told us with much merriment about killing all the chickens and pigs in the villages they raided in Vietnam and "fucking all the bitches." It was a bad place to wake up in the morning. But I'm glad I went. It challenged me harder than anything ever had up to that time. I would've probably stayed in if I hadn't gotten into some trouble near the end of my enlistment that was none of my fault. There was a life there, but I decided it wasn't the one I wanted. I missed home too much. But I certainly understand why it's the only life for some people, women and men both.

Day: When did you realize you wanted to write about working-class people?
Brown: I don't guess that was a conscious decision. Or maybe it was already an ingrained decision. I don't remember ever thinking about it. I wrote

about what I knew, country people, rural people who were working people. And I set them within a geography I knew. It was the natural thing to do.

Day: Did your family encourage you to seek security in life or go all out to follow your dreams?
Brown: It wasn't either way, really. It was just something I did in my spare time for years (while working as a firefighter) and they were probably surprised when I stuck with it. I know my wife was. She thought it was one of my whims. The last whim had been completely disassembling a '55 in very bad shape and putting it back together, which I never finished and sold for junk. It was a pretty big day around here when I went up to Square Books in Oxford for my first book party in 1988. I became an official writer then. And my whole life changed.

Day: How does a working-class background help and hinder a writer?
Brown: Well, one way it helps is to make things realistic. I'm talking about these big presses and stuff in this stove factory in this novel, and I've got one that's twenty-two feet high, and you can make car fenders with it if you've got the proper dies. And I used to change the dies in those things. They'll smash your fingers off in a second if you forget what you're doing for just one moment. And I also know what kind of people work there, so it surely helps to make the characters real. The food they eat, the cars and trucks they drive and the things that are wrong with them, the kind of beer they drink, the music they listen to. What they do on the weekends. Not just the way they talk, but that's important, too. Real dialogue. Those people have hopes and dreams, too.

About the hindrances I'm not so sure. Maybe they're just personal ones. I rub shoulders with wealthy people sometimes and I'm not completely comfortable with some of them because we don't have much in common. They like my books, yeah, and buy them all, and have for years, but beyond that, what do we talk about? So maybe my working-class background separates me from some people. I don't seek a lot of company uptown. The main thing I want if I go out to a bar is to be left alone, but that's hard around here these days. So most times I just stay home and work. I've found out that I'm more comfortable with musicians than just about anybody, including other writers, but at the same time I've got a lot of friends who are writers. I've found that the better the person, the better the writer. It makes sense if you think about it.

Day: Why is it important that there even be a working-class literature?
Brown: To document these lives and the times these people lived in and to tell who they were. To leave something indelible behind. To let people know other people they would have never come to know personally in their lives. To let them know they are human beings just like everybody else.

Day: Do you think that writers with more prosperous backgrounds misrepresent the working class, including the jobs they perform? If so, how?
Brown: I can't think of anybody in particular who's doing that. If it's inaccurate or fake, I think that would come out on the page. Just like in anything else.

Day: Currently who are your favorite writers whose subject is the working class?
Brown: Brad Watson, Harry Crews, Raymond Carver, Charles Bukowski, Kent Haruf, Tim Gautreaux. There's probably some more I've left out. Hard to make a complete list. There are so many people I haven't read that I've heard are good. But it's difficult for me to get enough time to read to stay halfway current.

Day: What has been the reaction of readers to your work?
Brown: I get all kinds of comments. I truly cannot remember how many times I've been told by somebody (*always* a woman) that she's my number one fan. Makes you think of *Misery*, of course. I swear before God, I was in a mall parking lot in Jackson last weekend, going to put some stuff in the 4-Runner, when a woman in a white car slowed down, rolled down the window, and said, "Brown. I'm your number one fan." Don't know who in the hell she was. Generally, I'd have to say that I've had a very positive reception. I've won some prizes and grants, for which I've been very grateful. I've always had good reviews. Out of a hundred, I'll see two bad ones. People will usually turn out if you're not in the crappiest bookstore in the crappiest city they can send you to, which does happen. I've got an Absolut Brown ad up here on the wall. I've got a real movie poster of *Big Bad Love* up on the wall. I've been in a couple of other movies. Just got the parts because of who I was. I've read at the Folger-Shakespeare Library in D.C. and talked to inner-city school kids

there. I've had some great things happen. I've turned some of my work into plays and seen them done onstage after a three-week rehearsal. I've had lots of opportunities. And writing brought all of it. And of course some people are just the opposite of number-one fans, will walk up and say something like: "Well, I just read *Father and Son* and it just depressed the hell out of me." You can't have a comfortable conversation with somebody like that. Some people will just be rude. The old ladies will ask why are there so many cuss words in my books. Or they won't like the ending of *Fay*. They'll want to know why I ended it that way. What they mean is why did I kill Sam? And how do you explain all this shit when you know you went through all the revisions and different endings long ago and made all these decisions? There are a lot of different reactions to my work. I've never gotten used to all of them. I'm not comfortable around a whole bunch of people any more. I like things quiet and I don't like to talk to people I don't want to. Many of them are well-meaning, but I've gotten to where I almost flinch if some stranger starts coming over smiling. I know he's recognized me. Many of them are very nice. But I just don't get out much. I prefer to stay with my growing family and my work and my pond and my little house I built in the woods behind it. That's plenty of life for me.

Index

Brown, Larry (*continued*)
178, 182, 191–92; awards, xxiii, xxiv, 44, 45,
51, 62, 70, 99; childhood in Memphis, xii,
xxi, 9, 16, 30, 39, 79–80, 100, 102–4, 111,
118, 119, 153, 164, 191; childhood in
Mississippi, 9, 60, 81–82, 101, 102, 105–7,
110–11, 145, 153; drinking, 131, 159, 161,
164; fame, 136, 159; firefighting career, vii,
ix, xi, 5–6, 30–32, 49, 72, 93–94, 148, 153,
164; hunting, love of, 60, 110–11, 191;
marriage, xi, xxii, 8, 114–15, 148–49,
154–56, 158–59, 161–62; reading, early love
of, xvi, 9, 16, 46, 47, 80–81, 100–1, 135, 151,
191; storytelling tradition, 38–39, 48, 71,
106–8, 110, 116; teaching, 44, 76–77, 182;
work history, 10–11, 86, 88, 148–49, 154,
165, 190, 192–93, 194; writer, late start as,
vii, 3, 15, 45
Themes and techniques: autobiography, 13,
28, 42, 50, 54–55, 57, 84–85, 140, 156–57,
174; character, importance of, 76, 141, 156;
comedy, 174, 182–83; community, 86, 90,
92–93; craft of fiction, xiv–xv, 33, 40,
50–51, 94, 118, 187; dialogue, 22, 43, 51, 56,
66; evil, 35, 36, 69, 101, 122–23, 141; family,
89; firefighting as subject, 49, 72, 130;
landscape, 43, 51, 64–65, 81, 87, 144–45;
poetry, 52–53, 74, 142; "sandbagging,"
xvii–xviii, 36–37, 43, 52, 53, 67–68, 75, 97,
156; spiritual elements, 28–33, 35–36, 54,
63–64, 69, 97–98, 144; tragedy, 47, 90–91,
101, 129; voice, 19, 42, 51, 56, 66, 72–73;
working-class emphasis, 6–7, 15–16, 42–43,
53, 56, 93, 113–14, 190–91, 193–95; writing
schedule, 5–6
Works: "The Apprentice," 56; *Big Bad Love*
(collection), xxiii, 40, 45, 50, 54, 56–57, 67,
69, 99, 70, 78, 79, 166, 181; "Big Bad Love"
(story), 65; *Billy Ray's Farm* (essay
collection), xxiv, xxv, 170, 171–72; "Billy
Ray's Farm" (essay), 115, 171–72; "A
Birthday Card," 57; "Boy and Dog," xi, xxii,
13–14, 73–74, 152–53; *Dirty Work* (novel),
viii, xi, xiv, xv, xvii, xviii, xxi, xxii, xxiii, 8,
16, 21–23, 28, 35, 38, 40, 43, 45, 46, 50, 51,
58–59, 65, 67, 69, 70, 73, 74, 79, 82, 95–98,
99, 109, 151, 166, 167, 177; *Dirty Work*
(stage adaptation), xxiii, xxiv, 44, 49–50, 99;

"Discipline: The Trial of a Plagiarist," 55,
77–78; *Facing the Music* (collection), vii,
xxiii, 3, 20–21, 34, 40, 42, 45, 47, 50, 52, 67,
69, 70, 74, 79, 99, 126, 127, 158, 165;
"Facing the Music" (story), xi, xvi, xxii,
xxiii, 26, 27–28, 44, 55, 78, 125–26, 160,
165–66; "Falling out of Love," 56; *Father
and Son*, ix, xi, xxiv, 92–93, 99, 116–18,
120–22, 126, 128, 140–41, 167, 196; *Fay*, ix,
xv, xvii, xxiv, 79, 163, 166, 167, 180, 182,
192, 196; "The Indonesian Subterranean
Termite Soldier Blues" (novel manuscript),
179; *Joe*, xii, xviii, xxii, xxiii, 27, 35, 37–38,
40, 43–44, 45, 50–51, 59, 67, 68–69, 70, 74,
79, 85–92, 95–96, 99, 113, 120, 144, 167, 169,
177, 181, 188; "Kubuku Rides (This Is It),"
xxiii, 44, 51–52, 66, 72–73; "A Late Start"
(address), vii, xxiii, 15; "The Miracle of
Catfish" (novel manuscript), xxv, 178;
"92 Days," xviii, 54–55, 77; "Old Frank and
Jesus," 14, 28–29, 55, 150; "Old Soldiers," 80,
84; *On Fire*, xxiv, 30, 70, 71, 72, 73, 88, 93,
99, 116, 156, 157, 167, 169; "Plant Growin'
Problems," xxii, 99, 135; *The Rabbit Factory*,
xxv, 173, 174–78, 180, 181–85, 187; "The
Rich," 55; "A Roadside Resurrection," 30,
34–35, 37, 62–64, 65, 73; "Samaritans," xvii,
29, 35, 55, 67, 139, 160; unpublished fiction,
xiii–xiv, 8, 34, 88, 95, 178–79; "Waiting for
the Ladies," 39; "Wild Thing," xviii, 156–57
Brown, LeAnne (LB's daughter), xxii, 100, 116,
118, 154, 161–62
Brown, Leona Barlow (LB's mother), xxi, 9, 46,
57, 60, 80, 100, 108, 135, 150–51, 190
Brown, Mary Annie (LB's wife), x–xi, xvi,
xxi–xxii, 26, 41, 80, 94, 99, 100, 104, 109,
114–15, 116, 164, 165
Brown, Shane (LB's son), xxii, 100, 103, 105, 116,
118, 162
Bukowski, Charles, xvi, 41, 57, 142–43, 145, 177,
195; Henry Chinaski character, 57
Burke, James Lee, 189; *Last Car to Elysian
Fields*, 189
Burnside, R. L., 189
Butler University, 70

Camp Electric Company (Memphis), xxi, 103, 190
Camp Lejeune, North Carolina, xxi, 16, 79, 82